THE VIOLENCE OF THE BIBLICAL GOD

The Violence of the Biblical God

Canonical Narrative and Christian Faith

L. Daniel Hawk

WILLIAM B. EERDMANS PUBLISHING COMPANY
GRAND RAPIDS, MICHIGAN

Wm. B. Eerdmans Publishing Co.
4035 Park East Court SE, Grand Rapids, Michigan 49546
www.eerdmans.com

© 2019 L. Daniel Hawk
All rights reserved
Published 2019

ISBN 978-0-8028-7244-9

Library of Congress Cataloging-in-Publication Data

Names: Hawk, L. Daniel (Lewis Daniel), 1955- author.
Title: The violence of the biblical God : canonical narrative and Christian faith / L. Daniel Hawk.
Description: Grand Rapids : Eerdmans Publishing Co., 2019. | Includes bibliographical references and index.
Identifiers: LCCN 2018026326 | ISBN 9780802872449 (pbk. : alk. paper)
Subjects: LCSH: Violence in the Bible. | Bible. Old Testament—Criticism, interpretation, etc. | God (Christianity)
Classification: LCC BS1199.V56 H39 2019 | DDC 220.8/3036—dc23
LC record available at https://lccn.loc.gov/2018026326

Abbreviations in this volume follow *The SBL Handbook of Style*, 2nd edition.

For my sons, Danny and Andrew,
who are not impressed by easy answers

Contents

Foreword by John Goldingay	ix
Preface	xiii
Acknowledgments	xvii
1. The Problem of the Violent God	1
2. Creation Ruined and Remade	23
3. Yahweh's New Approach	45
4. The Grand Entrance	66
5. A Covenant Made and Remade	90
6. God and Kings	109
7. The Land Promised and Taken	140
8. God Moves to the Outside	169
9. Interpreting Divine Violence	194
Select Bibliography	209
Author Index	215
Subject Index	216
Scripture Index	219

Foreword

I am bored by the topic of the violence of the biblical God—just not when Dan Hawk writes about it.

I am bored by it because people who ask or write about it are inclined to give the impression that we all know that Jesus is obviously against violence, so the question is how can we explain (away) the manner in which much of the Bible speaks about war and violence. In this connection as in others, it's easy to make allowance for the Bible's being culturally rooted. It's harder to work with the extent to which our Christian views are culturally rooted. After all, we're Christians and we accept the Bible's authority, so our instincts must be basically right, mustn't they? We don't realize the extent to which our framework for thinking about the Bible and violence (among other topics) is culturally determined.

But I am not bored when Dan Hawk writes about this subject. There are biblical scholars who through their lives flit from one subject or one book to another; when they are "done" with Psalms they move on to Isaiah and then on to Genesis and then on to the next thing. I am one of those scholars. There are other biblical scholars who worry at a particular topic or book for most of their academic lives. They keep coming back to it, they keep looking at it from new angles, they keep chewing over it, they keep wrestling with it. Dan Hawk is that kind of scholar. He has been badgering the topic of war and violence for forty years.

Every Promise Fulfilled, his first book on the subject, showed what insight can emerge if we lay aside for a moment our assumptions about a subject (in this case, "the book of Joshua is all about violence") and just pay attention to the text and read it carefully. It turns out that Joshua is "all about" God's promises and Israel's promises and about how far either side fulfills them and what the implications are.

Dan Hawk knows that the central truth about God is that he is good-natured and patient and always on the run with his arms open like the prodigal father, and he knows that the central truth about human relationships lies in harmony and forbearance and mercy. But he also knows that there is a lot in the Scriptures that reflects other noncentral truths about God, such as God's willingness to say "Okay, that's it" and humanity's obligation to echo that declaration. And in this book he shows that he knows there is a narrative shape to God's working at God's purposes in the world and that this narrative shape helps us understand and work with some of the tensions in the perspectives the Scriptures hold before us.

My students have often come to seminary hoping to find answers to questions that have troubled them. Sometimes over the years they have been given straightforward answers to such questions, but they have come to see that these straightforward answers don't work. Often they have questions I have wondered about, too, and sometimes I think I have an answer and can give it to them. In working as a seminary professor, one experience I love is the occasional moment when I give students such an answer and a light comes into their eyes as they see that the answer works. On other occasions they don't like my answer or they are not convinced by it. And on yet other occasions I invite them to see that Christian faith is often about living with questions rather than having answers. The "problem" of evil and suffering is an example, as is the relationship between God's sovereignty and human responsibility. Dan Hawk starts this book with a comparable observation about violence, that it may be more important to think biblically than to seek biblical answers.

My stepdaughter and her husband, Katie-Jay and Gabriel Stauring, have given the past ten years of their lives to taking political and practical action on behalf of victims of violence, in particular as it has decimated and traumatized the Darfuri people of Sudan who are now in refugee camps in Chad. A couple of years ago I was asked to talk about the Bible and violence in a "Bible-believing" church. What people wanted, and what I tried to give them, was some understanding of how to think about the way the Bible talks about violence. But my wife and I also showed them videos of the lives of the Darfuri and of the work that Katie-Jay and Gabriel have been doing, and we challenged the congregation regarding whether their concern about violence was just something in their heads or whether they expressed that concern in their lives. I believe this is consistent with Dan's message in this book. He encourages us not only to be ready with a biblical answer when confronted with violence, but to respond redemptively in a way informed by the Scriptures.

There is an approach to Ecclesiastes that uses the book as a way of getting people to see how empty life is, so that one can then tell them about Jesus who is the "answer" to this emptiness. I don't believe that this use of Ecclesiastes corresponds with how it got into the Scriptures, but I don't imagine that God minds much if the approach leads people to trust in Jesus. In an analogous way, I'm not wholly sure why God inspired the biblical authors to talk so much about the violence of God and the violence God commissions, but I suspect that God will be glad if wrestling with the question and facing the reality of violence drives us to stop just discussing violence and to do something about it.

JOHN GOLDINGAY
Fuller Theological Seminary

Preface

I have been thinking about the violence of the biblical God for a long time. While attending Asbury Theological Seminary, I had the privilege of participating in a small group led by Dr. Robert Lyon, late Professor of New Testament Interpretation, which convened in his home. Bob called the group The LO Society—"LO" standing for "Loyal Opposition." Bob envisioned a prophetic evangelicalism that pursued a path of peacemaking, justice, and nonviolence, in opposition to American evangelicalism's infatuation with power, nationalism, and materialism—a vision that, in the 1970s, was well ahead of the evangelical mainstream. Bob's teaching, by example and instruction, convinced me to pursue a nonviolent ethic that embodied the self-giving love of Jesus Christ. I entered the pastorate and traveled through subsequent academic contexts with every confidence that this ethic was the authentic way to follow the example and teachings of Jesus.

Since then, however, I have been unsettled by two challenges to my LO-instilled convictions. The first has to do with the magnitude of violence that swirls around God in the Bible, particularly in the Old Testament, and the difficulty of making sense of the violence in light of God's revelation of the divine self in Jesus Christ. The book of Joshua has been an especially vexing challenge. Why is it in the canon? What positive role, if any, can such a brutal book play in shaping Christian thinking and witness? The second arises from the many conversations I have had with thoughtful and mature Christians who have not been enlightened or convinced by what I had regarded as the clear message of Scripture on the topic of violence, which only needs to be identified and explained. These include Christians of deep faith who serve in law enforcement and the military, who have responded to my arguments by explaining what they do as a calling from God. I have known many of these friends deeply enough to realize that they respond to the work of the Holy Spirit as readily as I—often more so. A few have shared how profoundly torn they are by the violence they have been a part of and which they felt was necessary to prevent greater violence. If their acceptance of and participation in violence simply results from the undue influence of erroneous biblical teaching, why doesn't the Holy Spirit illumine their understanding and guide these faithful listeners otherwise? Finally, there are the students and colleagues who have lived in violent and unstable places and have pressed me to consider that my views might be more nuanced if my experience with violence was more immediate.

The cumulative result of these interactions, along with my own deliberations, has left me less confident about the unassailable certitude of my convictions. And while I have gained valuable insights from recent studies on the topic of divine violence, I remain generally dissatisfied. The reason? I have come to the conclusion that the Bible does not offer any clear-cut, definitive template on the question of divine violence and how it should inform Christian faith and practice. I want to suggest instead that it may be more important to think biblically than to seek biblical answers. In other words, the Bible shapes thinking and action most effectively when it informs how we see and respond redemptively to the violence that saturates our world. It does so by proclaiming the love of God, the brutal brokenness of the world, and the complexity of life. The canon's own testimony of God at work in multiple places in human communities draws faithful readers into a canonical conversation generated by a multiplicity of diverse and conflicting voices. The canon of Scripture mirrors the diversity of locations and perspectives that comprise the church and so may effectively guide Christian decision-making in any given instance by framing a conversation that speaks to all participants. I have written this book, therefore, not so much to present definitive answers on the topic as to contribute to the conversation through a focused study that explores the way the Bible addresses the issue of violence by the way it tells God's story.

The Bible has a narrative spine. That is to say, the diverse contents of Scripture are united by and find their meaning by virtue of their connection to the story that the Bible tells about God's work in the world. Both testaments begin by telling God's story in multiple renditions (Genesis through 2 Kings and 1–2 Chronicles in the Old Testament and the four gospels and Acts in the New). The prophetic books of the Old Testament are anchored in the narratives, and the wisdom books take up the thread either by embedding discourses in narrative (as in Job) or referring back implicitly or explicitly to

Solomon (as in Proverbs and Ecclesiastes). References back to the story occur in Psalms in the form of superscriptions and retellings of the story (as in Psalms 105 and 78). The epistles of the New Testament likewise presume and extend the narratives of God's work through Christ and the apostles, while Revelation finishes and summarizes the story through the use of metaphor.

I follow the story through the narrative that begins the Bible (Genesis-2 Kings) and the two-part narrative that extends it in the New Testament (Luke-Acts). The former tells God's story from creation to the exile of Israel (as opposed to Chronicles, which effectively begins the story with David), while the latter situates the story of Jesus and the apostles within the broad sweep of the former narrative and accounts for God's continuing work in the world past the resurrection of Jesus.

I base my reading on the Hebrew Bible and Greek New Testament, which means that I translate as well as interpret. All translations of biblical texts are my own. Relating to this, I also draw on historical material when doing so aids understanding, as if I were asking the narrator, "Could you explain what this is or why so-and-so was doing this?" I attempt to read the text in its own right—which does not means that I take everything as it is plainly rendered. There are instances when a clever narrator or narrators signal that what we read should be taken with a grain of salt, and I take note of those instances.

The thread of these narratives, as I read them, presents God as resolutely and relentlessly at work to renew a world gone bad. The narratives explain God's involvement with violence as a consequence of the divine decision to step into the world and renew it from the inside out—that is, to enter the maelstrom of a violent, chaotic world with the intention of utilizing restored relationships to set things right. The story tells what this decision costs God. As it unfolds, we see that a developing identification and relationship with human partners entangles God within mechanisms of violence that configure the warped systems that rebellious humanity has created. The story tells of the decisions God makes to adapt to the circumstances and actions of God's human partners, pulling God at each step more deeply into the world of violence.

The narrator alerts us to this dynamic early on in the story, by reporting five instances in which Yahweh is said to "come down" into the world. The first instance, at Babel, portrays Yahweh coming down in response to a worrisome plan being concocted by a unified humanity. Subsequent descents report Yahweh's decisions to enter into an authentic relationship with a human being (Abraham), announce Yahweh's supremacy in the world through the defeat of the mightiest human powers (Pharaoh and Egypt), identify Yahweh fully with a nation (Israel at Sinai), and commit Yahweh to the nation even when Israel forsakes its part in the relationship (when worshiping a golden calf).

Yahweh's decision to identify the divine self and work with the nation of Israel brings more challenges. Yahweh acquiesces to Israel's demand for a king, adjusts divine plans to accommodate the monarchical system that the people requested despite Yahweh's opposition, and finally abandons the project in the face of Israel's persistent intransigence. After a period of disengagement, God enters the world a final time but steps outside the system to fulfill the renewal of creation through an alternative monarchy established through Jesus, God's son.

Taken as a whole, the narratives vividly depict the complexity of God's decision to renew a violent world in partnership with human agents and the decisions human beings must make to live faithfully in this world. They set before Christian readers multiple ways of navigating complicated circumstances and, in so doing, call Christian readers into dialogue with each other about how God is calling them to continue God's renewing work in their places and times.

Acknowledgments

I have had the privilege, over the last twenty-three years, of teaching at Ashland Theological Seminary, a community of theological educators related to the Brethren Church and shaped by the Brethren practice of hearing every voice in the processes of communal decision-making and biblical interpretation. I have been influenced and challenged by countless conversations with colleagues and students that, while strident at times, have been undertaken with respect and a deep commitment to maintaining our relationship as brothers and sisters in Christ. The approach to communal interpretation that I commend in this book owes much to this ethos and to what I have learned and experienced as part of this community. I am also grateful to the Faculty Development Committee of the seminary, to the president and Advisory Board for a study leave that enabled me to get a good start on the manuscript, and to faculty and student friends who have encouraged me as I have worked out the contours and content of the book.

I have greatly benefited by the comments and support I have received from Dr. Allan Bevere and Bishop Joey Johnson. Allan gave me a listening ear and valuable encouragement early on and throughout this project. His invitation to submit guest posts for his blog (http://www.allanbevere.com/) gave me an early opportunity to put some ideas together and get important feedback. Bishop Joey, whose breadth of reading, interests, and thought are remarkable, listened to my ideas during our wide-ranging conversations over coffee and responded energetically and thoughtfully. I owe to him the suggestion that Said's notion of contrapuntal reading works better among biblical interpreters if conceived more in a jazz mode than one associated with seventeenth-century music.

My thanks go to Allen Myers, who encouraged my ideas on this topic early on and led this project from proposal to acceptance. Andrew Knapp has provided exceptional editorial initiative, oversight, and feedback, both in his careful work on the manuscript and through timely communication that moved the project speedily to publication. It has been a pleasure to work with the entire team at Wm. B. Eerdmans, and I am deeply appreciative of their creativity, professionalism, and collegiality.

Finally, as ever, I am grateful for the patience and forbearance of my wife Linda, who has been the best of all good gifts to me and whose wisdom and love have given me the soil my ideas have needed to take root and develop.

1

The Problem of the Violent God

You are not to kill.
                                               DEUTERONOMY 5:17

Yet from the cities of these peoples that Yahweh your God gives you as an inheritance, you shall not spare anything that breathes. You shall wipe them out—the Hittites, Amorites, Canaanites, Perizzites, Hivites, and Jebusites—as Yahweh your God commands you.
                                               DEUTERONOMY 20:16–17

The modern quest for an all-encompassing explanation for the disparate and violent portraits of God in the Bible is akin to physicists' quest for a Theory of Everything. Just as contemporary physicists seek a theoretical base that integrates all known phenomena of the physical universe, from the complex interactions of elementary particles to the operations of the fundamental forces of the universe, so contemporary biblical interpreters have been on a quest for an explanatory framework that unites all aspects of the canonical testimony—from the myriad, diverse chaos of elemental texts that testify of God's violence, to the broad theological themes that span the biblical corpus—into a single system of meaning. The challenge is daunting. One must find a way to reconcile texts such as God's command that the invading Israelites slaughter the indigenous peoples of Canaan with texts that speak of the self-giving, saving love of God for the sake of the world, displayed most vividly by the Cross. One must account for a loving God who saves by killing Egyptians in one part of the Bible and by being killed by Romans in another.

This quest has pressed itself with particular urgency in the first decades of the twenty-first century. The rise of violent religious extremism has challenged Christians to come to grips with the role that religiously sanctioned violence plays and has played in the life and mission of the church. The ripple effects of waves of genocidal violence, coupled with the disintegration of empires and colonial regimes, has raised the issue of Christianity's complicity with programs of conquest, oppression, and the erasure of indigenous cultures—and the role the Bible has played in justifying them. The specter of nuclear annihilation has taken up new haunts in rogue regimes. Old ethnic and religious antagonisms coupled with new nationalist sentiments gain momentum in all parts of the globe.

The question of what role the Bible has played in justifying and generating violence presses for a response from followers of the Prince of Peace. How have the violent acts of the God of the Bible influenced Christian faith and practice? What impact has divine violence had on the way Christians conduct themselves in a world saturated with violence? How do the warrior God of the Old Testament and the self-giving God of the New Testament reflect the same deity? How are Christians to understand the person and work of a God who calls for the death of lawbreakers in one part of the Bible yet forgives sinners in another? A God who commands his people to show no mercy to enemies in one text and to love one's neighbor in another? What biblical images and teachings are faithful readers to appropriate in response to the manifestations of violence in their own times and circumstances? If God takes up violence in certain ways and for certain reasons, should not those guided by the Bible do the same?

These and associated questions concerning the violent God reflect one of two primary and related concerns. First, there is the task of determining what to make of the paradoxical nature of the biblical God's participation in violence. What are faithful followers to make of a God who declares "Thou shalt not kill" and yet commands killing, in some instances on a massive scale? Related to this is the question of how the violent depictions of the biblical God influence, or should influence, Christian thinking, and how they have played out and continue to play out in distinct Christian practices. The connection between interpretation, practice, and witness has driven the impulse to develop a comprehensive and trustworthy explanation since the early centuries of the church's existence.

THE PROBLEM OF THE VIOLENT GOD

Early Christian Approaches

The quest for a sound, all-encompassing framework for interpreting divine violence has long been elusive. Patristic interpreters were concerned to clarify that God's anger and violence do not flow from impulse or caprice, as is the case for the deities that populate Greek and Roman mythology. Some argued on philosophical grounds that God is above anger, or that anger is inconsistent with the immutable character of the divine. Others argued that anger and hostility are divine practices that are necessary for the maintenance of justice and divine law, or that divine love and goodness presume divine indignation as well. Tertullian pointedly brought the two streams together by declaring that God "can be angry without being shaken, can be annoyed without coming into peril, can be moved without being overthrown."[1]

Two early ways of addressing divine violence were advanced by the Gnostic teacher Marcion and the Alexandrian teacher Origen. Both considered the depiction of God in the Old Testament as incompatible with the God revealed in Jesus Christ and in the New Testament. Marcion insisted that a supremely good God could not act like the violent God who is depicted in the Old Testament. On the basis of Gnostic ideas of the imperfection and mutability of the material world, Marcion argued that the God portrayed in the Old Testament is an evil God, an imperfect and flawed deity who created a miserable world, imposed a covenant of law, and cruelly judged those who transgressed it. The New Testament, on the other hand—and particularly selected epistles of Paul—speak of a good God who was revealed in Jesus Christ, proclaimed a gospel of love, and intended to destroy the evil God and his works. In a nutshell, then, Marcion held that the Old and New Testaments testified to two different deities. Because the Old Testament concerned the savage God of Israel and not the good God who sent Jesus, Marcion rejected the Old Testament in its entirety, along with a large part of the New Testament.

Although Marcion's teachings prodded the church to think more deeply about the connection between the Old and New Testaments, they were emphatically rejected. His opponents recognized that Jesus explained his ministry and grounded his teachings in the Old Testament, and that the writers of the New Testament followed suit. The vast preponderance of Christians, therefore, viewed the gospel as an extension and fulfillment of what God

1. Michael C. McCarthy, "Divine Wrath and Human Anger: Embarrassment Ancient and Modern," *TS* 70 (2009): 861.

had done through Israel; the entirety of God's revelation spanned both testaments. The church's decision to recognize both testaments affirmed that the God who created the world and entered into a covenant with Israel is one and the same God who was incarnate in Jesus Christ.

Origen took a different approach. Although he viewed the Old Testament as Scripture, Origen believed that the violent and unsavory portraits of God, when taken at face value, could not be reconciled with the God who, in the person of Jesus Christ, taught his disciples to love others. To hold the incompatible portraits of God together, he adopted the approach that much of the Greco-Roman world used to interpret the myths they told about their gods. The widespread turn to philosophical systems throughout the classical world had created a problem for those who adhered to the old myths, which were populated by unseemly, lascivious, and capricious deities unworthy of emulation and sometimes devoid of morality. As a means of retaining and rehabilitating the myths, interpreters transformed them into allegories that conveyed moral messages. The allegorical approach to myths was subsequently appropriated by Jewish interpreters in the Greek colony of Alexandria as early as the second century BCE. Most prominent was Philo, who, two centuries prior to Origen, used allegorical interpretation to integrate Platonic philosophy with Jewish thought and to present Moses as a great and ancient philosophical teacher.

Origen was a head of the prominent catechetical school at Alexandria, which drew from the allegorical interpretation of Philo. In contrast to the other prominent school, in Antioch, which focused on the grammatical and historical meaning of biblical texts, Origen looked for the deeper spiritual meaning that he believed could be discerned through allegory, in consonance with a typological view of the Old Testament. His hermeneutical approach thus joined messianic interpretation with a philosophical vision that viewed the entire biblical canon as a single coherent system of truth. On this basis, Origen was able to interpret accounts of divine violence in the Old Testament in a way that rendered their meaning consistent with the life and teachings of Jesus. Arguably the most impressive and persuasive application of his method is the series of homilies he wrote on the book of Joshua. Observing that the Greek form of the name Joshua is identical to the Greek form of the name of Jesus, Origen interpreted the entire book of Joshua as an allegory of Christ's saving work in the life of the believer and of the believer's work with Christ to defeat the powers of sin that hold sway in the human heart.

The allegorical method that Origen and the Alexandrian School practiced was eventually embraced by the Western Church. It had the benefit of promoting reverence for the Bible as divine revelation, rendered that revelation coherent and edifying, supported the teaching of the church, and provided a powerful response to critics who seized on the violence of the biblical God as a means of discrediting the church.

The Protestant Reformation, however, saw a return on the part of Protestants to a realistic, grammatical approach, similar to that taught by the ancient academy at Antioch. The Protestant turn to the literal sense opened the way for a critical reading of Scripture which, as advanced by the Deists, expressed sympathy for Marcion's dismissal of the violent God. The Deists held that the Bible's depictions of divine violence could not be true, although they argued their point by asserting that a holy and perfect God must act in conformity with the dictates of reason and the Law of Nature. For this reason, Deists rejected the Bible's wrathful and violent depictions of God as irrational and unworthy, useful only to priests who sought to exploit superstition and fear in order to control adherents. In addition, they argued that the Bible's anthropomorphic rendering of God, who expresses both anger and repentance, and who both swears and breaks promises, could not be reconciled with God's eternal changelessness. The willingness to accept these deficiencies in the Bible, they asserted, resulted in zealous violence in the name of God. Deist writer Matthew Tindal quotes Archbishop John Tillotson to summarize the matter:

> According as men's notions of God are, such will their religion be; if they have gross and false conceptions of God, their religion will be absurd and superstitious. If men fancy God to be an ill-natured Being, armed with infinite power, who takes delight in the misery and ruin of his creatures, and is ready to take all advantages against them, they may fear him, but they will hate him; and they will be apt to be such towards one another, as they fancy God to be towards them; for all religion doth naturally incline men to imitate him whom they worship.[2]

Tindal later elaborates:

> Since there can be nothing in God but what is God-like; he either must be perfectly good, or not be at all. It would be well, if all who

---

2. Matthew Tindal, *Christianity as Old as Creation; or, the Gospel, a Republication of the Religion of Nature* (London, 1730), 75.

in words give this character of the Deity, were consistent with themselves, and did not impute such actions to him, as make him resemble the worst of beings, and so run into downright demonism.[3]

The view that violent images of God are unreasonable, contradictory, and inflammatory led some Deists to follow Marcion's lead and reject large segments of the Bible altogether.

Although the Deists did not succeed in winning the theological day, their criticism impacted how the violence of God would be addressed and explained in subsequent Protestant interpretation. Contradiction and paradox, in the first place, could not be accepted by interpreters, as neither conforms to the dictates of reason. Paradoxes had to be resolved, and contradictions had to be harmonized, since both reflect irrational modes of thought and therefore do not speak truthfully about God. Likewise, biblical texts that impute emotions to God (such as anger or jealousy) were seen to portray God as irrational or impulsive. As God is presumed to be a rational being, such embarrassing depictions might be regarded as metaphors or human attributions but certainly not aspects of the divine.

Historical-Critical Approaches

The development of a critical and descriptive approach to biblical interpretation shifted the focus of interpretation significantly toward the human composition and character of the Bible. The historical-critical method situated the production and meaning of biblical texts within the context of human experience, setting them within discrete places, societies, and points in time. Discerning the influence of events and culture on the thinking of biblical authors became definitive for determining what the biblical writers wanted to say. The focus of interpretation, therefore, fixed on what the human authors intended to communicate, within the context of a specific time and culture, as a means of discovering how the divine voice spoke through the human authors of Scripture.

Setting the entire span of biblical revelation within an evolutionary framework suggested a new way to explain violent portrayals of God. Older biblical literature could be cast as primitive expressions of Israel's religious

---

3. Tindal, *Christianity as Old as Creation*, 78. See also Henning Graf Reventlow, *The Authority of the Bible and the Rise of the Modern World*, trans. John Bowden (Philadelphia: Fortress, 1985), 289–410.

consciousness, which evolved over time into a mature ethical and theological perspective that found its full expression in the teaching and ministry of Jesus Christ. The flood, the exodus, the slaughter of the Canaanites, and other violent texts could be regarded as necessary steps on the way to the revelation of God's vision through Jesus. As more was learned about the cultural milieu of the ancient Near East, it became possible to set Israel's developing consciousness over against the thinking and practices of other societies of the time. Comparing Israel's theological and moral sensibility to those of its neighbors allowed interpreters to present the violent depictions of God as products of the time, while simultaneously exhibiting ethical advancements over the brutal practices of other peoples. So, for example, it could be argued that biblical wars were actually more humane or were constrained by higher ethical dictates than those conducted by the other powers of Israel's time.

Set within a theological framework, this thinking led to the idea of progressive revelation, which holds that God met the Israelites and their forebears at the level of their understanding and progressively revealed truths that lifted Israel to a higher and truer vision of God and human dignity. It could be argued that God progressively led Israel from polytheism to an ethical monotheism that prepared the way for God's full revelation in Jesus Christ. At every point, God accommodated the values and perspectives of the people at the time, utilizing familiar forms to convey new truths. Directed toward the prosecution of war, the scheme could explain God's involvement in Israel's wars both as a sign of accommodation to Israel and as a means of teaching Israel. By commanding the Israelites to follow divine directives and initiative in battle, God took decisions about war out of human hands. Prohibitions against taking plunder taught that war could not be justified by the lust for booty. Even commands to slaughter entire populations could be explained as lessons about human dignity, in that summary killing implicitly preempted practices of torture.[4]

Progressive revelation as an explanatory grid for divine violence highlights an important thread in the incarnational character of God's relationship with Israel and therefore has much to commend it. God appropriated the suzerain-vassal treaty from the sphere of international relations to enable Israel to understand the covenant relationship that bound the nation to God at Sinai. God appropriated and historicized agricultural festivals so that they became occasions to remember what God had done for Israel as they marked the cycle of seasons. God acquiesced to Israel's demand for a

---

4. For more information, see Eryl W. Davies, "The Morally Dubious Passages of the Hebrew Bible: An Examination of Some Proposed Solutions," *CBR* 3 (2005): 199–208.

king and accommodated his working through Israel to a monarchical system that resembled those of the surrounding nations. The incarnation of God in Jesus Christ indeed represents the quintessential act of divine revealing within the context of human experience.

The evolutionary approach, however, whether framed as progressive revelation or the historical development of Israelite religion, fails to offer a comprehensive explanation for divine violence in the Bible. It is not clear, for one thing, that Israel's God was any less violent than the gods of the surrounding nations, nor that the nations were more savage than Israel. The Bible's account of the annihilation of Canaanite populations goes beyond what is attested in the military literature of other nations, where mass killing was generally undertaken against rebellious cities but not entire people groups. Then there is the question of the developmental framework itself. Dating the composition of biblical texts to particular points in time is a notoriously slippery enterprise. In many instances, it is difficult to know with any degree of confidence whether a given text reflects a primitive or a later mode of thought. Furthermore, many texts that likely reflect later expressions of Israelite thought contain some of the most violent imagery and sentiments: Isaiah's prophecy of God coming up from Edom in garments spattered with the blood of the nations he has trampled is a salient example (Isa 63:1-6).

Representative Contemporary Approaches

The last decade has seen a proliferation of studies that address the problem of divine violence through a framework that joins historical analysis to Christian theology. In light of the sheer number of book-length and shorter studies, a review of three of the most prominent works affords the best way to get a sense of the contemporary biblical discussion. The works I review below, while different in the particulars of their proposals, hold similar assumptions and look to historical factors to help explain some of the more troubling aspects of divine violence. Each approaches the problem of divine violence, not to mention Scripture itself, from the context of faith and with a determination to deal with violent texts forthrightly and faithfully for the sake of the Church. The authors practice a critical approach that challenges conventional interpretations, refuses simplistic responses, and takes into account the diversity of ethical perspectives expressed in the Bible.

In *The Violence of Scripture*, Eric Seibert undertakes a comprehensive treatment of those Old Testament texts, images, and themes that implicate

God in violence, either directly or through human agents. He aims to shift Christian interpretation and practice away from sanctioning violence in the name of God toward a nonviolent reading stance that conforms to the image of the loving and just God revealed through Jesus Christ.[5] Seibert bases his approach on a simple premise: "the Bible should never be used to inspire, promote, or justify acts of violence."[6] The premise is based on the conviction, which Seibert discusses in *Disturbing Divine Behavior*, that God's moral character is expressed most clearly and fully in Jesus Christ.[7] A second premise holds that God's character remains consistent over time.

On the basis of these premises, Seibert employs a Christocentric hermeneutic, which holds that "the God Jesus reveals should be the standard, or measuring rod, by which all Old Testament portrayals of God" should be evaluated.[8] Since the God revealed by Jesus rejects violence, Seibert argues that violent depictions of God in the Old Testament cannot be true. They should instead be understood as the products of human writers who expressed their experience of God according to ancient Near Eastern conceptions of the gods. The warrior God of the Old Testament, incompatible with the God revealed in the New, reflects "culturally conditioned explanations of divine involvement in warfare" that express the violent thought-world of the ancient Near East but which do not reflect "what God actually said and did."[9] In short, violent images represent a textual depiction of God that must not be confused with what God really said and did. When measured by the revelation of God in Jesus Christ, biblical images of violence are erroneous and distorted, and must not be accepted as reflecting who God truly is.

Like Seibert, in *The Violence in Scripture* Jerome Creach advocates reading the Bible with the conviction that "the Bible is a work that points to Christ."[10] Unlike Seibert, however, he does not reject violent depictions of God outright but rather views them as "an integral part of the Bible's authoritative word to the church."[11] For Creach, reading the Bible with Christ as

---

5. Eric A. Seibert, *The Violence of Scripture: Overcoming the Old Testament's Troubling Legacy* (Minneapolis: Fortress, 2012).

6. Seibert, *The Violence of Scripture*, 148.

7. Eric A. Seibert, *Disturbing Divine Behavior: Troubling Old Testament Images of God* (Minneapolis: Fortress, 2009).

8. Seibert, *Disturbing Divine Behavior*, 185.

9. Seibert, *The Violence of Scripture*, 117–18.

10. Jerome F. D. Creach, *Violence in Scripture*, Interpretation: Resources for the Use of Scripture in the Church (Louisville: Westminster John Knox, 2013), 5.

11. Creach, *Violence in Scripture*, 3.

the organizing center of the canon prompts interpreters to discern aspects of violent texts that reflect what is central or normative for the whole. When set within the context of the entire sweep of Scripture, many violent texts may be recognized as actually condemning violence, teaching that violence is an affront to God and pointing to a nonviolent ideal.

Creach's approach to interpreting violent texts incorporates five components. First, the biblical canon, taken as a whole, presents violence as a human activity that opposes the reign of God. Second, many difficult passages that appear to endorse violence contain self-correcting features that undercut the violence they report. Third, attention to the historical circumstances within which the biblical texts were composed must be taken into account in order to resist simplistic interpretations; the writer's intention is to be taken into account particularly in the case of narrative texts. Fourth, the figural reading practiced by the early church illumines the symbolic character of much of the biblical canon; Pharaoh and the Amalekites may assume greater significance within the context of the whole canon, becoming symbols of evil and depravity. Finally, the Bible sanctions violence when violence advances God's work of justice and liberation, but such instances also convey that the execution of violence in the service of justice lies within the purview of God and not humans.

Creach skillfully applies the historical-critical method to a number of key texts and in the process demonstrates both the diversity of canonical perspectives and the importance of addressing various genres appropriately. While attentive to the ways that violent Old Testament texts point to God's restorative acts and ends as revealed in Jesus Christ, he does not attempt to reconcile the discrepancies that arise when the texts are put into conversation with each other. Creach does not summarily reject texts and imagery that associate God with violence, calling instead for reading each depiction in light of the biblical whole.

Gregory Boyd's two-volume *Crucifixion of the Warrior God* has recently offered a third approach for interpreting violent depictions of God.[12] Boyd shares with Seibert the conviction that the God revealed in Jesus Christ is altogether nonviolent and so sees violent depictions of God, when taken at face value, as incompatible with God's revelation through Christ. On the other hand, he shares with Creach the conviction that the whole biblical corpus comprises an inspired, authoritative revelation to the Church. The challenge

---

12. Gregory A. Boyd, *The Crucifixion of the Warrior God: Interpreting the Old Testament's Violent Portraits of God in Light of the Cross*, 2 vols. (Minneapolis: Fortress, 2017).

as Boyd sees it is to discern how those texts that implicate God in violence "actually point to Jesus, whose identity, life, and ministry are centered on the revelation of the self-sacrificial, *agape*-love of God most fully disclosed on the cross."[13] Drawing on the allegorical method advocated by Origen, Boyd suggests that violent depictions of God present invitations to discern a deeper message that witnesses to God's self-giving love. He therefore proposes that we read violent texts with the assumption that "'something else is going on' when we encounter violent divine portraits in the OT."[14] The interpretive task, when dealing with texts of divine violence, is therefore to discover how the text reflects a meaning worthy of God.

To discern this worthy meaning, Boyd proposes that we read texts of divine violence through the supreme revelation of the self-giving, unconditionally nonviolent love that God displayed through Jesus Christ on the cross. At the cross, God condescended to bear the ugliness of human sin. Texts that impute violence to God, in a similar way, manifest God's love that condescends to take on and mirror the ugliness of human sin. Faith is required to lift the veil of ugliness that clothes these texts, so that the beauty of God's self-giving love may be revealed. Violent texts therefore become "literary crucifixes" that take on the appearance of human sin but reveal self-giving love as it is manifested through divine condescension.

To guide readers from mirror to message, Boyd advances a "Cruciform Hermeneutic" comprising four principles. The first, which he calls the "Principle of Cruciform Accommodation," proposes that God breathed on the human authors of Scripture the same divine love displayed on the cross, but their fallen and culturally conditioned human minds got in the way of what God was breathing through them. Boyd commends the doctrine of progressive relevation as an apt way of recognizing the extent to which God accommodated to earlier human perceptions along a trajectory that culminated in God's self-revelation at the crucifixion. God condescended to be portrayed in deficient human modes throughout the Old Testament, as well as to take on the appearance of sin on the cross. The cross, then, becomes both the revelation that God was working toward all along and the means by which we realize the shortcomings of the violent depictions that came before.

> With the cross as our criterion, we can assess that, insofar as any canonical divine portrait reflects the true cruciform character of God, it

---

13. Boyd, *The Crucifixion of the Warrior God*, 1:xxxii.
14. Boyd, *The Crucifixion of the Warrior God*, 2:633.

participates in the beauty of the cross that reflects God acting toward. But insofar as any divine portrait falls short of the true cruciform character of God, it participates in the ugliness of the cross that reflects God humbly allowing the sin of the world to act upon him.[15]

Boyd argues that God accommodated to the extent that he allowed himself to be depicted as saying and doing things inconsistent with his character; in so doing, God took on the ugly character of his people's sin and curse. Just as we look past Jesus who became sin for us on the cross to see the self-giving love of God, so we must listen through the sin-stained testimonies of the biblical God in order to hear the true, revelatory voice of God.

The "Principle of Redemptive Withdrawal," secondly, is based on the recognition that the wrath suffered by Christ on the cross for our sin was expressed by the withdrawal of God's protective presence in response to Jesus's willing submission. Boyd takes from this that God is not a God of coercion but of persuasion. He therefore directs readers to regard all biblical texts that report God's direction of violent punishment as occasions when God undertook similar withdrawals from sinful subjects in order to accomplish redemptive ends. In other words, although many texts report that God acted violently, they recount in fact instances in which God did nothing more than withdraw divine protection.

The "Principle of Cosmic Conflict" sets the cross, as well as biblical revelation as a whole, within the framework of God's ancient struggle with Satan and fallen spiritual powers. The principle of God's redemptive withdrawal thus means that many instances of divine violence (such as killing of the firstborn in Egypt) were actually perpetrated by Satanic powers who brought suffering and destruction on the unprotected objects of God's judgment. The "Principle of Semi-Autonomous Power," finally, holds that the biblical God entrusts agents with supernatural authority but chooses not to control how they wield that authority. While Jesus constitutes the epitome of faithful use of divine authority, fallen human agents characteristically use divine power imperfectly. Thus, some violence attributed to God actually constitutes imperfect exertions of divine power by those entrusted with it.

My brief summary of these important studies cannot adequately express my appreciation for their acumen and candor. I select these three works because each of them incorporates an approach that appears prominently in the contemporary discourse about divine violence in the Bible. Each strives

---

15. Boyd, *The Crucifixion of the Warrior God*, 1:495.

to take into account the whole of the biblical canon and the diverse literature that comprises it. Each presents a set of guidelines or principles designed to explain the disparate portraits of the violent God of the Bible. Finally, each in various ways incorporates the historical-critical paradigm to support its proposals. In particular, the writers focus on the composition of the texts, which lies at the center of the historical-critical project. Each takes a historical turn to defuse the offense of the violent God by claiming to know what biblical authors thought and intended.

Approaches to the conquest of Canaan—arguably the most disturbing of the texts that implicate God in violence—demonstrate the particular historical-compositional move each author makes. Both Seibert and Creach follow the mainstream of modern scholarship and affirm that the conquest never actually happened. Instead, they view the narrative as a pious fabrication composed during the reign of King Josiah in order to inspire devotion to Yahweh. The violence of the book, therefore, reflects the violent world of Assyrian imperial domination and its traumatic effects on the people of Judah. Seibert notes that recognizing the fictitious character of this and related narratives "effectively exonerates God from certain kinds of morally questionable behavior" and frees interpreters from the plain sense to explore other alternatives[16] (although he also comments that the move does not ultimately resolve the offense).[17] Creach suggests that the book of Joshua is best read in a figurative sense, while Seibert suggests ways that a plain reading of Joshua may be taken up to expose and challenge religiously sanctioned violence.[18]

While also adopting the idea that texts of divine violence reflect the impact of cultural ideas and motifs, Boyd adopts a "Conservative Hermeneutical Principle" that inclines him to accept the essential historicity of the conquest narrative. As a result, he asserts that cultural filters distorted the way the characters in the drama understood what God was saying to them. Based on the fact that the use of the verbs for "wiping out" and "removing" describe what Israel does or is to do in the book of Joshua, Boyd argues that God's original intention was to remove the Canaanites nonviolently. This, he suggests, would be accomplished by Yahweh using insects ("sending the hornet") and other means to make life in the land so intolerable that the Canaanites would finally leave of their own accord. This nonviolent plan,

---

16. Seibert, *Disturbing Divine Behavior*, 112.
17. Seibert, *The Violence of Scripture*, 98.
18. Seibert, *The Violence of Scripture*, 95–112.

however, was reworked by Israel, who misunderstood what Yahweh revealed in light of their "fallen, untrusting, disobedient, and culturally conditioned hearts and minds."[19] The misunderstanding extended to Israel's leaders.

> It should not surprise us if the low spiritual state and high degree of cultural conditioning of Moses and the people . . . caused them to distort Yahweh's word by conforming it to what they expected to hear. While Yahweh had said, "you will possess the land," Moses and the people heard, "you must mercilessly destroy the indigenous population." And while Yahweh had said, "I will drive out the inhabitants," Moses and the people heard, "I will deliver the inhabitants over to you." . . . As is true of all violence, therefore, the violence that God's people engaged in as they entered this territory originated not in the will of God but in the fallen desires of Moses.[20]

The massacre of the Canaanites, in a nutshell, took place because "Moses and the people he led were incapable and/or unwilling to completely trust God and thus incapable and/or unwilling to hear, let alone obey, God's plans to have them take possession of the land nonviolently."[21] What ensues is a colossal misunderstanding of God's will by Israel and Moses. Yahweh is off the hook.

Although I practice historical-critical interpretation and agree that we can detect biblical authors' intentions to a certain extent, I do not believe that historical criticism can bear the theological weight placed on it by these and similar studies. While historical inquiry has proven a valuable tool for understanding the biblical text through its capacity to explain the worlds that produced the Bible, historical reconstructions fall short when they displace the biblical text as the basis for theological reflection. It is one thing to draw upon the fruit of historical research to elaborate aspects of the world presented by the biblical text. It is quite another to construct a hypothetical historical scenario in support of a theological reading, to set that scenario over against the biblical narrative, and then to use it to judge the theological witness of the biblical text as plainly rendered.

My concern here is not whether the conquest actually happened in something like the way Joshua reports it. That is a question that must be ad-

---

19. Boyd, *The Crucifixion of the Warrior God*, 2:974.
20. Boyd, *The Crucifixion of the Warrior God*, 2:979–80.
21. Boyd, *The Crucifixion of the Warrior God*, 2:971.

dressed by literary as well as historical modes of interpretation. Rather, I am concerned with the displacement of theological reflection from the biblical text and onto a platform of historical speculation. There are problems here simply on procedural grounds. For one thing, the hypothesis of a fabricated conquest narrative is itself a matter of conjecture—informed conjecture, to be sure, but conjecture nonetheless. While we have gained significant understanding, in broad strokes, of the societies, events, and cultural milieus that defined the ancient Near East in the Iron Age, we still have precious little to build on to assess and reconstruct accurately what shaped the thinking of Israelite priests and scribes during the reign of Josiah. We lack hard evidence to confirm the fabrication hypothesis, and there are no other known instances of an ancient society making up an origin narrative of conquest to connect it to the land. Conjecture proposes historical fabrication, which in turn removes the offense of massive, divinely orchestrated violence.

While I appreciate the thoughtfulness of Boyd's approach to the conquest, I find it particularly problematic. To assert that Moses (for one) distorted or misunderstood what God communicated runs afoul of the Pentateuch's insistence on the unique status of Moses as one who had direct access to and spoke directly with Yahweh. Moses's singular status is emphasized during a dramatic scene at the Tent of Meeting, when Yahweh informs Miriam and Aaron that God speaks with Moses in a way that provides perfect clarity about divine intentions:

> When there are prophets among you, I, Yahweh, will make myself known to them in visions and speak to them within dreams. Not so with my servant Moses. He is dependable amongst my entire house. Mouth to mouth I speak to him. In plain view and not in obscurity. He observes the very form of Yahweh. (Num 12:6-8)

The Pentateuch reinforces the dependability of Moses's words by declaring that he spoke to God "face to face," that is, directly and with full comprehension of the divine word (Exod 33:11; 14:14; Deut 34:10). This assertion is the foundation for Mosaic authority. Yahweh spoke to Moses with complete clarity. It is quite a stretch to assume anything different.

To ground theological conclusions on historical reconstructions or proposals about what ancient people were thinking— and then reject what the Bible plainly says on the basis of those reconstructions— situates theological conclusions on an unstable foundation. I am equally uncomfortable with the theological counterpart of this approach, the premise that divine revelation was flawed by its transmission through human authors, so that, in the words of Kenton Sparks, the Bible is "evidence that our fallen condition is so serious that it warps not only the cosmos but even the written word itself."[22] The strategy seems to me too simple a way to respond to the complex canonical testimony, because divine violence constitutes so much of that testimony, particularly in the Old Testament.[23] Does not the sheer scope and ubiquity of God's violence in the Bible demand that it be taken seriously as a significant element of God's interaction with a violent world?

Appealing to the New Testament to invalidate divine violence in the Old, whether with reference to the crucifixion narrative or the Sermon on the Mount, does not settle things because, as I will argue later, the meaning of the relevant texts is open to interpretation. Before adopting any approach that attempts to resolve the canonical contradiction, we should make every effort to understand the Bible in its own right. The impulse to unify, allegorize, or reject offensive texts flattens the Bible's complex and contentious theological witness. It leaves us, as Walter Brueggemann has written, "trapped in an interpretive practice that refuses to struggle with the deep complexity of the character of God. The question is exceedingly hard, and easy answers will not suffice."[24] The refusal to struggle, I suggest, goes hand in hand with an aversion to paradox and an impulse to resolve the tensions and contradictions that the canon, as a whole, sets before its readers.

Back to the Book

I believe we cede too much when we accord the narratives of history a primary role in constructing a theological program or assessing the theological veracity of biblical texts. The truth the Bible speaks comes by way of the biblical text itself. Basing theological reflection on the canonical text accepts that the Bible as a whole, and even particular biblical texts, presents diverse and sometimes clashing depictions and claims about God. Rather than approaching the Bible as a book from the past and about the past, I will approach the Bible as a revelatory text that speaks the truth about God, hu-

---

22. Kenton L. Sparks, *Sacred Word, Broken Word: Biblical Authority and the Dark Side of Scripture* (Grand Rapids: Eerdmans, 2012), 157.

23. I borrow this idea from Peter C. Craigie's fine little book, *The Problem of War in the Old Testament* (Grand Rapids: Eerdmans, 1978), 11-12.

24. Walter Brueggemann, "Warrior God," review of *Violence in Scripture*, by Jerome F. D. Creach, *Christian Century*, December 25, 2013, 30-31.

manity, and the world in the here and now. The Bible explains who we are, who God is, and how we are to live with God in the world. In this capacity, it enables Christian readers to see as God sees and to so order our lives by that vision that we may participate in what God is doing in the world we live in.

I therefore seek to address the violence of the biblical God by reading the canonical text with a focus on how it narrates God's experience of and work in a violent world. In this, I follow the work of such Old Testament scholars as Walter Brueggemann, Terence Fretheim, and John Goldingay,[25] who have recentered theological reflection on the biblical text's rendering of God, as opposed to hypotheses about what ancient writers were thinking or saying about God. I regard the following as aspects of the Bible's testimony about God.

- The biblical God is *personal*—"a fully articulated personal agent, with all the particularities of personhood and with a full repertoire of traits and actions that belong to a fully formed and actualized person."[26] God is known to Israel, and later to the followers of Jesus, as an embodied being who possesses both rationality and emotion.
- The biblical God is a profoundly *relational* deity—"relationality is basic to the very nature of God."[27] God seeks relationships, makes the divine self known through relationships, and enlists human partners as participants in the divine work in the world. God creates humanity to care for the earth and manage a burgeoning creation (Gen 1:28; 2:8). The covenant that God establishes with Israel formalizes a relationship of reciprocal choosing, in which Israel becomes God's treasured possession and God becomes the sole divine object of Israel's devotion. The God incarnate in Jesus seeks and calls disciples and shares the divine life with them.
- God's decision to form authentic relationships with human partners means that *God freely decides to give up a measure of control*, for "any re-

---

25. See, among many works, Walter Brueggemann, *An Unsettling God: The Heart of the Hebrew Bible* (Minneapolis: Fortress, 2009); also Walter Brueggemann, *Old Testament Theology: An Introduction* (Nashville: Abingdon, 2008); Michael J. Chan and Brent A. Strawn, eds., *What Kind of God? Collected Essays of Terence E. Fretheim*, Siphrut 14 (Winona Lake, IN: Eisenbrauns, 2015); and Terence E. Fretheim, *God and World in the Old Testament: A Relational Theology of Creation* (Nashville: Abingdon, 2005); John Goldingay, *Old Testament Theology*, 3 vols. (Downers Grove, IL: InterVarsity Press, 2003-2009).

26. Brueggemann, *An Unsettling God*, 2.

27. Fretheim, *God and World*, 16.

lationship of integrity with a sharing of power means that God will have to make adjustments to what God plans to do in the world. Each party to the relationship must give up any monopoly on power for the sake of the relationship."[28] This means that, although God has goals and ends in mind that will be accomplished, the manner and means by which God's ends are met have much to do with the actions and responses of the human partners. As a result, God adapts what God is doing in the world in response to the actions and words of human partners.

- God's relationship with humanity and the world, finally, means that *what happens in the world affects God deeply*. God's decision to form relationships and work with human partners means that God's life is bound closely with the life of the world and with those God befriends. This involves both risk and vulnerability. The language of emotion, as it is manifested through God's actions and words, conveys the intensity of God's involvement with humanity, whether expressed by rejoicing or anger.

A Narrative Approach to the Violence of the Biblical God

As may be apparent by now, I do not believe that there is a definitive, all-encompassing explanation for the problem of divine violence in the Bible. No template, unifying paradigm, or set of principles can fully account for the diverse array of divine depictions in the Bible. Nor does the Bible, as I read it, provide categorical and unquestionable guidelines that can be called upon to demarcate clearly how to respond faithfully to every instance or context of violence. I feel deeply the attraction of the quest for a Theory of Biblical Everything and recognize that it arises from a faithful desire to be holy people in the unholy mess of our world. We want to know what the boundaries are, and we seek unambiguous moral mandates so that we can know what is right to do and have the confidence that we are doing it.

Yet the quest for certitude comes with a price. It presents the illusion that ethical decisions are always clear-cut and that what is primarily required, in any situation, is the correct application of the right principle. It does not acknowledge the complexity of ethical decision-making that must be undertaken within a world that sometimes allows *no* good answers, where

---

28. Terence E. Fretheim, *The Suffering of God: An Old Testament Perspective*, Overtures to Biblical Theology 14 (Philadelphia: Fortress, 1984), 36.

the conditions of endemic global brokenness can sometimes tinge even the most ardent efforts to do the right thing with the stain of sin, and where pure intentions may not necessarily find opportunity for holy expression. The pursuit of certitude also has the capacity to generate divisive sentiments that dismiss or exclude fellow Christians who come to different conclusions that stand outside principled boundaries.[29]

I do not aspire, therefore, to offer yet another comprehensive study of divine violence but rather will inquire into the role violence plays in the story the Bible tells about God's involvement with the world. The Bible's testimony to God, I propose, is fundamentally a *narrated* testimony. While the Bible is not a narrative *per se*, the structure of the biblical canon—beginning with creation in Genesis and ending with a renewed creation in Revelation—signals that the contents are joined together by an underlying story. Both the Old and New Testaments reinforce the primacy of the narrative vision by opening with narratives and narrative complexes. The Christian Old Testament begins by relating God's work from creation to exile (Genesis through 2 Kings) and then rewinds to tell and extend the story again through different voices (1 Chronicles through Esther). The New Testament begins by narrating the story of God's work through Jesus Christ from four different perspectives. By situating narratives at the beginning of both testaments, the Bible presents the testimonies of God's saving work as the first order of biblical business. One must know the story in order to interpret what follows.

The biblical narratives, furthermore, reinforce the primacy of the story by serving as the medium within which most of other forms of literature are embedded. Genealogies, laws, songs, liturgical instruction, and other types of literature are interspersed at strategic points throughout the narrative of the Pentateuch. The law codes are a particularly striking example. The so-called Covenant Code (Exod 20:1–23:33) is situated within the story of the covenant-making at Sinai. Its placement within the story demonstrates that Israel's laws are not self-standing entities but rather arise from and serve the purposes of God's saving work in and through the covenant people. Jesus's teachings likewise are customarily embedded within brief narrative contexts, which occasion his words. We may therefore think of the Bible

29. On this matter John J. Collins presses even further in a challenge to biblical critics. He writes, "The Bible has contributed to violence in the world precisely because it has been taken to confer a degree of certitude that transcends human discussion and argumentation. Perhaps the most constructive thing a biblical critic can do toward lessening the contribution of the Bible to violence in the world, is to show that that certitude is an illusion." "The Zeal of Phinehas," *JBL* 122 (2003): 3–21.

as having a narrative spine. All other forms and genres of biblical literature are to be interpreted with reference to their connections to the story of God's work in the world.

The Bible's narrative vision resists the imposition of a principalizing hermeneutic. Conventionally speaking, narratives make sense of human experience in space and time by rendering a vision of the world that connects a series of events into an explanatory whole. The content may be fictional or historical, this-worldly or otherworldly, but to be effective a narrative must convey some insight into life as it is experienced by its audience. Narratives work by constructing a world and inviting readers, viewers, or hearers into that world—to walk around in it, experience it, try it on, try it out, and see if it fits and brings insight or confirmation. Bundled into the mix is a complex of convictions, values, images, and perspectives that influence what parts of the story a narrative tells, how it tells it, and why it tells the story in a particular way.

The act of telling stories constructs, negotiates, and reinforces a sense of identity—the idea of who I or we are in relation to others and to the world that forms the basis for our moral vision and actions. Every exercise in storytelling is in some way an act of identity formation and maintenance. This can be illustrated by the stories that families commonly tell when they gather. If your family is like mine, family get-togethers often lead to telling stories we've told and heard many times before. Sharing the stories is not only entertaining but also binds us and reminds us of who we are as a family, what we regard as our distinctive attributes, what values we hold, the people with whom we associate, and so on. Certain stories are told often, not because we are worried we will forget them, but because those stories in some way express the essence of how we see ourselves in relationship to each other and the world.

Every group, whether a family or a nation, tells its stories in its own way. Group narratives in particular not only encode values and perspectives but also the customs and motifs that express the group's distinctive ways of thinking and knowing. In the case of narratives like those in the Bible, which were written in a culture we no longer have access to, the insights offered by historical study can provide valuable insights into symbols, motifs, and customs that configure the world the narrator presents.

I use the word "narrator" rather than "author" intentionally. "Narrator" identifies the voice that tells the story as opposed to the "author," the person who actually composed the narrative. The distinction is important because it alerts readers to the possibility that the voice presenting the story world is not necessarily that of the individual who wrote it. So, for example, a wide range of factors persuade many biblical interpreters that the visions narrated by a person named Daniel were not composed by an exiled Jew living in the time of Nebuchadnezzar, whose story is recounted earlier in the book. The authorial distinction is important when exploring the question of how and why the book of Daniel was composed but is not decisive when the task is determining how the book works as a whole.

Narrators tell their stories from particular perspectives and in order to convey a particular sense of what their story means. If you have ever been asked to share your story—perhaps as a testimony to God's work in your life—you have an idea of how this works. Important decisions have to be made so you can convey to your audience the meaning of your story. Where and how should I begin? What events must be told? Which to summarize or expand? Which people have played a significant role in my story, and how do I talk about them so that others will grasp the role they have played? How can I draw and keep people's interest, so that they don't check out before I'm done? And so on. Narrators shape their stories so that hearers or readers will grasp the meaning they see in them.

Biblical narrators tend to value brevity and subtlety. They often leave big holes in the story that invite speculation. (Where did Cain's wife come from? Who on earth were the Nephilim?) They appear to tell their stories not so much to provide answers and certitude for life's questions as to present the complexity of life in relation to God and in the midst of the maddening confusion of a world where answers are not always self-evident. Biblical narrators tell their stories to give readers a vision of the world, to provoke reflection, response, and perhaps even prayer and so ultimately direct faithful readers to the One to whom the stories point.

Not all biblical stories, moreover, are related by a single narrator. Some biblical stories are told as if by a panel, with a boisterous and contentious assemblage of voices vying with each other to tell their side of their story, carrying the thread of the story at times, and interrupting, interjecting, correcting, and commenting at others. Some of the most pronounced of these narration-by-panel texts cluster around those stories that implicate God in the most massive manifestations of violence, that is, the narratives about the flood, Israel's exodus from Egypt, and Israel's invasion of Canaan, as if explaining the import of violence on this scale could not be meaningfully rendered by just one narrating voice.[30]

---

30. One of the most important contributions of historical-critical research on the biblical text is the recognition and description of the multi-voiced narration of many biblical narra-

Readers and listeners, on the other hand, bring their own experiences, values, and perspectives with them as they enter and engage the narrative. They see different things, gravitate toward different parts of the story, and identify with different characters. Some don't even care to follow the narrator's clues and make of the story what they will. I take it for granted that Christian readers do not populate this last group (at least not intentionally) and want not only to engage the story but also to ascertain the meaning the narrator sees in the story. I raise the reader's engagement, first of all, as a way of pointing to the openness and fluidity that mark the interpretation of narratives. The narrator, by configuring the story in a certain way, suggests a trajectory of meaning but leaves significant latitude for filling in the gaps and shaping the contours according to experience and perspective. Equally important is to note that what a reader brings to the story plays a significant role in what the reader observes and what the reader makes of the story. And that includes people who are writing books about biblical narratives and divine violence! Reading biblical narratives, then, calls for a particular interpretive posture. It entails, for Christian readers, embracing them as testimonies that speak truth about God, humanity, and the world—as a definitive truth that contests the competing narratives that clamor to define reality and human existence.

The world depicted in the Bible's narrative literature is uniformly violent. It permeates human dispositions and interactions in relationship to others and to the world's creator. Violence, the narrative testifies, arises organically from the world that human beings make for themselves. This world is not, however, the world that God made or intends. That world is glimpsed briefly at the beginning of the story, but is quickly lost. In what follows, God enters the world to recover the world, only to be drawn into the mechanisms and systems of violence that God seeks to overcome.

---

tives. Historical criticism has been interested in how these voices reflect different authors and editors who have shaped the narratives over the course of time, revising the story in light of Israel's experiences. This interpretive trajectory continues today in projects defining who these writers were, what historical and social circumstances prompted their revisions, and the perspectives they wished to add to the stories. Where narrative critics see narrators, historical critics see authors and editors.

2

Creation Ruined and Remade

> Yahweh came down to look at the city and tower the human beings had constructed.
>
> GENESIS 11:5

Violence is not natural. While it is an element of the world as we know it, violence was not present at the beginning. The creation myths that explained the world for Israel's neighbors describe creation as the forceful subjugation of destructive powers. In these stories violence is the generative power that orders and reorders the world and protects the creation from chaos and destruction. Violence, therefore, is viewed as part of the warp and woof of creation—a force that defines relationships in the world and a necessary measure to ensure that order prevails. Israel's creation stories, however, present a God who creates and orders through the act of speaking. There is no hint of resistance or threat as God calls the world into being. Violence has no role and no place in the world that God speaks, nor in the interactions of the creatures that populate the world. Genesis instead explains violence as the product of humanity's determination to make the world in its own image and likeness. It is a destructive contagion that, once initiated, overwhelms the world and disintegrates the good work the Creator has made.

God's creating is a work of ordering, of setting the boundaries in place that provide space for life to flourish (Gen 1:1–2:4a). Beginning with a void of nothingness, an undifferentiated sameness, God creates a framework by dividing the daylight from the dark night, the waters above from the waters below, and the dry land from the seas. Then God fills in each space, creating the sun, moon, and stars for the dome that separates the waters; birds and sea creatures for the sky and waters; and animals to inhabit the land, culminating in the creation of humanity. After each stage God reviews the work and pronounces it good. The notion of the "good" has acquired a great deal of philosophical and theological freight, but in simple terms this "good" can be regarded as a description of the world as God created it to be. "Good" signifies whatever is in harmony with the design of creation as originally set in place.

The first creation story also reveals key attributes of the Creator. These set the trajectory for interpreting God's activity throughout the whole of the biblical narrative. I have already mentioned God's creation by speaking. The repeated act of speaking accentuates God's supremacy, power, and separation from the created world. There are no rival deities or powers to combat. God speaks and the world comes into being. God's speech is the mechanism for ordering the universe and bringing forth life. God's supremacy and God's speaking are thereby presented as essential components of an ordered, harmonious world. The Creator, furthermore, cares about the good, that is, the well-being of the creation. From this we may infer that God is concerned with maintaining the good, the original harmony and unity, for the sake of the creation.

God creates humanity to resemble the divine, apparently with the participation of a retinue of spiritual beings ("Let *us* make humanity in *our* own image, according to *our* likeness," v. 26). The idea of the image of God, like the notion of the good, has generated a vast discussion that we cannot engage here. It is sufficient to note that the phrase includes the idea that humanity is to function as the representative of the Creator's authority. This is made plain by the purpose God assigns to them: "Let them govern the fish of the sea, the birds of the sky, and every crawling thing that crawls on the land" (v. 26). Human beings are given an exalted place by way of a divine mandate to extend God's authority and dominion on the ground. This mandate reveals, as Terence Fretheim has observed, that God is willing to place limits on God's own activity with respect to creation. The Creator "chooses to share power in relationship, with a consequent self-limitation in the use of divine power and freedom."[1] The Creator thus is rendered as a God who prefers to work with creaturely partners and who willingly acknowledges limitations to divine power and activity as a collaborator.

---

1. Terence E. Fretheim, "The Self-Limiting God of the Old Testament," in *What Kind of God? Collected Essays of Terence E. Fretheim*, ed. Michael J. Chan and Brent A. Strawn (Winona Lake, IN: Eisenbrauns, 2015), 161.

God's speech to the human beings in vv. 28-30 both confirms their elevated status and the divine conferral of authority and also expresses the Creator's beneficence:

God blessed them and said to them, "Bear fruit and multiply. Fill the earth. Exert power over it and govern the fish of the sea, the birds of the sky, and every animal that crawls on the earth." Then God said, "See, I have given you every plant that bears seeds, on the surface of the earth, and every tree that yields fruit containing seeds. This shall be your food. And to every wild animal, every bird of the sky, and everything that crawls on the earth, everything that has the breath of life, I have given every green plant for food." And it was so.

The blessing and command express God's desire for human flourishing, as does the declaration that God has given seed-bearing vegetation to humans and animals alike for food. The addition of a second verb to the mandate to govern (Heb. *radah*) suggests that the application of force will be necessary for the task of governing creation and thus, on its face, hints that violence may in fact be required. The verb is commonly used to denote the subjugation of land or people (Num 32:33; Josh 18:1; 1 Chron 22:18; 2 Chron 28:10) and is conventionally translated "subdue." Yet it is difficult to see how this sense fits the context here. There has been no hint of any resistance or opposition to either God or humanity anywhere in the story, no opponent or obstacle that needs to be conquered. The action denoted by *radah* appears rather to signify the application of force in the service of authority. In context, and by virtue of its pairing with a verb signifying governing, the action is best understood as a notice that humanity's governing will require exertion. Creation is now self-generating, with burgeoning life ready to cover the earth. It will take some energy on the part of God's representative to manage the explosion of life in the world.

The second creation story (Gen 2:4b-25) elaborates the Creator's decision to create humanity as an agent of God's oversight of creation. In the account, the Creator—here bearing the name Yahweh God—is present within the creation that he has spoken. Adam, on the other hand, is distinguished both by his connection to and distinction from both the earth and the divine. Like the sprouting vegetation, Adam is a creature drawn from the earth, an association marked in the Hebrew text by his name; Yahweh God molds *Adam* from the *adamah*, "ground." (The name "Earthling" captures the Hebrew pun.) Yet Adam also receives the divine breath, reinforcing the first story's depiction of humanity's resemblance, as the image of God, to the Creator. Adam's mandate, as a creature who brings together the material and divine in his own person, is conveyed here not through divine command, as in the preceding account, but through a narrative report: he is to work the soil from which he was taken and care for the garden in which he has been placed (v. 15). In this sense, the story identifies humanity with reference to its connection to the land.

As in the first story, the declaration of Adam's role on the earth is followed by the Creator's generous provision (2:16-17; cf. 1:29-30). Yahweh God's directive conveys an expansive generosity and freedom to Adam in the context of creation:

> Yahweh God gave this command concerning Adam: "From every tree of the garden you may freely eat. But from the tree of the knowledge of good and bad you may not eat anything, because on the day you eat from it you will surely die." (2:16-17)

"Good and bad" is a figure of speech (like "heaven and earth") that conveys totality. Here, as elsewhere in the Bible, it refers to the decision-making categories of what is right and fitting (Deut 1:39; Lev 27:12, 14) and in conformity with creation (Eccl 12:14). Through this pronouncement, Yahweh God makes all creation available to humanity but reserves the right to determine what is good and what is bad for creation. Taken in this sense, the declaration plainly articulates the one thing necessary for creation to flourish. Only the one who created the world and all that is in it, who called that world "good," knows how to maintain that "good." Only the one who created the world has sufficient knowledge and wisdom to determine how it should be ordered.

Yahweh God reinforces the intention to employ Adam as an agent of dominion when Adam is enlisted to name the animals that have been created to populate the earth. Determining the identity of each creature asserts Adam's authority—and Yahweh's, by extension—over all the animals, in much the same way that Yahweh's later renaming of Abram to Abraham, Sarai to Sarah, and Jacob to Israel demonstrates the reestablishment of Yahweh's authority and the beginning of Yahweh's work to renew the world through human agents. The account is bracketed by references to Adam's solitary existence on earth and Yahweh's determination to bring a helper for him. It begins with Yahweh God deeming Adam's solitary existence as "not good" and declaring that a suitable partner will be made for him (v. 18), and it concludes with the narrator stating that no partner could be found for Adam among the animals (v. 20b). The narrative framing directs the reader to see the parade of animals and their naming as a process that Yahweh undertakes to alleviate Adam's solitude. Yahweh brings each animal to Adam to "see what he would call it" (v. 19), as if the process also enables Yahweh to learn about Adam based on Adam's responses. The naming then not only demonstrates Adam's role as the Creator's on-the-ground authority, but also Yahweh's interest in working with and getting feedback from Adam, in the spirit of a true, collaborative relationship.

The two creation stories, in sum, render a vision of the Creator's character and involvement in creation, and humanity's role within it. Yahweh is presented as simultaneously apart from yet deeply involved in the world that has been created, particularly in the relationship with Adam, whom Yahweh God has designed to manage a robust diversity of creatures. The stories highlight the Creator's beneficence, generosity, and concern for the world. Human beings bear the stamp of the Creator, embody aspects of the divine and the earthly, and are given the task of establishing and maintaining the Creator's dominion. Their relationship with the Creator involves a measure of give and take, yet is defined by their dependence on Yahweh's provision and blessing—a dependency that restricts them from making decisions about what is good for creation on their own initiative.

The Creator's commitment to creation, humanity's role as divine agent, and the relational nature of Yahweh's interaction with the incipient human community orient the reader to the explanation of the world that follows in Genesis 3:1-24. This account begins with a subtle shift in humanity's perception of the Creator, suggested by the craftiest of all creatures. The serpent suggests that the Creator is someone other than the generous being portrayed in the previous accounts: "Did God say, 'You must not eat from any tree in the garden'?" (v. 1). The negative rendering of Yahweh's original commandments ("You may freely eat . . . but not") suggests an entirely different divine persona. By rendering into the negative what the Creator originally spoke in the positive, the serpent implies that the Creator is demanding rather than beneficent. The serpent's version of the command intimates that the Creator cares primarily about keeping the rules and that humans are not in fact given access to what they need to flourish. As the "any tree" of the serpent's question corresponds grammatically to "the tree of the knowledge of good and evil," the serpent also suggests that the Creator cares more about preserving boundaries than about caring for the creation. A "you-must-not" God is a very different kind of deity than a "you-may-freely" one.

Eve is not easily persuaded. The serpent, however, continues to paint the Creator in dark hues. The crafty creature brazenly disputes Yahweh's warning that death will result from eating the tree, insinuating that Yahweh has misled the two humans. The serpent then suggests a reason for the deception: Yahweh knows that eating from the tree will bring insight, which will elevate the man and woman to godlike knowing and, by extension, to godlike authority. The irony is that, as bearers of the divine image, Adam and Eve are already like God. The serpent's words intimate, however, that Yahweh has misled them in order to protect divine supremacy over creation. We are left to ponder why Adam and Eve take the bait at this point, but whatever the case, the serpent's words reveal what lies at the core of a mangled creation, that is, humanity's desire to be God's equal and so to take the role of determining what is good for creation. The narrator confirms this state of affairs by identifying the tree's desirable wisdom as the enticement that draws Adam and Eve to defy Yahweh's commandment (3:6).

The impact is immediate. The original openness is lost and vulnerability enters human interactions. Each human being now hides a part of themselves from the other; Adam and Eve sew fig leaves together to cover their loins—the parts of their body that generate life (v. 7). They then hide from Yahweh God and, when discovered, engage in a sequence of recriminations that manifest each one's refusal to acknowledge their own responsibility for what has transpired (vv. 8–13).

Yahweh's response to the serpent, the woman, and the man has traditionally been interpreted as laying out the punishment for each of the offending creatures: the snake is condemned to eat dirt and be crushed underfoot, the woman receives intensified pain in childbirth and is relegated to a subordinate position to the man, and the man is doomed to wear himself out toiling on ground that resists him. Yet, while one cannot dismiss an element of punishment in the response, the portrayal of the Creator in the previous stories offers little support for the view that Yahweh's response is primarily punitive. Nor does the passage itself suggest that Yahweh responds out of anger or offense; Yahweh's speech to each party is introduced simply by "(Yahweh) said to . . ."

For these reasons, it seems better to read Yahweh's words more as description than decree. That is, Yahweh's words elaborate the contours of the world that the aspiring deities make for themselves. In the world that human beings make, there will be hierarchies of power; some (mainly men) will rule over others, and people will labor arduously to eke out a living, with constant exertion and disappointing results. The world that humans will make is incompatible with the world the Creator called good. Yahweh therefore sends Adam and Eve from the garden and from the life-sustaining tree within it. The original Eden becomes a foreign and inaccessible place, and human beings enter a broken world in which they function as gods, deciding for themselves what is good and evil.

Making Babies and Killing Brothers

The narrator presents the making and taking of life as the two basic elements of the human condition outside the garden. Immediately following the report of the couple's expulsion from the garden, we are told that Adam "knew" Eve and that Eve conceived and bore a son, whom she named "Cain." The explanation Eve gives for the name of Cain, the first human to be born, is cryptic: "I acquired (*qaniti*) a man with Yahweh" (4:1). The verb she employs (*qanah*) generally refers to the acquisition of property. Does the first mother, now living outside the garden, regard children as property? And what about the phrase "with Yahweh"? Most translators assume that Eve is acknowledging Yahweh's participation in the birth and thus supply the phrase "with the help of" Yahweh (e.g., NRSV, TNIV, ESV). The phrase, however, is ambiguous and could as easily refer to joint ownership, thus intimating that Eve views the child as Yahweh's property as well. The birth of Abel follows, at which point the narrator sets up the ensuing conflict by describing Abel as a shepherd and Cain as a farmer (4:2).

Also cryptic is the story that follows (4:3-17). Why does Yahweh accept Abel's offering of fat, which requires the killing of an animal, but disregard that of Cain, who tills the ground as Yahweh had directed Adam to do (3:23)? Our interest, however, is drawn to the story's reflection on the nature of violence. This first act of violence issues from anger and jealousy. Destructive impulses arise within the context of human interactions and differences and in response to divine inscrutability; Cain is incensed that Yahweh accepts Abel's offering but not his own (v. 5b).

Yahweh's response to the murder of Abel presents a marked contrast to Cain's impulsiveness. Yahweh hears about the death from the ground, which opens up to receive Abel's blood, and responds not with anger but with mercy. Yahweh does not kill Cain or decree that he should be killed for what he has done. Instead, Yahweh banishes him. When Cain protests that the banishment may result in his own death at the hands of another, Yahweh assures and protects him by putting a mark on him that will prevent him from being killed (vv. 14-15).

Most significant for our purpose is how the story addresses the topic of violence. First, the story associates violence with religious experience. Cain and Abel experience God in different ways, and as a result, one child kills the other. Second, the story presents violence as endemic to the human condition and a direct consequence of human sinfulness. This is communicated through the placement and the structure of the story. Murder is the topic of the first story about the first children. The narrator draws a direct connection with the defiant human autonomy that broke creation in the garden by casting Yahweh's response to Cain in the manner of Yahweh's response to Adam and Eve (3:17-24). As in the preceding story, Yahweh approaches Cain with questions (4:9-10; cf. 3:9-13), even repeating to Cain his question to Eve: "What have you done?" Yahweh also declares that Cain will be alienated from the ground, and there is an additional curse associated with the earth this time, though with Cain rather than the earth as the subject. Finally, Yahweh banishes Cain just as Adam and Eve were banished. By alluding to the garden narrative in this way, the narrator invites the reader to view the human violence in this story as something characteristic to all humanity.

Although Yahweh condemns Cain to wandering, Cain finds a place to settle down and builds a city (4:17). A brief genealogy follows, which expands in the sixth generation with Lamech. The list of names pauses at this point to report that two of his sons, through his wife Adah, established the way of life defined by tents and flocks (4:20) and developed instruments to play music (4:21). A third son through his wife Zillah, we are told, worked with all kinds of bronze and iron implements. The generation of Lamech and his children thus is linked with basic elements of human culture and society: livestock management, the arts, and technology.

The note expands even more, however, to report Lamech's boast that he killed a man for hitting him and that, if Cain was to be avenged sevenfold, he will be avenged seventy-sevenfold (4:23-24). The world that human beings make is thereby manifested, in the person of Lamech, with an escalation of violence and presumption. God is nowhere in the picture.

Wiping the Slate Clean

Given the escalation of violence in the human community, it comes as little surprise that humanity develops a deep-seated propensity for destructiveness that eventually warps every thought and action (Gen 6:5). The narrator begins by drawing attention to the impact that the situation has on Yahweh by bracketing Yahweh's resolution with statements of remorse for having made human beings:

Yahweh was sorry that he made humanity on the earth, and his heart was in turmoil.

Yahweh said, "I will erase humanity, whom I created, from the surface of the ground—humanity as well as the beasts, and creeping things, and those that fly in the sky—

because I'm sorry I made them." (6:6-7)

The bracketing comments lead us to see Yahweh's massive response to human wickedness as an expression of sorrow rather than anger or caprice. What humanity has become affects Yahweh deeply. The Hebrew verb *nacham*, here translated "sorry," holds together the human emotions of grief, regret, and a change of heart.[2] Yahweh's first *act* in response to human violence, the banishment and protection of Cain, is mercy. The first *emotion* attributed to Yahweh in response to human violence is sorrow. Together, these responses to human violence establish an important basis for viewing subsequent expressions of divine violence. First, Yahweh is emotionally invested in what happens to humanity; humanity's descent into destructiveness provokes turmoil in the Creator. Second, sorrow as the first divine response to human wickedness provides an important interpretive perspective for the occasions of divine anger that occur throughout the rest of the Bible. Divine anger, in other words, must be understood against the backdrop of divine sorrow.

A second overview clarifies why God decides to take the biblical version of the nuclear option. Humanity's pathology has infected the whole of creation. The earth is utterly ruined. All living things are utterly ruined. The entire created order is hopelessly in the grip of violence (6:11-13).

God announces the divine plan to Noah with words, in the Hebrew text of v. 13, that echo the narrator's description of the ruinous creation that God observes in v. 11. There are parallel references to what has come before (*lifne*) God (i.e., the ruin of creation in v. 11 and the end of all flesh in v. 13), to the earth being filled with violence, and, in an intriguing wordplay, to the ru-

---

2. John Goldingay, *Old Testament Theology*, vol. 1: *Israel's Gospel* (Downers Grove, IL: InterVarsity Press, 2003), 168.

ination (*shakhat*) of creation—something that God observes in v. 11 and sets into motion in v. 13. Most translations take God's opening words in v. 13 as a declaration of intent and attempt to preserve the wordplay in English. So, for example, "I have determined to make an end of all flesh, for the earth is filled with violence because of them; now I am going to destroy them along with the earth" (NRSV). The conventional translations, however, override the grammar of the Hebrew text, which makes a statement of fact rather than a declaration of intent. The construction suggests that God has seen where the ruination of creation is headed and has decided to accelerate the process to its completion. Barry Bandstra, in a recent grammatical study, captures the meaning of God's declaration succinctly:

> Deity is not the Subject of the clause, nor is a verb of cognition (determine or decided) used. Instead, the meaning of this clause is encoded with a material process that expresses movement, as if the notion of the demise of all flesh passed before deity and so made itself evident. In fact, the Hebrew construction distances deity from the decision making process, almost as if this outcome was inevitable.[3]

A wooden rendering of the Hebrew for vv. 12-13, in this sense, reads: "Yahweh looked at the earth. Look! It was ruined, for all flesh had ruined its way on the earth. God said to Noah, 'The end of all flesh has arrived right in front of me, for the earth is saturated with violence before them. Look! I'm going to ruin them with the earth.'"[4] The plain sense of the Hebrew text thus conveys something very different than English translations, which are perhaps influenced by the view of an angry, punitive deity.

God later specifies how the ruination will take place: "I am bringing a flood of water to ruin all flesh" (6:17). The flood, an ancient symbol of destruction and disorder, is a fitting medium for the dissolution of creation, as it overwhelms every boundary and returns creation to the primordial, undifferentiated "deep" that existed before Yahweh spoke boundaries into being. In the mythologies of the ancient Near East, the flood was a terrifying, uncontrollable force and the epitome of the threatening, anti-creation power of chaos (cf. Pss 69:2, 15; 124:4; Nah 1:8). In the hands of Israel's God,

---

3. Barry Bandstra, *Genesis 1-11*, Baylor Handbook on the Hebrew Text (Waco, TX: Baylor University Press, 2008), 358.

4. The phrase "the end has come" signifies the endpoint of a process of degeneration and thus a return to chaos (cf. Jer 51:13; Ezek 7:2-7; Amos 8:2).

the flood is likewise an anti-creation force that dissolves the ordering mechanisms and structures that allow life to flourish in the world. Yet, it is also an instrument of the Creator, wielded now against a creation already well on its way to oblivion. Yahweh, as the psalmist proclaims, sits enthroned over the flood (29:10).

We are left with the sense that God is not so much sending the flood to punish the world as facilitating, through the flood, the inevitable descent into chaos caused by human destructiveness and violence. God ruins an already ruined creation, and in so doing creates the conditions for a reordering and a renewal to take place.

This more restrained view of Yahweh's decision to send the flood finds support from the way the narrator relates what God does in the story. The narrator relates no *action* on the part of Yahweh other than seeing (vv. 5, 12) and saying (vv. 7, 13). God *says* a lot about the flood, but, at least the way the narrator tells it, God doesn't *do* much. There is no direct report that Yahweh sent the flood or caused the waters to rise. We are simply told that the floodwaters came and water burst out of the earth and rained down from the sky (7:10-12). Aside from a note that Yahweh closed the hatch for Noah (7:16), God remains out of the picture when the action takes place.

God only reenters the narrative after the flood has done its work, and then only by way of a summary that repeats what Yahweh said at the beginning of the account. The summary simply confirms that Yahweh acted as foretold: "He erased every living being on the surface of the ground, from humanity to the beasts, creeping things, and those that fly in the sky. They were erased from the land. Only Noah and those with him in the ark were left" (7:23; cf. 6:7).

The summary leads into the next scene, which begins with two divine actions: "God kept Noah in mind, as well as every animal and beast with him in the ark. Then God made a wind blow across the earth, and the water receded" (8:1). The two sentences—the first about thinking and the second about doing—echo the divine thinking and doing that began the episode. They also signal how we are to understand what has happened and how we are to view what will ensue. The first sentence employs a verb generally translated by the English verb "remember." It is the first of many occasions in the Old Testament in which God "remembers" a person during a time of trouble and intervenes with an act of deliverance. Such remembering presupposes a prior relationship that God values, on the basis of which God acts. So God remembers Abraham and spares Lot from the destruction meted out to Sodom and Gomorrah (19:29). God remembers the childless Rachel, listens to her plea, and opens her womb (30:22). God hears the groans of the Israelites in Egypt and remembers the covenant with Abraham, Isaac, and Jacob (Exod 2:24).

The sentence prompts us to view what God does next as an act of deliverance. The particular action, sending wind across the water, evokes a conventional motif in ancient creation narratives and alludes to the biblical creation account, which begins with a divine wind hovering over the surface of the primeval water (Gen 1:2). The connection is more easily seen in Hebrew than in English translations, which typically render the Hebrew *ruakh* "wind" in the flood story but "spirit" in the creation story. The report signals, at this strategic juncture, that we are to understand what happens next as an act of creation, or, perhaps better, re-creation. The floodwaters have returned the earth to its pre-creation state and so have generated the condition for a reboot of the creation project. The slate has been wiped clean and is now ready for a new design. God remains passive as the flood covers the earth but intervenes in a saving way once the old world has been submerged.

That Yahweh is at work re-creating the world becomes clear when Noah and his family disembark from the ark. After dry ground appears again, God tells Noah and his family to leave the ark and release all the animals inside it "that they may be fruitful and multiply across the earth" (8:17b). The declaration echoes a similar command in the creation story (1:22). The command is later repeated directly to the human characters, in the context of blessing, just as it is in the creation narrative: "God blessed Noah and his children and said to them, 'Be fruitful and multiply, and fill the earth'" (9:1; cf. 9:7; 1:28). Furthermore, Yahweh affirms that the order of creation, marked by its cycles and seasons, has been reestablished and will continue into the future (8:22).

This is not, however, an entirely new creation. The waters that cover the world carry a remnant of the old creation, namely Noah's family and the animals with him in the ark. To be sure, the creation has been renewed, but the original harmony between the Creator, humanity, and creation has not been completely restored. This is apparent first of all in what Yahweh says to Noah and his family after he blesses them and commands them to be fruitful and multiply. In the creation story, God tells the man and woman to subdue and exercise dominion over the creatures of the earth, and he gives them the plants for food (1:28–29). To Noah and his family, however, God follows the blessing and the command to fill the earth with the declaration that all animals will be terrified of human beings, yet are nonetheless given into their power (9:2).

CREATION RUINED AND REMADE

God grants the humans permission to eat animals and then comments on the shedding of blood: that of animals (vv. 3-4) and then of humans (vv. 5-6). In the latter instance, God pointedly declares that God will hold accountable anyone or anything that sheds human blood and that anyone who spills human blood will have his or her own blood shed. The reason: God made humanity in the divine image (v. 6). The reference to humanity as the divine image-bearer here turns the creation declaration on its head. In the creation story, the creation of humanity constitutes the capstone to a diverse, unified, and harmonious creation, and the image of God ennobles humanity (1:27). In the aftermath of the flood, however, the image of God is associated cryptically with the extremity of violence that haunts human affairs after humanity has been expelled from the garden. Violence will be as endemic to the post-flood world as it was to the world the flood wiped away. Erasing all that lived and breathed in the old world, in other words, has not put an end to human violence and the damage it does to the creation.

Yahweh appears to acknowledge and accept this reality and decides to continue working in and through creation in spite of it. Yahweh will not ruin the world again through a flood. The change in Yahweh's disposition seems to come as a result of the offerings that Noah makes after leaving the ark. The narrator informs us that the smoke of the offerings pleased Yahweh and then gives us a window into Yahweh's thoughts: "I will never again curse the ground because of humanity, for humanity is predisposed toward destruction from an early age. And I will never again strike every living thing as I have done" (8:21). Yahweh realizes that human beings are violent beings, but Yahweh's first inclination is to refrain from violence in return. Noah's expression of gratitude and respect seems to have given Yahweh hope that human beings are not entirely ruined.

Noah may even give cause for optimism. He seems originally to have drawn Yahweh's attention by the fact that he was a man of moral integrity (6:8, 9). He lived in the old saturated-with-violence world and yet did not succumb to it. Noah, unlike Adam and Eve, is not innocent or naive. He is battle-tested. Immersed for his entire life in a world hell-bent on destruction, he has experienced the full force of human wickedness and successfully resisted it. This certainly presents a more hopeful scenario as creation is reset. Noah knows well the twisted operations of human wickedness. Adam and Eve may have been taken in by a slick-talking serpent, but Noah knows the end of that path. What better person to start over with?

Yahweh responds to Noah's sacrificial expression of respect and gratitude by making a unilateral covenant with Noah and his descendants, and with all of creation. The terms bind Yahweh never to ruin the earth with another flood (9:8–17). We cannot here address the complex of issues that has fascinated interpreters of this passage. Sufficient for our purpose is to note that, in establishing this covenant with creation, Yahweh binds the divine self to humanity and creation. Yahweh in other words is "all in" with creation despite all its violent messiness. This is a significant move for the Creator, who now understands the futility of trying to eradicate violence within creation itself. At this point, we do not know how Yahweh will deal with the world as it is. But we do know, through Yahweh's declaration, that Yahweh will not again bring about the disintegration of the entire created order. In binding the divine self to humanity and creation, Yahweh has placed a limit on how Yahweh will respond to human wickedness from this point on.

The second creation is distinguished from the original creation because it is also an act of salvation. We are not told what prompts God to speak the original creation into being. Such is not the case, however, with the creating that God does after the flood. God undertakes a new act of creation for the sake of Noah and the remnant of the old world with him in the ark. Saving coalesces with creating. God's creative work sets a precedent for Yahweh's activity in the world that follows, in which creation will take place through acts of salvation.

Even so, Yahweh remains distant from creation. The narrator's depiction of Yahweh's involvement in the course of events, as we have noted, conveys a sense of detachment. Yahweh's role in the narrative mainly comprises speaking as opposed to direct action. In this respect, Yahweh resembles the transcendent Creator presented in the first creation story, to which the present account alludes. Yahweh speaks from a distance, and things happen as a result. Yahweh cares for creation, yet remains above it.

We may pause at this point to summarize the main points of this discussion of the flood narrative. First, there is little to suggest that a vindictive or angry God decides to send the flood in order to punish human wickedness and the unfortunate creatures affected by it. Rather, the narrative depicts Yahweh as deeply affected and troubled by the violence that ruins creation. Yahweh sees where creation is headed and steps in to bring about the end; Yahweh wrecks an already-wrecked creation. Second, Yahweh's decision to bring the old world down does not succeed in eliminating the presence and influence of violence within creation. Yahweh acknowledges that violence infects every human being and appears to accept the condition. Yahweh, however, does not abandon what has been made, but, on the contrary, binds the divine self more tightly to humanity and the world as it is. Third, Yahweh remains at a discreet distance from the world and the violence that fills it. Aside from seeing that Noah is safely shut within the ark, Yahweh does not make an appearance as the waters cover the earth and wipe away all flesh. To put it another way, Yahweh is not in the world when the flood rages, but outside of it. As in the first creation account, Yahweh remains aloof, all-powerful, and detached, primarily dictating what will be through words rather than actions. Finally, Yahweh intervenes directly to bring salvation and renewal, setting the world aright. Despite having participated in violence, Yahweh expresses in turn an inclination to turn away from such violence in response to Noah's sacrificial act of gratitude and respect.

The First Descent

If there is any cause for optimism that Noah and his family will bring a better beginning, it is quickly dashed. Like Adam and Cain before him, Noah works the soil (9:20; cf. 3:23; 4:2), but it doesn't end well. The vineyard he plants leads to a troubling end (9:20-27). What happens as a result of Noah's drunkenness is obscure, but the effects are clear: a curse enters the human community again (v. 25), strife besets the family, and inequities of power and blessing configure the future that stretches out before humanity (vv. 26-28).

The final segment of the primeval narrative—the scattering of humanity at Babel (11:1-9)—must be understood as a narrative capstone that depicts the intransigent human dispositions and practices that configure the world. The story focuses on what human beings make: bricks and mortar, a city and tower, and a name. The setting of the story is apt. Babylon was one of the great cultural, political, and technological centers of the ancient world, and so serves as a fitting example of the original human impulse to take dominion over the earth.

The story depicts a unified human community, bound by a common language and vocabulary, that decides to cease wandering and claim a place for its own. Making follows settling. Whereas Yahweh had made a garden for humanity's dwelling place, human beings now aspire to make a city for themselves, and a big one at that: "a city and a tower with its top in the sky" (v. 4). While this phrase may be idiomatic for a large city, the context suggests something more than a building project. Humanity wishes to extend its dwelling place vertically as well as horizontally. The plain on which they plan to build the city provides a level space with plenty of room to spread out, but unified humanity wants to claim the sky as well.

The twofold rationale assembled humanity gives for the city-building enterprise is telling: "so that we make a name for ourselves and are not scattered over the surface of the earth." Building the city and the tower will accomplish one thing (make a name) and prevent another (scattering). On the surface of things, this is a strange reason for building a city! Why is humanity concerned about making a name? How will a city ensure that they will stay together?

The reason becomes clearer when we read this passage in light of the texts that surround it. The story of unified humanity's quest to make a name for itself is set within a neatly segmented sea of names. Preceding it is a list of the nations that emanated from the three sons of Noah, each one grouped "according to their families, their languages, their lands, and their nations" (10:5, 21, 31). The genealogy of nations begins and ends by announcing the divided character of the human race, first by noting the spread of the descendants of Japheth into their respective lands and then by concluding that "from these the nations were separated throughout the earth after the flood" (v. 32). Following the story of Babel, another genealogy connects the time of Noah to the time of Abram.

The so-called Table of Nations (Gen 10:1–32), which interrupts the prior genealogy, draws a direct connection to the story of Babel. When the genealogy comes to Nimrod the succession of names is suspended and the name of Nimrod expounded:

> He was the first to become a powerful man on the earth. He became a powerful hunter before Yahweh. That's why it is said, "Like Nimrod, a powerful hunter before Yahweh." The beginning of his kingdom was Babylon, Erech, Akkad, and Calneh, in the land of Shinar. (10:8b–10)

This terse expansion provides a critical context for the Babel story. Nimrod has a name, which is to say, he has a reputation. The reputation he gains from his exploits and power is so great that his name is remembered proverbially. And in addition to a reputation, Nimrod has a kingdom. This is the first mention of anything associated with kingship, which may be regarded as the flawed human imitation of the original relationship between Yahweh, humanity, and creation. Like Yahweh, a king has the power to dictate and demand, to receive honor and obedience, to be feared and reverenced. Human kings, however, occupy the pinnacle of a hierarchy of power that can be maintained only by perpetuating a system of inequity that divides, oppresses, and deprives. The last sentence of the account refers to a vast realm that is "the beginning of his kingdom," intimating that he aspired for more power over more lands. Nimrod's identity, reputation, will to power, and persona transcend the ages.

The textual connection between the Babylon of Nimrod and the Babel constructed by the human community (the names are identical in Hebrew) suggests that the latter's determination to "make a name" for themselves expresses a fundamental human impulse to establish one's own identity, attain standing, honor, and power, and ultimately to achieve a transcendent, larger-than-life everlastingness. This is evidently what gets Yahweh's attention. The human community settling on the plain of Shinar wants to establish its own identity on its own terms and in the service of its own aspirations. It wants to be honored and esteemed. It wants to extend its dominion across the earth and into the heavens.

Human beings therefore continue to do what Yahweh has created them to do; that is, to take dominion. But in the post-garden world, that impulse has turned inward, creating a world of inequity and rivalry where human kings, rather than the cosmic sovereign, establish identities and dictate reality. As Yahweh remarks, the city and tower are only the beginning. If something isn't done about it, there will be no stopping the people.

Yahweh, therefore, makes a momentous decision. Yahweh decides to *come down* into the world that humans have made. In contrast to the divine response to humanity's pre-flood condition, Yahweh does not remain above the situation but enters the human world. It is a tentative move, as if Yahweh is only dipping a toe in troubled waters. Yahweh does not interact with any human beings. But it is a momentous entering nonetheless, and the retinue of spiritual beings that was present at the creation appears again to witness it (cf. v. 7). From this point on, Yahweh will work within the world as it is. It is the first in a series of descents that will draw Yahweh deeper into the maelstrom of human violence, while simultaneously pulling humanity outward from its captivity to destructive narcissism.

The narration of the story is tightly crafted and economically told. A series of repetitions casts the human community's actions and aspirations as provocations that lead to a divine response in kind. The first half of the story (vv. 1-4) relates people's actions in a sequence that begins with references to "one language and unified speech" (v. 1), then relates their discovery of a plain and settling "there" (v. 2), their speaking "to each other" (v. 3), and their determination to "build a city" and "make a name" for themselves so that they will not be "scattered throughout the face of the earth" (v. 4). Yahweh's response follows a similar sequence. Yahweh observes that all humanity is "one people and one language" (v. 6) and decides to confuse their language "there" so they cannot understand "each other" (v. 7). As a result of Yahweh's intervention, the people stop "building the city" (v. 8), which is called by the "name" of Babylon and is remembered as the place from which Yahweh "scattered them throughout the face of the earth" (v. 9). The pivot upon which the sequence turns is v. 5, which relates that "Yahweh came down to look at the city and the tower which the children of Adam had built."[5]

An elaborate symmetrical construction draws attention to the report of Yahweh's descent into the world. Gordon Wenham offers the most succinct description (italics are mine):

    A "For *the whole earth* had one language" (v. 1)
      B "*there*" (v. 2)
        C "*each other*" (v. 3)
          D "*Come let us* make bricks" (v. 3)
            E "let us *build* for ourselves" (v. 4)
              F "*a city and a tower*"
                G "*the Lord came down*" (v. 5)
            F' "*a city and a tower*"
            E' "which mankind had *built*"
          D' "*come . . . let us* mix up" (v. 7)
        C' "*each other's* language"
      B' "from *there*" (v. 8)
    A' "the language of *the whole earth*" (v. 9)[6]

The structure reinforces Yahweh's descent as the central element in the story and highlights the factors that define humanity's agenda and Yahweh's response: scope ("the whole earth"), a sense of place ("there"), human reciprocity ("each other"), decision ("come, let us"), human production ("build"), and intended result ("a city and a tower"). Together, the elements reveal that the magnitude of the project is of such concern that it prompts Yahweh to enter the world to ascertain what is happening and then to respond by reversing the human operations. The story begins with human plans, but concludes with divine action.

---

    5. Gordon J. Wenham, *Genesis 1-15*, WBC 1 (Dallas: Word, 1987), 234-36.
    6. Wenham, *Genesis 1-15*, 234-36. A more elaborate description of the symmetries that configure the passage is presented by J. P. Fokkelman, *Narrative Art in Genesis: Specimens of Stylistic and Structural Analysis* (Assen: Van Gorcum, 1975), 11-45.

What of humanity's plans is of such gravity that it pulls Yahweh down from heaven to the earth? The plans entail the construction of bricks, a city, and a tower. The construction, however, serves a nonmaterial end, expressed positively as making a name and negatively as not being dispersed throughout the world. Humanity not only seeks to settle in its own place, but to elevate that space heavenward—to remake the flat, nondescript space that they inhabit so that they may reconnect that space to the place of Yahweh's abode, as if to repair the divine-human connection by their own efforts and on their own terms.

"Let us make a name for ourselves" articulates the gist of the problem; the action continues and extends the building project ("let us do x") but is set in opposition to an undesirable end ("so we won't be scattered"). A name can signify any number of things. In this instance, it is often understood to refer to permanence or immortality; continuing or remembering a name is a way for someone to live on into future generations, as is illustrated by the genealogy of names that surrounds the passage. Naming, however, can also signify identity and standing in the world. It brings recognition and establishes reputation. In the garden, as an expression of Adam's collaboration with Yahweh, Yahweh created the animals and birds and brought them to the human, who gave them their names (2:19-20). Adam identified animals at the time, acting not as Yahweh's equal but as Yahweh's representative tasked with extending the deity's dominion over the created order (1:28). Conferring an identity on the creatures, in other words, established Adam's standing and authority over creation. In this way the creation narratives affirm that human identity is not autonomous but derivative; human beings draw their identity from the Creator and are not to inhabit the earth as free agents.

The human community on the plain of Shinar, however, is intent on making a name for *themselves*, that is, establishing their own identity on their own terms and apart from any apparent relationship with the Creator. In this sense, the sea of names that connect the Babel story back to the creation represents the broken system of human relationships established by men outside the garden, a system inaugurated immediately after the expulsion, when Adam names his wife "Eve" (3:20). Unlike the original design of creation, where diversity and order were bound together as a unity under the sovereign work of the Creator, the diversity of names that comprise the genealogies instead conveys the divisions within humanity that define one's family, friends, and opponents. In the human world, divisions separate and divide rather than bind and order.

On the plain of Shinar, however, the human community is unified and anxious that they shall be separated from each other and scattered abroad. The thread that unifies them is their language, their ability to express themselves and be understood. Like the Creator at the beginning of the story, they use their speech to construct an ordered world in which to live and flourish. Yet, although what they build extends to heaven, the world that they make is for themselves. Restless humanity aspires to stop wandering, make their own space, and establish their own identity apart from a relationship with the Creator. They aspire, on their own terms and by their own ingenuity, to make the world from the ground up, intending to extend their world as far as the abode of God. The project, in sum, aims to create a counterfeit Eden—a human society with a place of its own, but which is oriented toward its own ends rather than toward executing a mandate conferred by the sovereign of creation.

This is what gets Yahweh's attention. It is the beginning of a false unity, resting on a false foundation, and directed toward an arrogant end. It must not be allowed to take root. Yahweh quickly realizes that the preparation for building is the start of something big and that, without intervention, rebellious humanity will continue, unrestrained, with their program (v. 6). So Yahweh upsets everything. In response to their determination to build toward the sky, Yahweh comes down to earth. Humanity aspires to maintain unity and establish its own identity through the power of speech, so Yahweh mixes up the speech so that there can be no conceptual common ground. The human community, estranged from its Creator, fears the loss of identity and power if dispersed, so Yahweh divides and scatters. Babylon, the epitome of human achievement and culture in the ancient world, becomes a confusing cacophony of contesting speech.

Yahweh intervenes to reduce humanity's construction project to chaos. As noted above, this represents a new stance for Yahweh in relation to the world. In the aftermath of the flood and the failure of Yahweh's plan to restore creation from a distance, Yahweh comes down into the world to frustrate humanity's attempt to remake the world in its own image. The story thus casts the human system, as reflected in the genealogies, both as a divisive world, in which diversity brings separation and disorder rather than unity and flourishing, and as the medium with which and within which Yahweh will work to restore creation. The genealogies going forward lead to Abram, who will be Yahweh's partner in a new strategy for renewing the earth (12:1-2).

CREATION RUINED AND REMADE

Primeval Violence

The early chapters of Genesis present a vision of the world as Yahweh created it: a carefully ordered space populated by a diversity of creatures, all bound together in an original harmony. Human beings are created to manage and care for the creation as representatives of the Creator's authority in the world. Yahweh gives them the opportunity to act in the Creator's stead by naming the animals that had been made from the same ground from which humans were formed. As represented by Adam, human beings are unique in the created order. They are creatures shaped from earth but bearing Yahweh's image and animated by Yahweh's breath. Yahweh also makes human beings the object of divine care and concern, forming an authentic relational bond that gives them a measure of freedom in the exercise of their mandate and a measure of give-and-take in the relationship.

The two accounts of creation present the Creator as supremely powerful, outside, and unapproachable, yet willing to share power, present within creation, and deeply engaged with humanity. The narrative accentuates Yahweh's beneficence and generosity towards creation and Yahweh's satisfaction with the creation. Yahweh calls each aspect of creation "good" and the completed project "very good." The creation flourishes under the care of Yahweh and the work of human beings on the earth.

Adam and Eve, however, overstep their mandate and their position in creation and decide that they themselves can determine what is good for creation. The decision immediately throws the created order out of joint. Humanity is intended to draw its identity from God; humans are not meant to inhabit the earth as free agents. The effects reveal divisions once held together in a unity blessed by the Creator, which now separate and fragment the world. Human beings hide parts of themselves from each other, and all of themselves from God. Hierarchies of power enter human relationships, and the original unity shatters into a world of alienation. Yahweh must expel the two from the garden lest, by eating from the Tree of Life, their toxic influence permanently infects the whole of creation. In order to restore the world to its original state, Yahweh must expel them from the garden.

Violence is the immediate consequence of the incipient human community's decision to determine the good apart from the blessing of God. Yahweh responds to that violence with compassion and a determination to restore the damage human violence generates. There is little to support the notion that Yahweh strikes back at humanity because of caprice, vindictiveness, or personal offense. Nowhere in these opening chapters of Genesis is Yahweh said to be angry at what human beings do. Yahweh does not kill Cain for killing Abel. Instead, when Yahweh banishes the first murderer, Yahweh listens to Cain's protest that his banishment will subject him to possible murder by others. Rather than leaving Cain to his fate, Yahweh puts a mark on him to protect him from the violence he has meted out to his brother. When human violence intensifies to such a degree that the boundaries between heaven and earth begin to dissolve, Yahweh's response is sorrow. In this instance, Yahweh accelerates the inevitable death-spiral of creation and saves a righteous man and his family, along with pairs of every species of creature, with the intention of beginning anew once the world reverts back to chaos. Yahweh waits until the point of no return has been reached and then intervenes to bring about the ruination that human beings have generated.

The determination of the human community to re-create Eden on its own terms, through the construction of a city, draws Yahweh back down to earth. Yahweh enters the world again but works from a distance. The deity does not interact with any members of the wayward community that is intent on establishing a name for itself, but scrambles communication altogether. Yahweh thereby blocks the human impulse to assert its own identity, to make its own way in the world, to acclaim its preeminence in creation, to bring the whole earth into its sphere of control, and to construct its own continuity and future. The descent reveals a willingness on Yahweh's part to enter directly into the world that humans have made in order to bring about restoration within it. The question going forward is whether, and to what extent, Yahweh's entry into that world will affect how Yahweh will bring about this restoration in a world caught up in violence.

3

Yahweh's New Approach

> Yahweh said, "The outcry from Sodom and Gomorrah is loud, and their sin is very grave. I will go down and see if the outcry that has come to me is commensurate with what they have done. And if not, I will know."
>
> GENESIS 18:20–21

The genealogy of Shem (Gen 11:10–32) connects unified humanity's aspiration to settle, build, and make a name for itself to Yahweh's promise to make the name of a particular human being great. As at creation, Yahweh simply speaks to bring a new reordering of the world into being:

> Yahweh said to Abram, "Depart from your land, your ancestry, and your father's house to the land I will show you. I will make you into a great nation. I will bless you and make your name great, and there will be blessing. I will bless those who bless you and curse those who curse you. All the families of the earth will be blessed by you. (Gen 12:1–3)

During the span of time represented by the catalog of names, Yahweh appears to have decided to take a hands-on approach to the problem of human wickedness. That is, Yahweh will enter the world that humans have made and will work within the system to restore creation to a state of blessing and order, beginning with a single family and extending outward from there. The process will require restoring the divine-human relationship onto its original foundation, with the human partner subservient to and dependent on the direction and provision of the Creator.

Making a Name

The plan Yahweh announces to and through Abram directly counters the pretentions of wayward humankind and signals a reversal of the way of the world. Wandering humanity settled down on a plain in Shinar and started building a city. Now Yahweh calls a man, whose roots are in the same area (Ur of the Chaldeans), to leave his city and embark on a life of wandering, with no destination in sight as he begins the journey. At Babel, unified humanity manifests the spirit of Nimrod, aspiring to establish its own identity, build its own reputation, extend its own power, and ensure its own permanence, with no mention or acknowledgement of the Creator. Now Yahweh breaks into the life of a single human being with the promise of all of these things. Posterity and renown will come to Abram through the work of the Creator, not as a result of Abram's efforts. At Babel, a homogenous humanity feared being scattered and began to build. Now Yahweh calls a human family to separate itself from its land, ancestry, and kindred to enter the rootless existence of the perpetual outsider.

Yahweh enters carefully and cautiously. Remarkable in this momentous beginning is the sense of distance between Yahweh and this prospective partner. There is no context. No information about what draws Yahweh's attention to *this* particular human being. No visitation or vision. No account of Abram's situation or even how the initial contact is made. There is only Yahweh's voice, speaking something new into being and announcing blessing. Blessing is the focal point of what Yahweh intends for Abram and his family and, through them, for the nations of the world. Blessing reiterates Yahweh's first action toward the first human beings and expresses Yahweh's original disposition toward humanity, despite its intransigent arrogance (cf. Gen 1:28). Yahweh speaks the remaking of the world through Abram and his family. There is nothing but speech from Yahweh in this first encounter. Abram will receive divine blessing in order to extend the scope of blessing outward to the whole of humanity. In so doing, the family will restore and fulfill Yahweh's original mandate.

Yahweh's first response to human wickedness precipitated a massive overturning of the entire creation and a renewal through the battle-tested Noah, who alone among his peers was righteous. That program was not successful in restoring the world, and in its aftermath Yahweh now decides to start small. Yahweh enters the world to stay and begins to restore the world from the inside out in collaboration with a chosen human agent.

YAHWEH'S NEW APPROACH

So Yahweh resets the creation by resetting the relationship with humanity. The sequence of Yahweh's speech is telling: a command first, then a promise. Yahweh bids Abram to obey with blessing in view. The relationship begins distantly but develops into an abiding friendship. Yahweh, in short, chooses to *identify* with Abram. This is a decision of significant import. By undertaking the restoration of creation through a relationship with a particular human family, Yahweh takes on the obligation to protect and provide for Abram. In order to promote Abram, to make his name great and so to draw attention to what Yahweh is doing through Abram, Yahweh will take Abram's part in the world. Those who treat Israel well will be Yahweh's friends, and those who treat his family poorly will be opponents. Yahweh's work, in other words, will be determined and shaped by Abram's fortunes in the world. For his own part, Abram's ready obedience to the divine command to leave signifies the human partner's willingness to identify with Yahweh, which, as will become clear, puts Abram at odds with other claimants for his attention and respect.

From these unadorned beginnings a friendship develops over time and assumes a pattern. Yahweh appears unannounced, discloses new information about the plan, and at times asks more of Abram. Abram, for his part, continues to respond with the same show of respect and obedience he exhibited when Yahweh first called him. Little textual ground is traversed before Yahweh delivers a second bit of information in person. Upon Abram's arrival in Canaan, Yahweh appears to the traveler, now far from home, with a terse announcement that elaborates the initial promise—"I give this land to your descendants" (12:7)—whereupon Abram builds an altar to mark and honor the divine appearance. Following this divine visitation, Abram journeys to the region of Bethel, where he builds a second altar and calls on Yahweh's name (12:8).

It isn't long, however, before Yahweh is called upon to intervene on Abram's behalf. When famine strikes the land of Canaan, Abram strikes out on his own and settles in a place Yahweh did not direct him. Like his grandson Jacob will later do, Abram decides to make his own descent (the verb is the same employed for Yahweh's descent to Babel), from the land Yahweh just promised to give him, to the land of Egypt (12:10-20). Once there, Abram fears that his beautiful wife has put him in danger of being killed by someone in the country. We are not told if there is a valid reason for his fear or whether he has simply manufactured it. Significantly, Abram does not seem to give much attention to the promise that Yahweh has given to "curse those who curse you." Has he forgotten? Or does he wonder if Yahweh can and will defend him? Abram after all lives in a world of capricious deities. This promising deity has taken a liking to him, but will his new divine friend come through if there is trouble?

Abram complicates matters by passing Sarai off as his sister. And as he suspected, word gets to Pharaoh, who takes her into his harem. The narrator, however, makes a point of saying that Pharaoh treats Abram well for her sake—very well in fact, lavishing him with extraordinary wealth (v. 16). Pharaoh, it turns out, does not take on the persona that Abram feared. He does not act as an imperious tyrant who takes what he wants. Rather, Pharaoh respects Abram and the conventions of the culture, and he more than compensates Abram for the woman he believes to be Abram's sister.

This would appear to put Yahweh in somewhat of a bind. Yahweh has announced that Abram will be an agent of divine blessing, and that divine blessing will extend to those who bless Abram. Will Pharaoh receive a blessing, especially since he has elevated Abram's economic and social status? Or does the promise require Yahweh to take Abram's side and extricate him and Sarai, even though Pharaoh has to the best of his knowledge acted beneficently? Interpreters have commonly pointed to a different element of the divine promise as a reason for Yahweh's intervention—specifically the promise that Yahweh will make Abram a great nation and give his descendants the land of Canaan. On this view, the danger is that Pharaoh may sire children through Sarai, effectively destroying the divine plan for her to bear Abram's children. This surely is a key concern in the story, even though at this point Yahweh has not specifically revealed that the promise will be extended through Sarai (and, as David Clines has perceptively noted, there are other possibilities before Abram at this point in the story).[1]

The thread we are following, however, suggests that the situation confronts Yahweh, at this early point in the relationship, with the implications of befriending Abram. Yahweh must decide whether and how to take Abram's side when problems arise with others—even when the conflict arises from Abram's less-than-honest behavior. Pharaoh treats Abram honorably and generously, but Yahweh evidently decides that having a human friend in a wicked world requires a thoroughgoing commitment to the welfare of that individual, even when it works against the welfare of others. Standing

---

1. David J. A. Clines, "The Ancestress in Danger: But Not the Same Danger," in *What Does Eve Do to Help? and Other Readerly Questions to the Old Testament*, JSOTSup 94 (Sheffield: JSOT Press, 1990), 69–72.

with someone inevitably leads to standing against someone else. Yahweh, therefore, strikes Pharaoh and his household, even though the mess was made by Abram. Pharaoh had not acted maliciously, and his household was involved minimally if at all. To make matters worse, Pharaoh must also take on the additional vexation of trying to find out why his household has been stricken. Somehow, Yahweh gets the word to Pharaoh, who immediately confronts Abram with his deceit and demands that he take his wife and leave. Given the circumstances, it is difficult to know who the wronged party is in this sad state of affairs.

We are not told how Yahweh arrives at the decision to strike Pharaoh. We can surmise, however, that Yahweh has determined it necessary to reassure an insecure friend that his divine partner stands with him and will follow through on divine words of commitment. Whatever the reason, Yahweh's decision to plague the house of Pharaoh is momentous. The first act of divine violence after the flood is directed toward people who have not, to the best of their knowledge, acted wickedly or violently, for the sake of demonstrating solidarity with the family Yahweh has befriended.

The Relationship Deepens

Abram leaves Egypt a very wealthy man (Gen 13:2). With Sarai and Lot, he returns to the place in Canaan where he first built an altar to Yahweh. Wealth, however, provokes strife between his people and Lot's, leading Abram to propose that the two separate from each other. The scenario sets up another object lesson. Abram makes no reference to Yahweh's direction or gift of the land but rather invites Lot to choose for himself where he wants to live. Lot then chooses cities located in an Edenic setting and heads east. Abram remains in Canaan, the land of promise, while Lot settles near Sodom (13:2). There Abram receives another communiqué from Yahweh, this time elaborating upon the expanse of land that Yahweh will give to him and his descendants and inviting Abram to traverse the expanse (13:14-17). Abram responds by erecting another altar to honor Yahweh (13:18).

Whereas Yahweh used violent means to extract Abram from Egypt, Yahweh appears reluctant to assist Abram when the latter is embroiled in warfare and a contest of kings (14:1-24). When Lot and his possessions are carried off by a coalition of kings from the east, Abram jumps into action. We have been informed previously that he has made a pact with some of the Amorites in the area (v. 13b). Joined by his allies, Abram pursues the hostile kings as far as Damascus. He surprises their forces by night and succeeds in rescuing Lot and all the possessions that were carried off with him.

On the way back, Abram is greeted by another king, Melchizedek of Salem (14:18), who is also a priest of El Elyon ("God Most High"). Melchizedek attributes Abram's victory to the work of El Elyon. Abram does not disagree. Melchizedek's declaration, however, differs from the narrator's account of the event, which contains no reference to Yahweh or any other deity. Rather, the narrator attributes the victory to a divide-and-conquer strategy (v. 15). The narrative is noteworthy for two reasons. First, the association of Yahweh with warfare—the first of its kind—comes not through a narrative account of Yahweh's participation in battle but through a priest-king's attribution of victory to El Elyon, a later epithet for Yahweh. Second, as noted, Yahweh is conspicuously absent from the account itself, intimating that Yahweh's entrance into the world does not extend at the moment to participation in large-scale violence between kings and potentates.

When Yahweh makes an appearance again, the encounter comes by both vision and word, indicating a more substantial interaction in both form and content (15:1-21). Yahweh signals the purpose of the visitation with a greeting: "Don't be afraid, Abram. I am your shield. You'll have a very large reward" (v. 1). The first sentence addresses a lingering sense of apprehension on Abram's part, while the second two suggest what lies behind it. Yahweh invites Abram first to think of Yahweh as a piece of military hardware, an apt metaphor perhaps designed to redirect Abram's thinking in light of his prior campaign against the eastern kings. Then Yahweh speaks of reward. The Hebrew term here translated "reward" connotes compensation for services rendered or actions undertaken, for good or ill. The sense of recompense communicated by Yahweh's greeting intimates that Yahweh is cognizant that Abram may be wondering about the material benefit of the relationship.

Abram responds with a question that has obviously been weighing on him: "O Lord Yahweh, what will you give me? I'm walking along childless. The one who'll get my estate is Eliezer of Damascus" (v. 2). This is the first time Abram has responded verbally to Yahweh, and his comments lead to an interchange that moves the relationship from monologue to dialogue. The terse divine pronouncement followed by Abram's construction of an altar, which characterized earlier interactions, is absent here. Now there is a conversation founded on the relational capital that the two have developed together. Abram peppers Yahweh with questions, and Yahweh responds by further disclosing what Yahweh has in mind for Abram. Specifically, Yahweh puts to rest the idea that the promised descendants will emanate from someone else; they will descend from Abram himself. Yahweh then calls Abram to believe the audacious promise that the descendants from his own body will be as countless as the stars in the sky.

The narrator reports Abram's response with succinct poignancy (v. 6): "Abram trusted Yahweh, and Yahweh reckoned him righteous." The reference to righteousness links Abram to Noah (Gen 6:9). Noah's righteousness had been linked to his character, that is, to being "blameless in his generation" in the midst of a ruined world. Abram's association with righteousness, however, comes as a result of his trust in Yahweh's promise and so has a *relational* orientation; righteousness in this context points toward right relationship rather than right character. The pronouncement thus expresses Yahweh's judgment that the divine-human relationship has been reconstituted along the right lines, with the Creator as initiator and provider and the human partner responding with dependence and obedience.

Trust in Yahweh does not mean, however, that Abram does not look for assurance. This becomes clear in a second question wherein Abram asks, "How will I know?" Yahweh's response is surprising. Abraham is directed to bring five different animals. Abram for his part evidently recognizes what Yahweh is up to, cuts the larger animals in two, and keeps the vultures away from the carcasses. Darkness overcomes Abram when the sun goes down, and Yahweh speaks again with more information about his descendants. They will be aliens in a land that doesn't belong to them. They will be enslaved for four hundred years, but Yahweh will render judgment on the oppressing nation. They will depart with many possessions and return to the land of Canaan in the fourth generation. Yahweh also discloses that "the iniquity of the Amorites has not yet reached its full extent" (v. 16).

The interchange concludes with the strange sight of a smoking fire pot and a flaming torch passing between the pieces of the animals Abram had set opposite each other, followed by a reiteration of the land promise. Passing through severed carcasses evokes covenant-making, which suggests Abram understands the fire pot as connected with Yahweh's decision to make a covenant with Abram. The narrator confirms in fact that this is indeed what happened: "On that day, Yahweh made a covenant with Abram" (v. 18a; the Hebrew phrase is "cut a covenant").

We are prompted to see this entire sequence as Yahweh's response to Abram's "how will I know?" In this sense, we may perceive a greater engagement with Abram's world on Yahweh's part, as well as Yahweh's acknowledgement of the human partner's concerns. By making a covenant with Abram, Yahweh formalizes the relationship according to the social conventions that structure Abram's world and understanding. Yahweh, as it were, signs on the dotted line and so confirms the divine commitment to the relationship, come what may. Nothing requires Yahweh to do so. Ideally Yahweh's promise should be enough confirmation for Abram. Yahweh, however, realizes that Abram needs something more, a tangible expression of Yahweh's loyalty. So Yahweh adjusts to Abram's concerns, and confirms divine commitment in a way that Abram will understand. The relationship is maturing. The parties are interacting and recognizing mutual interests and concerns. Trust is growing.

It comes as no surprise then that during the next divine visitation Yahweh seeks assurances from Abram (17:1-27). This time Yahweh addresses Abram with an announcement of divine identity ("I am El Shaddai"), a command that Abram "walk before me and be blameless," and a declaration of Yahweh's intent to make a covenant between them (vv. 1-2). Whereas the previous interchange focused on Yahweh's response and accommodation to Abram's questions, these words signal Yahweh's interest in requiring a commensurate response from Abram. Up to this point, Yahweh has asked no more of Abram than that he trust in what Yahweh has promised. Now Yahweh calls Abram not only to relational fidelity ("walk before me") but to a moral fidelity that hearkens back to righteous Noah, who was blameless among his peers in a ruined world (6:9). Yahweh's declaration of intent to make a covenant with Abram seems redundant on first glance, as the narrator concluded the account of the last appearance with the declaration that Yahweh had done just that (15:18).

The ensuing dialogue, however, reveals that the covenantal emphasis on this occasion will elaborate what Yahweh requires of Abram. The first part of Yahweh's next speech interlaces reiterations of Yahweh's promise of descendants (17:4, 6, 8) with the bestowal of a new name on Abram (v. 5) and a declaration of covenant (v. 7). The bestowal of the name, which follows on Abram's prostration before Yahweh, confirms the contours of the relationship. Prostrating oneself in Abram's culture is what a person of lower social class typically does when making a request or receiving favor from a person in power. By doing so in response to Yahweh's declaration, command, and promise, Abram expresses his acknowledgement of Yahweh as cosmic sovereign and gives Yahweh due honor.

Yahweh acknowledges the relationship by renaming Abram: "Your name will not be called Abram anymore. Your name shall be called Abraham, for I have given you to be the father of a host of nations" (v. 5). The contrast between the world of Babel and the world Yahweh will inaugurate through Abram has now been made explicit. Unified humanity sought to assert its own identity, aims, and future apart from relationship with the Creator. Now the Creator bestows a new identity on the chosen friend, an identity that emanates from divine promises of a place, purpose, and posterity. The right relationship necessary for the right ordering of creation, expressed by the human partner's obedience, dependence, and acknowledgement of supremacy, has now been reestablished through Abraham and his family.

Yahweh, furthermore, seeks to formalize Abraham's commitment to the relationship as constituted, just as Yahweh had done during the previous interchange. Another command follows: "As for you: you and your descendants throughout their generations are to keep my covenant" (v. 9). Yahweh then explains what the command means. The covenant will require an act of violence against the body: Abraham is to cut off the foreskin of his penis. Circumcision, Yahweh declares, will be a mark of the covenant between the two. The mark carries a message and a reminder, for Abraham's descendants will proceed from that organ of his body. Abraham (and as it turns out, every male connected to him) will therefore carry a daily reminder of Yahweh's promise, power, and supremacy.

Yahweh concludes by bestowing a new name on Sarai as well and reiterating that nations and kings will derive from her. This appears to amuse Abraham. He raises questions that touch on the absurdity of old people having children (v. 18), and he attempts to resolve the absurdity by proposing his son Ishmael—born apart from Yahweh's initiative or involvement—as an appropriate candidate for the continuation of his line. Yahweh, however, immediately quashes the idea and emphatically declares that Sarah will bear the promised son. Yahweh will not bend to Abraham's feedback on this score.

At the same time, however, Yahweh makes a point of telling Abraham that he has been heard and that Yahweh will make an adjustment accordingly; Ishmael too will be the bearer of a divine blessing that approximates what Yahweh originally made to Abram (v. 20). But Yahweh will choose another son, yet unborn, to continue the work begun through Abraham. The response defines an important aspect of the divine-human relationship that will carry Yahweh's work forward. Yahweh welcomes and values the human partner's input—listening is an expression of respect—and may do something new and different in response.

Summing Up the Backstory

Our review of Yahweh's relationship with Abraham forms a long but necessary backstory to the second report of Yahweh's descent into the man-made[2] world (18:21). Yahweh's promise to Abram initiates a divine strategy to restore creation by working from within the system. Through Abram and his family, Yahweh will reestablish the right relationship necessary for ordering the world. Yahweh will start with Abraham and extend a renewed blessing of creation through this first family, as opposed to bringing everything down and starting over. Abraham's story depicts a relationship that begins with a divine promise and command met by acceptance and obedience from the human partner. Through multiple encounters, Yahweh and Abraham learn about each other and build trust. Brief monologic interactions—during which Yahweh alone speaks, while Abram responds in silence—give way over time to a dialogic relationship in which the two interact as partners and friends.

The narrative illustrates what being in relationship means for both partners. For Abraham, the relationship means a deepening experience of the faithfulness, power, and caring of Yahweh and a deepening dependence that accords with Yahweh's original plan and purpose for humanity. Abraham learns that Yahweh will stand with him and that Yahweh takes his concerns seriously. For Yahweh, the relationship means entering into and working within the structures and customs that configure Abram's world and appropriating them to advance relational and creational concerns. Yahweh is not compelled to accommodate Abram's world but decides to do so even when it means difficult adjustments. Yahweh's decision to identify with Abram and his family means in part that Yahweh has to work within the limitations and brokenness of the system.

---

2. The world that human beings create is indeed "*man*-made." The system that human beings construct to order their lives in the world sets men and the concerns of men at the center. It develops hierarchies of power in which some human beings rule over other human beings. The patriarchal system that configures the human world, in short, is a social manifestation of human brokenness that results from defiant humanity's insistence on making the world on its own terms. In this world, Yahweh God has declared, the man will rule over the woman (Gen 3:16). Yahweh's work to renew creation thus entails restoring interhuman relationships—as well as the divine-human relationship—to their original state.

YAHWEH'S NEW APPROACH

The Second Descent

Yahweh makes a second descent (18:21), as in the case of Babel, in order to investigate a bad situation on the earth. The descent takes the form of a fully embodied encounter with Abraham and Sarah (18:1–16) followed by a remarkable interchange between Yahweh and Abraham (18:17–33). It results in the destruction of Sodom, Gomorrah, and the surrounding area, which the narrator renders so as to evoke associations with the flood narrative.

Yahweh's appearance at Abraham's tent represents the fullest and most direct instance of divine disclosure Abraham has yet received. God appears to Abraham in human form, or perhaps better, human *forms*. The narrator introduces the encounter with the announcement that God appeared to Abraham while he sat at the entrance of his tent in the heat of the day, but then shifts abruptly to relate what Abraham saw when he looked up: three men standing in front of him (vv. 1–2). The ensuing encounter is both mysterious and matter-of-fact. Although we are left to wonder how Yahweh's appearing is to be associated with the three men, Abraham immediately recognizes them and responds with a similar show of obeisance as he did when Yahweh appeared to him previously (17:3). He welcomes the visitors with lavish hospitality, in stark contrast to the unhospitable response two of the men will receive from the men of Sodom.

The meeting provides the occasion for Yahweh to repeat the promise that Sarah will bear a son, and for the first time Yahweh interacts with her. In a playful, terse interchange reminiscent of Yahweh's interaction with Abraham, Yahweh first addresses Sarah from a distance but eventually speaks to her directly. After inquiring of her whereabouts, the men tell Abraham that Yahweh will return at the same time next year and that Sarah will have a son by then. Sarah, who was listening from inside the tent, laughs at the thought of bearing a child at her advanced age. When a fearful Sarah responds that she did not laugh, Yahweh speaks to her directly: "No, you did laugh" (18:15). The back-and-forth exchange sets the tone for the longer back-and-forth argument that Abraham will soon have regarding the destruction of Sodom and Gomorrah, and Sarah's laughing (Hebrew *tsakhaq*) evokes the cry (Hebrew *tsaʿaqah*) that has brought Yahweh down to the earth in human form.

The episode's oblique references to Yahweh's expansive knowing and power form the backdrop for an extraordinary window into the divine mind:

> Yahweh said, "Shall I conceal what I'm about to do from Abraham, since Abraham will certainly become a great and powerful nation,

and all the nations of the earth will be blessed through him? For I know him, that he might direct his sons and household after him to keep the way of Yahweh—to do righteousness and justice—so that Yahweh may fulfill all concerning Abraham that Yahweh has spoken about him." (18:17-19)

Yahweh is deliberating, weighing alternatives, developing a rationale. The right answer does not present itself immediately. This disclosure of Yahweh's thoughts points to the depth of relationship that Yahweh has formed with Abraham. Yahweh is pondering the implications and limits of the divine relationship with this human being in light of Yahweh's intention for the relationship. Yahweh is pondering, in other words, whether to take this human friend into Yahweh's confidence. The consequences are significant for their impact on how Yahweh will work within the world from now on. The matter needs to be thought through. Confiding expresses a deep friendship and an openness founded on the relational capital of trust and experience. It also invites a response. By confiding in Abraham, Yahweh implicitly solicits the human partner's input and signals that that input may influence divine decision-making. Yahweh looks to the partner for a perspective from the human side of the issue.

Yahweh's rationale for confiding in Abraham focuses on the reason that Yahweh has undertaken the relationship. Yahweh has come to know Abraham and to work with a human partner in the world. Yahweh has promised to exalt and expand his descendants so that, throughout the ages to come, Abraham's descendants will "do righteousness and justice"; that is, they will manifest the life and practices that "correspond to God's creational intentions for the world order, including blessing all nations."[3] But this plan will require cooperation and response on Abraham's part; justice and righteousness must be *practiced*. Abraham and his descendants are to establish among themselves an expression of the restored creation that Yahweh intends ultimately to extend to all the nations of the earth. It is possible that Yahweh intends the disclosure as a means of discerning Abraham's understanding of justice and righteousness, whether he understands its import, and whether he will act to live it out.

Yahweh's thinking then abruptly shifts to the outcry that has risen from Sodom and Gomorrah (18:20-21). In response, Yahweh descends into the

---

3. Terence E. Fretheim, "Genesis," in *The New Interpreter's Bible*, vol. 1, ed. Leander E. Keck (Nashville: Abingdon, 1994), 135.

world again, this time to a different urban context, but with the investigative intent that Yahweh brought to Babel. The decision is not unrelated to Yahweh's thinking about Abraham. The disclosure and the descent are the outcomes of Yahweh's conclusion that the relationship with humanity and the world will require Yahweh to enter the man-made world, experience that world, and coordinate divine objectives with the affairs of chosen partners in the world.

An outcry has risen from the earth to Yahweh. It is too intense to be ignored, and the fact that Yahweh decides to see what is happening indicates that the outcry voices a threat to creation so potent that Yahweh will have to do something about it. The reference to the outcry looks back to the original act of violence, when Yahweh confronted Abel after his blood cried to Yahweh from the ground (Gen 4:10). It also looks forward to future oppression, when the enslaved descendants of Abraham will cry out to Yahweh from Egypt (Exod 3:7-9). The outcry is great because the sin—the disordering, chaotic force being generated in the cities—is great. Yahweh's decision to ascertain what the cry means conveys the depth of Yahweh's concern to restrain human wickedness for the sake of creation. The gravity of the outcry once more pulls Yahweh into the arena of earthly wickedness.

As a whole, this window into Yahweh's interior speech represents the third instance in which we are given access to the divine mind. The previous two instances also take place when Yahweh is about to make a decision of crucial import.[4] The first instance entails Yahweh's grief at creating humanity prior to sending a flood that destroys all of creation, save for Noah's family and the animals sheltered in the ark (6:5-7). The second occurs when Yahweh observes the city and tower that unified humanity is building on the plain of Shinar (11:6-7). In all three instances Yahweh acts in response to an observed threat: the intransigent wickedness of humanity, unified humanity's decision to make a name for itself, and the outcry that has arisen because of Sodom and Gomorrah. Taken together, the windows into Yahweh's thinking convey, first of all, Yahweh's determination to deliver the world from the forces that threaten to overwhelm the creation originally labeled "good." Secondly, Yahweh's deliberations counter the notion that these dramatic responses arise out of momentary outbursts of anger. Yahweh is thinking about how to respond and, in the present instance, drawing the human partner into the process of deliberation.

---

4. David W. Cotter, *Genesis*, Berit Olam (Collegeville, MN: Liturgical, 2003), 119.

This third instance, then, also represents a progression in Yahweh's decision-making. Before the flood, there is only Yahweh, grieving and decreeing. At Babel, a retinue accompanies Yahweh to earth to investigate human building and name-making. Now Yahweh draws Abraham into the divine deliberations and entertains Abraham's responses. After closing the window into Yahweh's thoughts, the narrator reports that the men turn and go toward Sodom, while Abraham still remains standing before Yahweh. We are left to wonder again how Yahweh has manifested through the three visitors and how to comprehend the visitation in light of Yahweh's exploratory descent into the world. Despite the mystery, our attention is drawn to the two matters that Yahweh is thinking about in Abraham's presence: whether to take Abraham into Yahweh's confidence and what to do about Sodom and Gomorrah.

A question from Abraham confronts both issues. Abraham addresses Yahweh—the first time in the narrative that Abraham initiates a conversation with God—with a challenge: "Are you really going to sweep away the righteous with the wicked?" (18:23). Abraham knows what Yahweh has been thinking and that Yahweh intends a surgical strike against the cities. His challenge to the Creator is bold and could only be countenanced through the mouth of a creature whose relationship is valued and whose feedback is welcome. Abraham, who Yahweh has declared will do justice and righteousness on earth, now queries Yahweh on the topic of righteousness; Abraham asks no less of Yahweh than Yahweh requires of him. He presses his point:

> What if there are fifty righteous people in the city? Will you sweep it away? Would you not spare the place for the sake of the fifty righteous people within it? Far be it from you to do such a thing! To kill righteous people along with wicked people, as if the righteous are like the wicked. Far be it from you! Will the judge of the whole world not do justice? (18:24–25)

What generates such a bold interrogation? Indignation? Surprise? Horror? Whatever the case, Abraham speaks with a forthrightness born of confidence and knowledge, punctuating his plea with a direct challenge for Yahweh to do justice. The questions, and particularly the challenge, reveal that Abraham has understood something vital about the relationship. The man who just earlier fell on his face in the presence of Yahweh now stands up to Yahweh and enters into a debate during which both partners will determine together how Yahweh will respond to human wickedness.

This does not mean, however, that Abraham regards Yahweh as his equal. His response is more along the lines of an advisor who has been given the freedom to speak to a king. Throughout their interaction, Abraham signals that he knows his place. He knows who he is in relationship to Yahweh. As he presses his point with Yahweh, he prefaces his pleas with deferential language: "I have presumed to speak to my lord, though I myself am dust and ashes" (v. 27); "Please don't be angry, my Lord, and permit me to speak" (v. 30); "I have presumed to speak to my Lord" (v. 31); "Please don't be angry, my Lord, and permit me to speak" (v. 32). The exchange confirms that the relationship between Abraham and Yahweh exemplifies the partnership Yahweh intended in Eden; Abraham freely collaborates with God, all the while recognizing and honoring Yahweh's authority and standing.

Abraham finds Yahweh quick to respond affirmatively to his pointed questions and equally compliant when Abraham continues to press for sparing the cities for the sake of forty-five, then forty, thirty, twenty, and finally ten. Yahweh's acceptance at each point demonstrates Yahweh's disposition toward mercy and reinforces the sense that Yahweh is acting out of a sense of necessity rather than caprice. The exchange manifests Yahweh's desire to uphold and protect the righteous, even when they constitute a small minority of the population. No cataclysm will befall Sodom and Gomorrah without due consideration and concern. At the same time, Abraham's silence after Yahweh agrees to spare the city for the sake of ten righteous suggests that a critical mass of righteous people must exist in order to avert divine repercussions. The outcry must be addressed, and whatever contagion threatens the world from the cities on the plain must be eliminated. The presence of a few righteous people in a community is not sufficient to counter overwhelming wickedness, as the following story about Lot illustrates.

That story confirms that the world is falling apart at Sodom and Gomorrah (19:1-29). The town that the two divine emissaries enter is a macabre, degenerate space. Abraham's nephew Lot greets the men with the same reverent and generous hospitality his uncle had earlier displayed; he falls on his face and throws a feast for them (vv. 1-2). Yet the space Lot occupies is toxic. In the middle of the night at Sodom, the townsmen gather around Lot's house and demand that Lot release his visitors "so that we might know them" (19:5). Sexuality in this space is expressed through violence, humiliation, and dominance. The presence of guests elicits an impulse to harm and abuse rather than to welcome and respect. When a desperate Lot tries to protect his guests by offering his daughters to the crowd, the men display even greater animosity by singling Lot out as a foreigner and declaring that they will do even worse to him (v. 9). This last comment confirms that the entire fabric of human relationships has unraveled in this man-made community. The men of the town want to abuse and destroy those who are different. Sodom therefore represents the violent extremity of a defiant humanity that looks only after its own and whose deepest inclinations are only destruction (cf. 6:5). The city represents the sordid, twisted world that humans have made in opposition to the restored world that Yahweh wishes to bring about through Abraham and Sarah.

Sodom and its kindred city Gomorrah occupy only a small space within the world that Yahweh wants to reclaim, but its violence is so virulent that it represents a threat to the whole world. The urgency of the threat is communicated through the words of the emissaries, who describe Yahweh's decision to obliterate the city as an act of deliverance.

> We are going to ruin this place, because their outcry before Yahweh is great. So Yahweh sent us to ruin it. (v. 13)

The language of ruination recalls Yahweh's response to a wicked world by sending the flood. In that instance, the narrator uses "ruin" (Hebrew *shakhat*) to describe the state of the world but also to signify what Yahweh planned to unleash upon the world as a result.

> The entire world was ruined before God, and the earth was filled with violence. And God looked at the world and it was ruined, for all flesh was ruined in its way on the earth. God said to Noah, "The end of all flesh has come before me, for the world is filled with violence because of them. I am going to ruin the world." (6:11-13)

As we noted in the previous chapter, the use of the wordplay in reference to the flood framed Yahweh's sending of the flood as a consequence that a wicked world had brought upon itself. Yahweh ruined the world by bringing a ruined world to an end. In the lips of the emissaries at Sodom, *shakhat* suggests that the impending cataclysm is similarly an acceleration of a process of ruination that the citizens of the town have brought on themselves. As in the case of the world prior to the flood, human wickedness has so permeated creation that the end result is inevitable.

An exchange between Lot and the divine emissaries mirrors that of Abraham and Yahweh. The emissaries disclose to Lot what Yahweh is about to do and tell Lot to gather his family and leave (vv. 13-14). Unlike Abraham, however, Lot does not contest what Yahweh has revealed. Instead, he attempts to gather his family. When he dithers, the emissaries seize him and direct him to take refuge in the hills. Here Lot responds with a forceful protest and presses back at the emissaries, asking them to allow him to flee to a nearby town instead. The emissaries agree. Lot challenges the emissaries not on account of what they have said Yahweh will do to Sodom and Gomorrah, but rather to serve his own interests. He is frightened and not sure that the way Yahweh has made for him will actually be safe (vv. 18–20).

Although Yahweh is ruining an already ruined land, the narrator emphasizes that the fire that rains down on Sodom and Gomorrah was sent by Yahweh (vv. 24–25). As was the case with the flood, however, the narrator also gives no indication that anger in any way prompts Yahweh to destroy the cities of the plain. Rather, the account of the towns' destruction is told succinctly and matter-of-factly, save for a comment that Yahweh "overturned" the towns (v. 25). The narrator repeats the comment at the close, where it occurs in parallel with the assertion that Yahweh "ruined" the cities of the plain (v. 29). The use of both terms, as an explanation for what Yahweh did, further confirms the necessity of his drastic response to the anti-creation contagion that was breaking out, even as Yahweh was beginning to extend the creational blessing through Abraham. The "ruined" towns were turned upside down, thus neutralizing the contagion and setting the land right.

Yahweh's rescue of Lot and his family on account of Abraham caps the story with another ironic twist. Lot's lavish and respectful hospitality toward the two emissaries indicates that he is a good man. His decision to give up his daughters, however, indicates that the influence of the town has seeped into his way of thinking and acting. The difficulty the emissaries have extracting him reveals his attachment to Sodom, despite what has happened to him and how the men of the city have threatened him. We learn that he had even betrothed his daughters to men of the city (v. 14). Lot, in other words, felt at home in Sodom. This one (righteous?) man was not able to influence the town. Instead, the town shaped him. The last we see of him, his own daughters are bedding him while he is in a drunken stupor (19:30–38). His fate, and the influence of the city, sheds further light on Abraham's decision to hold Yahweh to ten righteous men as reason for sparing the towns; the excessive wickedness of "every last one" of the men of the town (v. 4) was so overwhelming that even Lot was affected.

Double Trouble

On the heels of his remarkable exchange with Yahweh, Abraham travels to Gerar, where old behaviors resurface. Once again, Abraham grows apprehensive about living in a king's domain and presents Sarah as his sister (20:1-18). Abraham's ruse is surprising given the maturity of his relationship with Yahweh, Yahweh's demonstrations of power and faithfulness, and the privileged access that Yahweh has given Abraham. When King Abimelech takes Sarah, Yahweh is put in the same difficult situation. For a second time Yahweh must take Abraham's part, though he is in the wrong, against a ruler who has acted honestly and in good faith.

The tension between Yahweh's commitment to act justly and Yahweh's commitment to Abraham comes to the fore when Yahweh confronts Abimelech in a dream. The sequence of their interchange echoes the earlier exchange between Yahweh and Abraham concerning Sodom. Yahweh begins by announcing a death verdict for Abimelech for taking Abraham's wife (alluding obliquely to Lot's ready presentation of his daughters to the crowd to save his guests): "You are a dead man, because the woman you've taken is a married woman" (v. 3). Abimelech, however, protests the judgment by raising a question that resonates with Abraham's challenge to God: "My Lord, will you kill an innocent nation?" (v. 4). He then continues with a defense that implicitly appeals to God's justice: "Didn't he say to me, 'She's my sister' and didn't she also say 'He is my brother'? I did this with complete integrity of intention and innocence of action" (v. 5). Yahweh recognizes Abimelech's intention to act with integrity and reveals that he has already intervened to prevent Abimelech from sinning by not allowing the king to touch Sarah. Then Yahweh allows Abimelech to escape the death sentence by telling him to return Sarah to Abraham and telling him that Abraham will pray for him. Abimelech responds by relaying what Yahweh has said to all of his courtiers, who respond appropriately with great fear.

A second confrontation then takes place between Abimelech and Abraham. The interchange enhances Abimelech's integrity as well as Abraham's timidity and defensiveness. An outraged Abimelech lays out the gravity of Abraham's offense against the king and people who have shown him hospitality:

> What have you done to us? How have I sinned against you that you would bring great sin upon me and my domain? You have done something to me that ought not to be done! . . . How did your perception lead you to do this thing? (20:9-10)

Abraham, however, is quick to excuse himself by projecting his fears onto his royal host. Despite evidence to the contrary in Abimelech's response, Abraham claims that he saw no fear of God in the land and that he therefore feared for his life. He then claims that Sarah technically *is* his half-sister, implying that he did not act deceitfully. Faced with the great offense he has caused, Abraham refuses to admit that he did wrong. Instead, he implicitly blames Abimelech and his people and deflects accusations of deceitfulness with a technicality. Like Adam and Eve in the garden, he blames others when confronted with his self-seeking actions.

Abimelech, by contrast, acts vigorously to make things right, even though he is not the offender. He gives Abraham extravagant gifts and allows him free rein to settle wherever he pleases. Abimelech also makes a point of telling Sarah that he has paid Abraham an enormous sum of money to restore her honor and reputation. The narrative closes with two significant comments. First, the narrator reports that Abraham prayed to God, who then healed Abimelech, together with his wife and his female servants, so that they could bear children (v. 17). Then the narrator reveals that Yahweh had previously made every woman in Abimelech's house infertile.

The encounter between Abraham and Abimelech shows how different Gerar is from Sodom. Unlike the men of Sodom, the king of Gerar and his people treat Abraham and Sarah with dignity and hospitality. Abraham, however, acts deceitfully and precipitates a divine visitation that brings suffering to his host's house and a death sentence upon the king and his people. Abimelech is a righteous individual who does not deserve what he receives from Abraham and Yahweh. Like Abraham with Sodom, the king responds with a protest that raises again the question of how God deals with the righteous. Abraham's deceit places Abimelech in grave peril, yet it is Abimelech who lavishes upon Abraham the kind of generosity Abraham showed to the visitors at his tent. In the end, Abraham again intercedes to lift divine punishment, but this time at Yahweh's initiative and as an expression of Yahweh's desire to lift the punishment from a righteous man.

What this all means for Yahweh can be appreciated by viewing the events from Abimelech's point of view. Although Yahweh has revealed divine faithfulness and mercy to Abraham, who is to bless other nations, Abimelech sees only a deity who protects a favored man and is willing to punish a righteous person for unintended offenses. Because of Abraham's and Yahweh's responses to him, Abimelech views Yahweh as a powerful deity who looks little different from the capricious deities that populate the world he knows, a deity who must be placated when one offends the deity or those with whom the deity is associated. Yahweh's decision to defend a deceitful Abraham, in other words, means that Yahweh is willing to be seen as other than Yahweh really is. Yahweh, the judge of all the earth, appears to a righteous person—one who shows respect to strangers—as a deity who is less concerned about doing what is right than defending a favored servant. Yahweh seems to have concluded, in short, that to identify with and coordinate divine objectives through Abraham, Yahweh will have to adjust to the foibles and waywardness of his partner and take actions that lead others to view Yahweh in ways that are inconsistent with divine objectives. Friendship and identity with Abraham means that Yahweh will have to act in ways that do not always represent Yahweh's life-affirming, just, and restorative character and commitments. The decision is momentous and opens the way for other, more significant accommodations to come.

Relationship and Violence

With Abraham, Yahweh initiates a new strategy for restoring creation. Yahweh enlists a human partner as an agent of divine blessing for the whole of creation in return for respect, obedience, and dependence on the part of the human. From the first calling, Yahweh makes clear that the relationship Yahweh establishes with this family will be a divine medium of restoration for all the nations of the earth. In so doing, Yahweh binds divine purposes and ends to a relationship with human agents who inhabit the world.

Thus far, we have tracked three threads in the narrative that have import for understanding Yahweh's participation in violence. First, in the course of developing a relationship with the human partner, *Yahweh is increasingly pressed to operate within the structures and processes of the human system that Yahweh opposes.* To identify with and execute divine purposes through Abraham and his family, Yahweh must provide for, protect, and promote the human partners. In order to make Yahweh's name great in the world, Yahweh must make Abraham's name great. As the relationship deepens, Yahweh discloses more to Abraham and gives Abraham a greater role in determining how Yahweh will respond to human wickedness. Yahweh looks to Abraham to give a perspective from within the maelstrom of the man-made world and dignifies that perspective by giving it due consideration in divine deliberations.

It becomes clear, however, that friendship with the human partner will entail more than making the future together. Although displaying due

YAHWEH'S NEW APPROACH

honor and trust in the Creator, the human partner is nonetheless caught up in a toxic world and sometimes reverts to its form. The failings of the human partner require that Yahweh at points act in ways incommensurate with the high plans and purposes Yahweh intends for creation. Standing with Abraham entails standing against others, even when the human partner is in the wrong. Yahweh, therefore, discovers early on that *Yahweh will have to adjust the ways of divine working for the sake of the relationship and what Yahweh intends to do through it.*

On the other hand, Yahweh continues resolutely to respond to and remove dire threats to the creation that arise from excessive human wickedness. Yahweh's back-and-forth with Abraham on the matter of Sodom and Gomorrah confirms that Yahweh undertakes serious deliberation about how to respond to threats. Yahweh does not inflict massive violence unless the threat has magnified to such an extent that destruction is the only foreseeable end. *There is no instance of mass destruction in Genesis that associates divine violence with divine anger.* Yahweh does not explode against the victims in a paroxysm of rage. Rather, Yahweh steps in, after careful deliberation, to do what must be done for the sake of the whole of creation.

4

The Grand Entrance

> I have come down to deliver them from the hand of the Egyptians and bring them up from that land to a good and expansive land, to a land flowing with milk and honey, to the place of the Canaanites, Hittites, Amorites, Perizzites, Hivites, and Jebusites.
>
> EXODUS 3:8

Yahweh's third descent draws the Creator directly into the power politics that configure the world that humans have made. The conflict with Pharaoh on behalf of Israel signals Yahweh's deeper and more comprehensive engagement with that world. It is a world, as we have noted, driven by the impulse to "make a name for ourselves" and a corresponding anxiety to maintain a false unity on human terms (Gen 11:4). Yahweh has responded to this world by initiating a relationship with a single individual and his family and setting that relationship on the right footing. Yahweh will *make* a name for his friend—a great name—and intends to use him as the agent of divine blessing for all the peoples of the earth (Gen 12:1-2).

Humanity's preoccupation with making a name for itself manifests a determination to assert human identity on its own terms, determine its own way in the world, extend its dominion over creation, and give itself permanence and preeminence. Yahweh's promise and work to make Abram's name great counters this determination. As expressed by Yahweh's bestowal of a new name, the relationship with Abraham and Sarah established the divine/human relationship as it was originally constituted. Abraham acknowledges Yahweh's initiative and authority, follows Yahweh's guidance, and receives Yahweh's provision and protection. He relies on the faithfulness of Yahweh over against human knowledge and planning. For this reason, Abraham like Adam receives Yahweh's blessing and becomes the agent of Yahweh's plan to bless the nations and so renew creation from the inside out.

The world that men have made and the world that Yahweh has begun to make clash as Yahweh steps in to rescue the descendants of Jacob. Names and naming are prominent in the early stages of the narrative. The book of Exodus begins by naming the twelve sons of Jacob (1:1–4). Lists of names occupy the seam between Yahweh's calling of Moses and Moses's mission to Pharaoh (6:14–25). The narrative devotes special attention to how Moses got his name and even more to Yahweh's self-identification and disclosure of the divine name (3:6–17; 6:1–8). We know the name of Moses's wife (Zipporah), father-in-law (Jethro), and son (Gershom). We even know the name of the two midwives who defied Pharaoh's orders so that Hebrew babies could live (Shiphrah and Puah).

We are *not*, however, given the name of Pharaoh or anyone connected to Pharaoh. This is not a coincidence. Pharaoh represents what it means to have a name in the violent world that men have made. He has standing and position. He claims dominion over a vast land. His speech directs the affairs of the people and beasts. He occupies the apex of a divisive system that privileges and oppresses. He unites all life through the exercise of his power. Yet in this story, Pharaoh, the personification of human power in defiance of the Creator, is a nobody—as are all those in his sphere of influence, including his daughter. This is a striking rhetorical move on the narrator's part, particularly given the fact that Egyptian Pharaohs were fond of plastering their names everywhere on victory columns, temples, and public works. Egyptian Pharaohs, like all ancient Near Eastern potentates, reveled in making names for themselves. The contrast in naming—between the sea of Israelite names and the desert of Egyptian ones—points to both the import and outcome of the conflict that will take place.

That Israel is a people with an identity in contrast to Egypt is signaled in a remarkable way early on in the narrative, when Pharaoh's daughter finds a baby floating in the Nile and takes him in. We are told that, after receiving him from his wet nurse, "she called his name Moses because, she said, 'I drew him out of the water'" (2:10). Scholars often note the cross-linguistic pun the name makes. The Hebrew name sounds like an Egyptian word used in the throne names of Pharaohs to designate them as the son of a deity (e.g., Thutmoses [begotten of Thoth], Rameses [begotten of Ra]). The pun notwithstanding, however, an association with Pharaoh is not the reason the *Egyptian* in the story bestows the name, nor is this the meaning she gives to it. Pharaoh's daughter gives Moses a Hebrew name and explains its meaning in Hebrew. An Egyptian cannot even bestow an Egyptian name on her adopted son.

The nameless Pharaoh stands in direct opposition to the work and will of Yahweh, epitomizing humanity's inveterate impulse to assert its own identity and make its own world. Like the human community that gathered on the plain of Shinar, he is a builder. The building activity here, however, is not undertaken by a unified humanity but rather through the forceful subjection of a different people who occupy the same space. Like assembled humanity at Babel, Pharaoh manifests an anxiety about holding together the human community occupying the area. The people of Babel build because they do not want to be "scattered over the face of the earth" (Gen 11:4). The new king who comes to power in Egypt observes the burgeoning Israelite population and subjects them to forced labor so that they will not "fight against us and escape from the land" (Exod 1:10). Pharaoh presides over a world that manages human differences through the exertion of violence.

Yahweh has blessed the descendants of Jacob during their sojourn in Egypt. The story begins by reporting that they have multiplied to such an extent that the whole land is teeming with them—an allusion not only to Yahweh's promises to the patriarchs but to Yahweh's original mandate to humanity as well (Exod 1:7; cf. Gen 2:28a). Pharaoh, however, attempts to stop the increase of population—and so opposes the outworking of divine blessing—by taking dominion over the Israelites, first by forcing them to build and then by ordering that male children be killed at birth. The actions succeed only in intensifying Egyptian anxiety: "But the more they oppressed them the more they multiplied and spread out, so they dreaded the Israelites" (1:12). The stage is set for a confrontation between the human who is at the apex of power and the human who is the agent of the Creator's work in the world.

As was the case at Sodom and Gomorrah, it is a cry that draws Yahweh back into the world to make things right. When a cry goes up against the two cities near the Dead Sea, Yahweh comes down to investigate and judge (Gen 18:20-21). There Yahweh confides in his friend Abraham. In Egypt, Yahweh discloses to Moses that the cries of the Israelites have drawn Yahweh back into the world. Yahweh has seen their oppression and suffering, has come down to rescue them from Egypt's power, and will bring them into a land of their own (Exod 3:7-9). Yahweh's plan to do so involves working through a chosen human agent in the person of Moses.

A good deal of attention is given, in two conversations between Yahweh and Moses, to Yahweh's identity and name. The first conversation takes place when Yahweh calls to Moses from a burning bush (3:1–22). There Yahweh initiates a relationship with Moses by recalling relationships with Moses's forebears: "I am the god of your father, the god of Abraham, the god of Isaac, and the god of Jacob" (v. 6). The epithet, repeated twice thereafter (vv. 15, 16), affirms Israel's history and future with Yahweh. History has prompted Yahweh to rescue the descendants of the patriarchs and to fulfill a promise to give them the land of Canaan. Sandwiched between the two references to the history and promise is another name, which Yahweh discloses in response to Moses's request to know the name by which he should identify Yahweh to the Israelites. The answer is mysterious, speaking as much about God's being as of God's relationship with Israel: "I Am Who I Am" (3:14). The name establishes Yahweh as the only self-existent One, the only being whose existence is not derived from another being.

The second conversation takes place after Moses and Aaron have met with and been rebuffed by Pharaoh (6:1–13). It comes as a reassurance and reiteration of Yahweh's power and presence. The key aspect of this conversation is the disclosure of the name "Yahweh" to Moses, along with a declaration that Yahweh was not known to the patriarchs by that name. As readers have recognized for centuries, the disclosure does not quite add up, as Yahweh is indeed addressed as such throughout the patriarchal narratives in Genesis. We only reiterate here that the disclosure of the name sets the Creator in stark opposition to the ruler of the human world, whose name is not disclosed. Furthermore, the disclosure of the divine name at this point signifies a deeper commitment of the divine self to Israel. This second conversation echoes the first in many respects, with one significant addition: "I will take you for my own people, and I will be your God. And you will know that I am Yahweh your God who brings you out from under the burden of Egypt" (v. 7).

The first sentence of this declaration represents a significant step for Yahweh. It is one thing to identify with a family, as Yahweh did in Genesis. It is quite another to identify with a people. To be sure, the declaration that Yahweh will take Israel as his own people is an extension of all that Yahweh practiced and promised to the patriarchs. It is nevertheless astonishing in its scope and implication. Yahweh here offers the divine self freely to the nation and expands the relational association to encompass the entire people; Yahweh's identification and solidarity with Abraham is now extended to a nation. This means among other things that Israel's friends become Yahweh's friends and Israel's enemies become Yahweh's enemies (cf. Gen. 12:3).

The second sentence of the declaration carries a different import. In a world preoccupied with making a name and achieving preeminence, Yahweh declares that Israel will know Yahweh's name and acknowledge Yahweh's supremacy. Yahweh will make the divine name preeminent to Israel by freeing the people from the burdens they bear in the man-made world and establishing them as a new people in a new land, in fulfillment of ancestral promises. Through these events, Israel will realize and acknowledge "I am Yahweh your God." Yahweh's self-disclosure and identification with Israel, as a people, signal that Yahweh is now prepared to step into the geopolitical arena. The mighty acts that Yahweh will do on Israel's behalf will reveal Yahweh to be the God of this nation and, by extension, the God of all nations.

Yahweh, however, begins with a public relations deficit. When Yahweh steps into the world on Israel's behalf and in response to Israel's cries, Yahweh enters as a newcomer into a world of well-established powers and deities. Pharaoh is the overseer of a world configured by structures, systems, and processes—an order that has been in place for centuries and by which stability and continuity are maintained. It is an order, as we have noted above, that is held in place by the application of power and by a willingness to resort to whatever violence is necessary to ensure domestic tranquility. Pharaoh is aided and legitimized by a panoply of deities who render cosmic stability and enable social stability. These deities and their interactions resemble powers in the man-made world. They have names (although none are named in the narrative). They elicit respect and worship. Their interactions with humans and other divine beings are well-known. Yahweh steps into this world unknown and unrecognized, and thereby easily dismissed.

The point is made vividly by none other than Pharaoh himself, who, when confronted with Yahweh's demand to release the Israelites to worship Yahweh, declares, "Who is Yahweh, that I should heed his voice and release Israel? I don't know Yahweh, and I won't release Israel!" (5:2). Even the descendants of Jacob—those whom Yahweh intends to liberate—do not appear to know who Yahweh is. When Yahweh commissions Moses to bring the Israelites out of Egypt, Moses replies, "If I come to the Israelites and say to them, 'The God of your fathers sent me to you,' and they say to me, 'What is his name?' what will I say to them?" (3:13). The people may recognize "the God of the fathers," but they don't appear to have a name for that God.

What does a new god—particularly a god who identifies with slaves—have to do to be taken seriously, to acquire recognition and standing, not to mention to stand apart and gain supremacy? Why should Pharaoh and his gods give the slightest notice to a new god who issues challenges? Why should an oppressed people trust a god who recalls promises but has seemingly bowed to the might of Egypt and its gods? In a world fixated on making names, what will it take to make this deity's name preeminent over the hierarchies of names that define power and place? What, in short, does the new god on the block have to do to get respect and gain credibility?

The directions that Yahweh gives to Moses reveal the answer. In the world that men have made, power brings notoriety. To gain prestige and credibility in this world, one must show oneself to be strong, and to gain preeminence one must show oneself to be the most powerful of all. Stepping into the world in solidarity with Israel means that Yahweh will enter and participate in the contests of power that define the world. The God of slaves must take on the alpha male who claims supremacy in Egypt and overpower him in his own land. Yahweh appears to see the raw exertion of power, and the violence that emanates from it, as the necessary means for accomplishing saving purposes: "I know that the king of Egypt will not let you go, except by a strong hand. I will stretch out my hand and strike Egypt with all my wonders, which I will do among them. After this, he will release you" (3:19–20).

Yahweh, therefore, intends to enter the world in a manner everyone will recognize—that is, through a superior demonstration of power, manifested by the subjugation of the present powers. The project will be directed primarily toward Pharaoh, the reigning king, and for the purpose of forcing him to acknowledge Yahweh's supremacy. By wielding power against power, Yahweh will compel Pharaoh and his people to recognize the power and character of the God of Israel: "I am Yahweh" (7:5, 17; 8:10, 22; 9:14, 29; 14:4, 18). The contest will be prolonged so as to break down delusion and resistance, and the demonstration of power will be so thorough as to remove any doubt. By overpowering Pharaoh and delivering the Israelites, Yahweh will confront the world with its Creator and humble all rulers and nations.

Yahweh's plan expands and redefines the divine/human partnership previously exemplified by Abraham's interrogation of Yahweh prior to the destruction of Sodom and Gomorrah. In that instance, the human partner took the role of confidant and sounding board. Now, in Egypt, Yahweh calls the human partner into active participation with the mighty acts that will subdue the oppressors of Israel. Yahweh will speak to Pharaoh through Moses, Yahweh's emissary, and through Moses's "prophet" Aaron (7:1). The role assigned to Moses sets another important precedent. Yahweh's demonstration of power will bring massive suffering to the Egyptian people, but the violence will be all Yahweh's doing. Moses will participate primarily by relaying Yahweh's demands and announcing what Yahweh will do.

Moses, as it turns out, is not quite as compliant as Abraham. He too asks questions, but his questions express reluctance and discomfort. "Who am I that I should go to Pharaoh and bring the Israelites out of Egypt?" (3:11); "When (the Israelites) ask me, 'What is his name?' what shall I say to them?" (3:13). Moses requires reassurance, prompting Yahweh to respond by momentarily turning his staff into a snake and his hand leprous. He looks for a way out, claiming faltering speech and finally pleading with Yahweh to get someone else (4:1-13). This is not quite the kind of give-and-take that Abraham and Yahweh engaged in over the destruction of Sodom. Moses's refusals smack of impudence. For the first time, we are told that Yahweh gets angry (4:14a). Yahweh's anger, however, does not lead to punishment but to an accommodation that addresses Moses's trepidation: "Isn't Aaron the Levite your brother? . . . You will speak to him and put words in his mouth, and I will be with your mouth and his mouth. I'll direct both of you what to do" (4:14b-15).

Yahweh Gets a Reputation

Yahweh reveals a two-pronged strategy for defeating Pharaoh, overturning the system Pharaoh governs, and firmly fixing Yahweh's name in the minds of Egyptians and Israelites alike. First, Yahweh will strike Egypt with many blows, thereby publicly exposing Pharaoh's powerlessness to maintain order and stability in the land. This Yahweh will do through Moses and Aaron. Secondly, Yahweh will tamper with Pharaoh's internal thought mechanisms so as to prolong the drama and prevent Pharaoh from making a decision on his own. If what makes a king is the free authority to issue decrees and execute them, Yahweh will remove Pharaoh's ability to do either effectively. Yahweh will harden Pharaoh's heart (7:3; cf. 4:21).

The execution of the first strategy takes place squarely within Egypt's world of understanding and brings the people, by steps, to the realization that one greater than Pharaoh is now in the land. Yahweh strikes Egypt with a succession of nine blows designed to bring about the release of the Israelites and demonstrate Yahweh's power. The disasters suffered by Egypt are known in the interpretive tradition as "plagues," but as Terence Fretheim has noted, the biblical text primarily refers to them as "signs" (Hebrew *'ot*, 4:17; 7:3; 8:23; 10:1-2) and "portents" (Hebrew *mophet*, 4:21; 7:3, 9; 11:9-10).[1] The

---

1. Terence E. Fretheim, *God and World in the Old Testament: A Relational Theology of Creation* (Nashville: Abingdon, 2005), 114.

use of these terms reveals that the disasters are designed to communicate something to both Israel and Egypt, namely Yahweh's supremacy over the forces of nature and Pharaonic power. The wonders that Yahweh performs in Egypt are intended to recast the vision of Egyptian and Israelite alike, to expose the power and claims of Pharaoh (and the human systems of oppression represented by Egypt), and to reveal the presence and supremacy of a Creator who has been all but forgotten.

The process is initiated, ironically, when Pharaoh demands that Moses and Aaron perform a wonder (7:9-10). The demand suggests that Pharaoh views the two men simply as magicians. Magic played a fundamental role in Egyptian religion, particularly to ward off disaster or attacks by evil powers. Aaron responds by throwing down his staff, which turns into a snake (cf. 4:2-4). Pharaoh then summons a bevy of magical practitioners, who throw down their staffs and produce the same effect. Aaron's snake, however, swallows the magicians' snakes, portending from the beginning of the ordeal the swallowing of Pharaoh's army by the Red Sea at its conclusion.[2] Pharaoh, however, remains unimpressed.

The contest between Moses and Aaron and the Egyptian magicians foreshadows events in the rest of the narrative. The swallowing serpent evokes a particular image in Egyptian mythology, namely the giant serpent Apep, who symbolized the threatening power of chaos and destruction. Apep was associated with darkness and was said to lurk at the horizon waiting to swallow Ra, the sun god. A variety of myths relate how helpers delivered Ra, but underlying all was the fear that failure would plunge the world into darkness. Viewed with this in mind, the swallowing of the Egyptian snakes by Aaron's serpent anticipates the ninth plague, in which the land of Egypt is plunged into darkness. A swallowing snake is thus associated, in Egyptian eyes, with the fearsome monster that threatens to destroy all.[3]

Yahweh subsequently tells Moses to intercept Pharaoh at the Nile (7:14-22). Yahweh's intent is to chide Pharaoh for not releasing the Israelites and to perform a wonder that will make Pharaoh realize who Yahweh is (v. 17).

---

2. Terence E. Fretheim, "The Plagues as Ecological Signs of Historical Disaster," in *What Kind of God? Collected Essays of Terence E. Fretheim*, ed. Michael J. Chan and Brent A. Strawn, Siphrut 14 (Winona Lake, IN: Eisenbrauns, 2015), 227; Jerome F. D. Creach, *Violence in Scripture*, Interpretation: Resources for the Use of Scripture in the Church (Louisville: Westminster John Knox, 2013), 82-83.

3. Fretheim also sees an allusion to the swallowing of Pharaoh's army at the Red Sea, thus setting the motif of chaos at the beginning and end of the contest (*God and World*, 115-16; "Plagues," 227).

Moses strikes the Nile with his staff and Aaron stretches out his hand as directed by Yahweh, and all the water in Egypt turns to blood. Again, the Egyptian magicians replicate the act and Pharaoh remains unimpressed. He goes home without giving the matter a second thought (7:22).

A third blow, a swarm of frogs out of the Nile, is also matched by the Egyptian magicians (8:1–15). But here a crack appears in Pharaoh's armor. He asks Moses to intercede with Yahweh to stop the amphibian onslaught. The Egyptian magicians, it turns out, are evidently good at producing frogs from the Nile but not so good at getting rid of them! They can bring chaos but cannot restore order. Pharaoh's request is an implicit acknowledgement that Moses has gained a measure of status in his eyes. Pharaoh agrees to release the Israelites to worship Yahweh in Egypt, only to renege when the frogs die out as the result of Moses's intercession.

The fourth wonder marks a turning point. This time Yahweh relays no demand to Pharaoh but simply directs Aaron to produce swarms of gnats by striking the dirt (8:16–19). This the Egyptian magicians cannot do. Their response reveals a dawning recognition: "This is the finger of God!" (v. 19). The magicians do not attribute their failure to the possibility that Moses and Aaron are superior magicians or that they possess superior magical powers. Instead, they realize that they are dealing with a deity. This sets the contest on an entirely different platform. A foreign deity wreaking havoc on Egyptian soil presents quite a different challenge than a couple of ragamuffin magicians who are trying to help their people escape bondage. Against this deity, the magic of the sorcerers has no effect. The magicians' reference to the "finger of God" is an ominous nod to the power of this deity. The hand and arm occur throughout the Bible as metaphors for power and strength. Yahweh, proclaims the psalmist, brought Israel out of the midst of Egypt "with a strong hand and an outstretched arm" (Ps 136:12). Jeremiah seconds: "You brought your people Israel out of from the land of Egypt with signs and wonders, with a strong hand, an outstretched arm, and great fear" (Jer 32:21).

Although the fifth blow (8:16–32) brings another swarm of pesky insects (flies instead of gnats), the setup contrasts significantly from the previous instances. The Egyptians now realize that they are dealing with a god. Yahweh, speaking through Moses, orders Pharaoh to release the people so that they might serve him. "Serving" in this context has to do with worship, but there is a deeper import in Yahweh's choice of words: Yahweh claims this people, who presently are Pharaoh's servants, as a divine possession. There is also an ultimatum. Pharaoh must comply, or

Yahweh will fill every nook and cranny of Egypt with flies. This, Yahweh declares, will be done to bring recognition of who Yahweh is. For good measure, Yahweh declares that the land of Goshen and the Israelites who live there will be exempted, so that the full extent of Yahweh's divinity may be realized—"that you may know that I, Yahweh, am in the midst of the land" (v. 18).

Pharaoh is not given much time. The flies swarm through Egypt the next day. Pharaoh responds swiftly but incompletely. He tells Moses and Aaron that they may offer their sacrifices within the land, perhaps a reasonable request in Pharaoh's eyes in light of Yahweh's demonstrations of power. The offer, however, is unacceptable to Moses, who declares that Israel must go three days' journey from Egypt to sacrifice. Remarkably, Pharaoh backs down, decrees that they may sacrifice in the wilderness, and then asks Moses to intercede again. Moses prays, Yahweh listens, the flies go away, and Pharaoh again reneges once the crisis has passed.

The sequence is repeated once more with yet another plague (9:1–7). Yahweh directs Moses to issue another ultimatum. In this case, Moses declares that if Pharaoh does not release the Israelites to serve Yahweh, "the hand of Yahweh" will bring a pestilence on all the livestock of Egypt. Once again, Yahweh acts swiftly. The pestilence strikes the next day, and the livestock die throughout the entire land, except for the livestock belonging to the Israelites. The finger of God brought a nuisance. The hand of God now strikes more powerfully at Egyptian life and livelihood.

A sixth blow against Egypt demonstrates vividly that Yahweh's supremacy extends over human life itself (9:8–12). Yahweh directs Moses and Aaron to throw handfuls of ash into the sky, where the wind will take it throughout the entire land. The sky, in Egyptian religion, is the domain of Horus, the patron and protector of the Egyptian people. Yahweh, however, now uses the sky as a conduit to carry material that brings horrible boils to both people and livestock. No one is protected, not even the magicians, whose purpose is to protect the people from such disasters by means of their magic. Even they, the narrator notes, suffer with boils and cannot stand up to Moses (v. 11). The oozing eruptions on the skin of humans and beasts manifest a cosmos in a state of disintegration, uncleanness, and defilement, for which no ritual can bring effective remedy.

With divine status, power, and supremacy fully on display, Yahweh strikes with another blow from the sky (9:13–35). Yahweh prefaces the blow by reiterating the demand that the Israelites be released in order to worship Yahweh. A declaration follows, which portends the intensification of violence against Pharaoh and his domain and discloses Yahweh's motive for prolonging the contest.

> This time I am delivering all my blows right to your heart and on your servants and your people, so that you may know that there is no one like me in the entire land. By this point, I could send my hand and strike you and your people with pestilence, and you would be erased from the land. Nevertheless, I have propped you up for this purpose: to display my power and in order to acclaim my name in the entire land. (9:14-16)

Yahweh, in short, tells Pharaoh that his tormentor could easily make an end of him and his people but has kept them from collapsing in order to reveal the full scope of Yahweh's power and gain a preeminent name in the land. Yahweh then identifies the root of Pharaoh's opposition: "you are still thinking too much of yourself regarding my people, in not letting them go" (v. 17a).

Following the rebuke, Yahweh declares that the next day will bring the heaviest hailstorm ever experienced by Egypt and commands those listening to shelter all livestock and human beings so they will not be killed. The narrator notes that some "who feared the word of Yahweh" listened and complied, while others left their livestock and laborers in the fields (vv. 20-21). The comment reveals that Yahweh's objectives are at least partially being realized. Yahweh's power and decrees are being recognized, and some in Egypt respect who Yahweh is and what Yahweh can do.

The hailstorm that Yahweh sends is massively destructive but does not reach Goshen, where the Israelites reside (v. 26). It provokes from Pharaoh a striking admission of defeat, an implicit acknowledgement of Yahweh's divine status and power, and a confession of Egypt's culpability: "I have sinned at this moment. Yahweh is righteous. My people and I are wicked" (v. 27b). Pharaoh again asks for Moses to intercede and once again declares that he will grant permission for Israel to leave.

This would seem to be a case of "mission accomplished," but Moses is not persuaded. He agrees to put a stop to the destructive onslaught of hailstones in order to demonstrate once again that Yahweh, not Pharaoh, is the true possessor of power in the land. Then he dismisses Pharaoh's promises by declaring that he and his retinue do not yet fear Yahweh. "Fearing" thus takes on two nuances. Pharaoh now fears Yahweh in the sense that he realizes what Yahweh is capable of doing and that he is powerless to stop Yahweh. Yet despite his confession, he has not, at least in Moses's estimation, come to the point of yielding to Yahweh's supremacy. The matter is confirmed when, after the storm ceases, we are informed that Pharaoh and his servants sinned again and refused to release the Israelites.

The next blow confirms the rules of the game as Yahweh had defined them previously (10:1-20). Yahweh has prolonged the contest (by hardening the hearts of Pharaoh and his officials) in order to work wonders among them, and Pharaoh still refuses to humble himself (that is, to adopt a subordinate posture toward Yahweh). In addition, Yahweh states that the signs are also being performed so that the Israelites as well will recognize who Yahweh is and recount how Yahweh thoroughly thrashed Pharaoh (v. 2). The episode subsequently reveals more recognition for Yahweh on the part of the officials and a widening divide between them and Pharaoh. Faced with another divine ultimatum, the officials appeal to Pharaoh to give in (v. 7). The appeal seems to be effective, as Pharaoh sets before Moses and Aaron a proposal for compromise: only the men may go to worship Yahweh. Moses refuses the proposal, however, setting in motion a third blow from the sky—a swarm of locusts that matches the intensity of the hailstorm. In keeping with the established pattern, Pharaoh relents and asks Moses to intercede. This time he asks specifically that Moses would forgive his sin and that Yahweh would do away with the deadly menace. Pharaoh, whose word in Egypt can bring life or death, cannot keep death at bay. The only thing left under his control is the community of Israelites living in Goshen, and, once again, he refuses to release them when the crisis has passed.

The ninth blow, a palpable darkness, comes without warning or fanfare. The darkness immobilizes the Egyptians. No one can see or move about for three days, except, as in the previous instances, in the region inhabited by the Israelites; there the light continues. The dense darkness directly challenges Pharaoh's role as the priest of the sun god Ra, one of the principal Egyptian deities. The darkness exposes the abject powerlessness of Pharaoh in the contest with the God of the Hebrews. Even so, Pharaoh clings to the notion that he can barter with Israel's God. He presents Moses with a greater concession than in the previous instance, decreeing that the people may go to worship Yahweh but that their livestock must remain. Yahweh, however, will give no quarter. It is all or nothing on the issue of leaving Egypt to worship Yahweh. With attitudes on both sides firmly set, the episode ends abruptly. Pharaoh dismisses Moses with a warning that any more meetings will bring Moses's death. Pharaoh no longer has any leverage, real or imagined. The only viable decision remaining for Pharaoh is to accede completely to Moses's demand, and that would be an admission of total defeat.

Who Controls the Forces of Nature?

A world in utter darkness evokes the precreation state of the world, when "the earth was completely without form, and darkness covered the surface of the abyss" (Gen 1:1).[4] It therefore signifies a land that has descended completely into chaos. The darkness is the final stage of a sequence of events that not only engulfs two peoples but the entire created order. The confrontation between Moses and Pharaoh is personal in character and cosmic in scope. The entire created order is caught up and involved in the contest. The reach of Pharaonic power extends beyond the control of peoples to the management and oversight of creation itself. The king's power in the ancient world was, most of all, employed for the purpose of maintaining social and cosmic equilibrium. The social and natural orders were understood to be interrelated. An imbalance in the social order affected the whole of creation and vice versa. Pharaoh, then, functions as the supervisor and guarantor of harmony, order, and balance. If the king is firmly on the throne, all is right with the world.

The plagues that beset Egypt present "a picture of creation gone berserk," of a world "reverting to its precreation state."[5] The entire created order is caught up in the struggle between Yahweh and Pharaoh over the title of superintendent of creation. By settling this question in this particular place and at this particular time, Yahweh settles it for all places and all times. Yahweh enters the world through Egypt in response to Israel's cry and in faithfulness to divine promises. Israel's God asserts supremacy and reveals an intention to restore creation by working within the mechanisms and structures of political power. "The deliverance of Israel is ultimately for the sake of the entire creation."[6]

The creation theology that forms the backdrop of the plague narrative has been elaborated by Terence Fretheim, who argues that the plagues result from the release of chaotic powers caused by Pharaoh's anti-life practices. He notes in the text the opposition of Yahweh's creation work—expressed by references to Israel's fruitfulness, increase, and filling of the land—and Pharaoh's anti-creation work, demonstrated by oppressive measures and his decree to kill Israelite males. Yahweh's intention is that the divine name be

---

4. Fretheim, "Plagues as Ecological Signs," 310.
5. Fretheim, *God and World*, 120.
6. Terence E. Fretheim, *Exodus*, IBC (Louisville: John Knox, 1991), 109; *God and World*, 119.

exalted and come to the attention of all the peoples of the earth. Pharaoh, however, resists at the very point that Yahweh actualizes the promise to restore creation's fruitfulness through Israel. Because the ethical and social orders are intertwined, Pharaoh's anti-life actions destabilize the cosmos and unleash the wave of chaotic powers that overwhelm Egypt. Pharaoh's oppressive and death-dealing policies, in short, subvert Yahweh's work in the world, and this brings consequences that threaten creation itself.

God is portrayed in these texts as active in judgment, that is, in the interplay of Pharaoh's sin and its consequence (though not without mediation), but in effect God gives Pharaoh up to reap the "natural" consequences of his anticreation behavior (hardening of the heart being one).[7]

Yahweh acts in the narrative to judge and restore, to set things right, manifesting not only power over creation but also the ability to re-create in the aftermath of the plagues.

The plagues, however, do not arise of their own accord. The narrative is clear that Yahweh sends the plagues as a sign of sovereign power and the determination to bring into being a new world through Israel. The plagues do not just reveal a creation in chaos. They represent a weaponization of creation that turns creation itself against the Egyptians and unmasks Pharaoh's pretension. Stability, continuity, and harmony are premium values for Pharaoh, Egypt, and indeed any society. Pharaoh, however, can do nothing to preserve the people from Yahweh's onslaught. Yahweh overpowers Pharaoh by systematically turning the powers of nature against the people of Egypt. In this grand conflict between the Creator and the embodiment of the manmade world, Yahweh becomes the chaos monster who plunges the whole world into a dark abyss. Yahweh turns creation itself into a malevolent force that torments Pharaoh, his people, and their cattle, and in so doing brings human alienation into full view. Adam was estranged from the creation he was created to care for. Creation is now openly hostile toward Pharaoh.

Yahweh thus enters Egypt as the agent of chaos who throws the ordered world of Pharaoh into disarray. Yahweh commands water, earth, and sky. The Nile turns to blood and becomes a lethal environment for the fish that live in it, forcing the Egyptians to dig along its banks for drinking water. Frogs spill out of the Nile into the houses of Egypt. Gnats come out of the

---

7. Fretheim, *Exodus*, 111.

dirt, and flies follow. Disease strikes the livestock in the Egyptian fields. Ashes tossed into the sky are carried by the wind throughout Egypt, bringing boils to humans and animals alike. Locusts descend from the sky and destroy the crops of Egypt, and hail completes the ruin, shattering plants and trees and killing both humans and livestock that have not taken shelter. Finally, the astral lights are swallowed up, darkness descends, and the order dissolves completely. Only Yahweh turns away the catastrophes and restores order.

Fretheim has called the plagues "hypernatural" manifestations of the forces of nature; that is, they break outside the normal bounds of natural forces within a harmonious, ordered creation. They reveal an increasingly unbalanced and distorted world. "Water is no longer simply water; light and darkness are no longer separated; diseases of people and animals run amok; insects and amphibians swarm out of control."[8] As the text makes very clear, it is Yahweh who, through the agency of Moses and Aaron, throws the cosmic order into turmoil, sets the forces of creation against the population, and plunges Egypt into chaos. Yahweh wields the powers of creation that Pharaoh and his officials claim to manage. In the hands of Yahweh, the forces of nature are weapons that can be dispatched and recalled with a word. Yahweh works weal and woe in creation and does so publicly for the purpose of establishing the Creator's supremacy over the whole of creation (cf. Isa 45:7).

Hardening Pharaoh's Heart

The outward expressions of Yahweh's supremacy, manifested in the plagues, work in coordination with the inner workings of Yahweh's supremacy, manifested in the hardening of Pharaoh's heart. Yahweh lays out the connection between the two operations just before sending Moses to address the Israelite elders. After telling Moses to go to Pharaoh with a request to release Israel for a three-day journey into the wilderness, Yahweh declares, "I know that the king of Egypt will not let you go without a strong hand. So I will send my hand and strike Egypt with all my wonders, which I will perform within it. After that, he will let you go" (3:19-20). Later in the conversation, Yahweh connects the working of wonders to what Yahweh will do within Pharaoh. "When you get back to Egypt, make sure you perform before Pharaoh all the

---

8. Fretheim, *Exodus*, 109; cf. Fretheim, *God and World*, 119-20.

portents I put into your hand. As for me, I will harden his heart, and he will not release the people" (4:21). Pharaoh's stubbornness subsequently provides the reason for Yahweh to afflict Egypt with disasters. Each time Pharaoh refuses Moses's request to release Israel, Yahweh strikes a blow in return.

The narrative complicates the scenario, however, by reporting that Yahweh hardened Pharaoh's heart (4:21; 7:3; 9:12; 10:1, 20, 27; 11:10; 14:4, 8, 17), that Pharaoh hardened his heart (8:32; 9:34), and simply that Pharaoh's heart was hardened (7:13, 14, 22; 8:13, 14, 19; 9:7, 35). The assertions are made without harmonization, creating a tension that affirms both as true. The reader is left to work out the paradox.

The idea that Yahweh might interfere with a human being's ability to make decisions freely has not been attractive to most modern interpreters. The most common approach to resolving the paradox takes a cue from Yahweh's declaration that he knows that Pharaoh will not release the Israelites (3:19-20). Yahweh's hardening, it is argued, is a judgment on or an acceleration of the arrogant disposition that characterizes Pharaoh prior to receiving the first challenge from Moses. Pharaoh's stubbornness is viewed as an expression of his arrogant sinfulness or a characteristic of human entities that wield power in defiance of God. Pharaoh's attitude is fixed against Israel and against Israel's God. The prophetic demands uttered by Moses only harden him. Fretheim puts the matter succinctly:

> *God as subject intensifies Pharaoh's own obduracy.* While initially this does not result in a numbing of Pharaoh's will, it begins to have that effect as events drive toward final disaster. Both need to be said: Pharaoh hardens his own heart, and so does God. . . Each refusal makes it easier for Pharaoh to refuse the next time. More and more, the end becomes a certain matter. As Pharaoh's resistance progresses, God's hardening enters the picture.[9]

A different emphasis emerges, however, if we take account of the number of times that we are told that Yahweh hardens Pharaoh's heart (ten) compared to the number of times we are told that Pharaoh hardens his own heart (two), without taking into account the eight instances in which we are told simply that Pharaoh's heart is hardened. When this is noted, the textual emphasis tilts towards Yahweh's working rather than Pharaoh's intransigence. The emphasis becomes more apparent when we note that the

9. Fretheim, *Exodus*, 98, 100.

instances where Yahweh is the hardener occur primarily at the beginning and end of the narrative (4:21; 7:3; 10:1, 20, 27; 11:10; 14:4, 8, 17), while the two instances when Pharaoh hardens occur at the onset of plagues and in the context of the plague of boils (8:32; 9:34). The declarations that Yahweh hardens Pharaoh's heart thus bracket the other reports of hardening, setting all intervening instances within the context of Yahweh's interference with Pharaoh's inner deliberations.

To complicate matters, the Hebrew text employs three different verbs to signify the hardening of Pharaoh's heart. The verb *qashah* ("harden") occurs only once but constitutes the second mention of Yahweh's hardening (7:3). Most frequent is its synonym *khazaq* ("stiffen," 4:21; 7:13, 22; 8:19; 9:12, 35; 10:20, 27; 11:10; 14:8). The third verb, *kabed*, does not signify hardness but heaviness (thus "his heart became heavy" or "Pharaoh made his heart heavy"). The verb is also employed to denote having honor or respect, and the noun formed from the common root (*kabod*) is often translated "glory" and associated with Yahweh. The root *kbd*, furthermore, shows up repeatedly as a thematic thread within the Hebrew text. Moses protests to Yahweh that he is "heavy of mouth and heavy of tongue" (4:10). Pharaoh decrees a heavy workload for the Israelite brick makers (5:9). When Yahweh's divine power succeeds in provoking Pharaonic response, the root occurs as an adjective to characterize the plagues: a heavy swarm (8:20), heavy pestilence (9:3), heavy hail (9:18), and the very heavy swarm of locusts (10:14).

The repetition of the root *kbd*, with reference both to what happens in the story and to Yahweh's work on Pharaoh's heart, directs our attention to the role of both in bringing Yahweh honor and glory. Yahweh, the divine newcomer, gains a reputation by striking Pharaoh repeatedly, by publicly exposing him as a pretender, and by rendering him unable to make his own decisions as sovereign. As we noted above, Yahweh makes this clear to Pharaoh during the seventh plague by declaring that he has been kept alive for the sole reason of demonstrating Yahweh's power and proclaiming Yahweh's name throughout the world (9:12).

Yahweh, the hitherto unknown deity, is intent not only on delivering Israel but also on being recognized as the supreme power in the world. Although divine interference with human decision-making chafes against modern convictions of free will, the tactic is uniquely appropriate in this instance. The supremacy of a king is demonstrated by his ability to decide whatever he wills and by the power to enforce his will. Assuming this, Yahweh delivers the ultimate *coup de grâce* by blocking Pharaoh's ability to decide and decree and by bending Pharaoh's will towards Yahweh's purpose. It is significant in this regard that the only two instances that report that Pharaoh hardened his heart both employ the verb *kabed* to convey that "Pharaoh made his heart heavy." Human agency is not dismissed, but it is diminished. Yahweh overpowers the will of the most powerful of all human beings in order to publicly reveal Yahweh's supremacy. What distinguishes Yahweh from Pharaoh, the narrative reveals, is that Yahweh has both the power and freedom to execute decrees. Pharaoh's power is limited to saying "no," and even in that he vacillates. His word and will are not stable. They bend as circumstance and opportunity dictate. As disaster follows disaster, Pharaoh becomes increasingly indecisive and powerless to influence events.

It is important to note here that Yahweh's hardening work is directed at the king, at a particular time and for a salvific purpose, and not presented as Yahweh's customary way of dealing with human beings. It is an apt and portentous way of dealing with arrogant power in defiance of God's supremacy and work, and it will not be the only time that Yahweh hijacks royal decision-making in order to accomplish divine purposes (cf. Josh 11:20; 1 Sam 10:9).

Death and Deliverance

Yahweh's final blow brings death itself to Pharaoh's doorstep and to the homes of the Egyptian people (11:1-10; 12:29-36). Moses announces that Yahweh will enter Egypt, and as a result every firstborn, of both humans and beasts, will die (11:4-5). The unusual wording of the announcement draws attention to Yahweh's presence among the Egyptians and what that presence will mean. Israel's God will now directly come into Egypt, rather than working through divine agents, and people will die.

Yahweh strikes this blow without human assistance. Moses is assigned only the task of interpreting what is about to happen, instituting the means of its ritual commemoration, and relaying instructions that will preserve Israelite lives. Whereas in the previous cases Moses served as Yahweh's mouthpiece to announce and explain Yahweh's wonders to Pharaoh and his officials, he now fulfills the same role for Israel. Moses plays no part in the horror Egypt will experience. Yahweh will not implicate Moses in the death of children.

Through Moses, Yahweh conveys succinctly what will happen and why it will happen.

> I will pass through the land of Egypt tonight, and I will strike every firstborn in the land of Egypt, from human to animal. And on all the gods of Egypt I will render justice. I am Yahweh. (12:12)

Yahweh here speaks of settling the score with the gods of Egypt, who have remained discreetly in the background during the contest between Yahweh and Pharaoh. We may think of the Egyptian gods as those powers that uphold and protect Egypt and that reinforce its claims of life and supremacy. They have remained in the background so as not to confuse the nature of the contest between Yahweh and Pharaoh. Yahweh's comment confirms that they have not been absent or disengaged. Executing justice on the gods of Egypt means executing justice on the system that they legitimize and reinforce; they are the powers to which both people and Pharaoh appeal for protection and livelihood.

The idea of rendering justice has less to do with punishment and vengeance and more with the idea of restoring equilibrium and balance. A just society, as conceived in the ancient world, seeks to avoid and redress breaches and imbalances in the social fabric. Pharaoh's subjection of the Israelites has created a massive imbalance in political and economic power, precipitating a response from Yahweh when the oppressed Israelites cry out (2:23). Rendering justice is a matter of evening out the scales. Yahweh will later encode the concept within Israel's legal tradition:

> You must not oppress a widow or orphan. If you actually oppress them, and if they cry fervently to me, I will certainly hear. My anger will burn and I will kill you with the sword. So your wives shall become widows and your children orphans. (Exod 22:22–24)

This particular law stands alone, among all the laws given at Sinai, by identifying Yahweh, rather than a human authority, as the one who will restore balance (cf. Prov 22:22–23). It directly articulates for Israel how central justice is to Yahweh's intention for humanity. If those who have much power subjugate those with little power, the law declares, Yahweh will step in and even things out.

The world that men have made is a world of hierarchy and power, concentrated in the person of the king and maintained by the threat and execution of violence. The early chapters of Exodus presented Egypt as one manifestation of this world, and Pharaoh and his officials as those who wield power in it. Israel cried out, and Yahweh stepped in to deliver Israel "with great acts of justice" (Exod 6:6; 7:4). Yahweh makes clear, at the beginning and the end of the affair, that the blows Egypt receives even things out between Israelites and Egyptians. Yahweh identified Israel as his firstborn son before Pharaoh and declared that Pharaoh's firstborn would be killed if Pharaoh did not release Yahweh's people. The cry that went up to Yahweh from the Israelite slaves (2:23) is now matched by a cry that goes up from Egyptian houses at the death of firstborn children (12:30).

Yahweh's judgment on the Egyptian leadership and Egyptian gods removes any doubt that the God of Israel holds the power of life and death. Pharaoh had dismissed the Israelites but now appeals for a blessing (12:32). The Egyptian people likewise get the message. They urge the Israelites to leave, fearing that "we'll all be dead" (12:33).

Yahweh, however, is not finished. Once the Israelites have reached the sea, Yahweh informs Moses that Pharaoh's heart will be hardened once again. Yahweh intends a final, complete defeat of the assembled might of Egypt and orchestrates events once more to destroy the Egyptian military, the instrument of Pharaoh's power. The main threads of the narrative now come together with dramatic intensity. We are told, not once but three times, that Yahweh hardens Pharaoh's heart (14:4, 8, 17). Each instance reiterates the same rationale: Yahweh will gain honor through combat with Pharaoh and his military minions (14:4, 17, 18). Two of the iterations declare that Yahweh intends for the Egyptians to acknowledge the divine name ("the Egyptians will know that I am Yahweh," vv. 4, 18). At the sea, Yahweh decisively asserts supremacy by delivering Israel and drowning Egyptian power. There is even a subtle linguistic flourish. Yahweh gains glory a final time (again, the verb *kabed*) by making the wheels of the Egyptian chariots "heavy" so they cannot turn (14:25).

It has long been recognized that the splitting of the sea evokes the imagery of cosmic creation (cf. Gen 1:6-10). Yahweh initiates a new ordering of humanity by sending a wind across an expanse of water and dividing the water from dry land (cf. Gen 1:2). Isaiah makes the connection directly by evoking a version of what is likely a Canaanite creation myth that portrays the abyss as a serpent named Rahab.

> Awake! Awake! Clothe yourself with power, O arm of Yahweh! Awake as in the long-ago, ancient times! Aren't you the one who cut up Rahab, who split the dragon? Aren't you the one who dried up the sea, the waters of the great abyss, who made the depths of the sea into a path for the redeemed to pass through? (Isa 51:9-10)

By splitting the Red Sea, Yahweh not only manifests divine power over creation but is revealed as the Creator who rightly orders all life.

Yahweh's creative work at the sea, moreover, is reported using the motif of combat. When the Egyptian military approaches, Moses allays the fears of the Israelites by telling them to stay calm, because "Yahweh will fight for you" (Exod 14:14). The Egyptians likewise try to flee from the Israelites (though too late), for they recognize that "Yahweh fights for them against the Egyptians" (v. 25). Yahweh's revelation as a victorious warrior thereby merges with Yahweh's revelation as Creator. Yahweh's creative work at the sea entails both the birth of a new people who will be ordered by God and the dissolution of the warped, imbalanced world that Egypt represents. As was the case with the flood, the destruction of the old makes way for the birth of the new.

A victory song punctuates the impact and import of Israel's passage and Egypt's demise (15:1-18). The song begins by exalting Yahweh and associating Yahweh's name with Yahweh's manifestation as a warrior: "Yahweh is a warrior! Yahweh is his name!" (v. 3). It then immediately reinforces the association of Yahweh as Warrior and Creator by expressing the destruction of the Egyptian army in language reminiscent of the destruction of the world through the flood, with the waters piling up and covering the Egyptian army, which sank like stone and lead into the deep (vv. 4-10). The central section of the song accentuates the point of the whole event, namely the victory's dramatic display of Yahweh's supremacy: "Who is like you among the gods, O Yahweh? Who is like you, glorious in holiness, fearsome in acclamation, working wonders?" (v. 11).

The final section of the song confirms that Yahweh's intention to establish a reputation in the world has indeed succeeded (vv. 14-18). The song reveals that the news of what Yahweh has done in Egypt has traveled to the other peoples and potentates of the region, who are awestruck. Philistia is queasy. Edom is alarmed. Moab trembles. Canaan melts. Thus it can be confessed: "Yahweh reigns forever and ever!" The song concludes by confirming that Yahweh has the entire world in view as he pummels and cows Egypt. Again, Fretheim offers an apt summary:

> *The deliverance of Israel is ultimately for the sake of the entire creation.* The issue finally is not that God's name be made known in Israel but that it be declared (*sapar*) to the entire earth (9:16; cf. Ps. 78:3-4; Isa. 43:21). God's purpose in these events is creation-wide, for all of the earth is God's. It is to so lift up the divine name that it will come to the attention of all the peoples of the earth (cf. Rom. 9:17). Hence the *public character of* these events is very important.[10]

---

10. Fretheim, *Exodus*, 108.

THE GRAND ENTRANCE

The song declares what the narrative depicts. If Yahweh is to create in the world, Yahweh must destroy what is corrupted. If Yahweh is to be esteemed, Yahweh must show unassailable power. If Yahweh is to be acknowledged by all the nations of the earth, Yahweh must work wonders on behalf of Israel.

Violence in Egypt

The descent into Egypt entangles Yahweh in the systems of power that configure the world men have made. Yahweh enters this world as an unknown deity and a god of slaves. To reset the divine-human relationship on its original foundation, Yahweh must achieve supremacy over human powers and over creation itself. Yahweh therefore is faced with the task of making a name in a world that takes great stock in names. In this world, names identify and differentiate. They define one's status and place within the power grid.

The scenario that begins the account portrays a world of oppression and violence born of insecurity. Yahweh is drawn into the world by the cry that emanates from Israel's suffering, selects an emissary, and reveals a plan to advance restorative purposes in the world through Israel. It is clear from the beginning that Yahweh has deemed it necessary to take on the attributes and actions that define those who wield power in this violent world. Yahweh must make the divine name known both to the people who will bear divine blessing and to the nation that attempts to exploit them; and Yahweh must do so in terms a violent world can understand. To be taken seriously, Yahweh finds it necessary to confront the worldly powers with a greater display of power. Yahweh makes a reputation by violently disrupting the social and cosmic order of Egypt and showing the nameless king to be powerless in the face of Yahweh's attacks. The narrative relates what the strategy entails for Yahweh.

First, *Yahweh finds it necessary to utilize violence to bring recognition of Yahweh's universal supremacy.* In the world that men have made, position and status are maintained by the exertion of power. Gaining preeminence thus requires the acquisition of power. Pharaoh and his officials understand only power. In order to deliver Israel and display sovereignty, Yahweh must bring superior power to bear, and this must be done publicly. If the world is to know who Yahweh is, Yahweh must beat Pharaoh on Pharaoh's own turf. "A king confronts Israel, so Yahweh becomes a king in order to confront this king and play him at his own game, as a king delivering Israel from Egypt with powerful decisive acts."[11] Yahweh appears to Israel first and foremost as a champion who fights and defeats the Egyptian menace. Yahweh strikes Pharaoh repeatedly with disasters in response to Pharaoh's refusal to release the Israelites. Yahweh also strikes Pharaoh by hardening Pharaoh's heart, so that Pharaoh's public refusals give Yahweh the opportunity to strike more intense blows.

Second, *Yahweh utilizes violence to destroy in order to create.* Pharaoh's world has an order and mechanisms in place to maintain it. Egypt's order, however, is neither equitable nor harmonious. It is maintained by violence and oppression, which, when given voice, prompts Yahweh to enter the world to set things right. Yahweh exposes the impotence of humans to manage the world by setting the forces of creation against the earthly powers. Yahweh becomes the overpowering force of chaos that Egypt and its religious and political functionaries strive to keep at bay. Pharaoh's continued defiance precipitates a disintegration of the human-made world, ultimately bringing death to those who were the instigators and agents of death to Israel. The end of Egyptian power, manifested by its forces being swallowed up by the sea, becomes at the same time the event that creates a new people through whom Yahweh's order will be reestablished on the earth. In the end, Yahweh overturns and equalizes.

> The inversion of Israel and Egypt, in terms of who cries now and those who cried earlier, suggests something like an eschatological proviso on any set pattern of power relations. At the beginning of the Exodus story, one might have thought Egypt would abuse forever, and Israel could cry in agony to perpetuity, but now in this narrative, Egypt becomes the voice of the most extreme cry. The narrative affirms that drastic revision does indeed take place in power relations where no revision seemed possible.[12]

At no point does Yahweh act out of caprice or anger. No emotion is attributed to Yahweh during the entire contest. Rather, the narrative emphasizes Yahweh's determination to free Israel and return cry for cry and death for death.

---

11. John Goldingay, *Old Testament Theology*, vol. 1: *Israel's Gospel* (Downers Grove, IL: InterVarsity Press, 2003), 311.

12. Walter Brueggemann, "Exodus," in *The New Interpreter's Bible*, vol. 1, ed. Leander E. Keck (Nashville: Abingdon, 1994), 772.

Third, *Yahweh finds it necessary to prolong the violence in order to achieve divine objectives*. The realization that their world is coming apart comes only gradually and grudgingly to Pharaoh and his minions. Those who have been accustomed to managing the world and enjoying a privileged place in it cannot conceive of a power greater than theirs or a world that is better ordered. Yahweh continues the blows until the principalities and powers are completely unmasked and exposed as helpless pretenders. Yahweh, however, is also implicated in the prolonged suffering endured by the Egyptians. Yahweh hardens the heart of Pharaoh in order to display divine power in no uncertain terms, leading ultimately to massive slaughters, first of the firstborn babies, children, and men of Egypt and then to the military implements of Pharaoh's power.

Fourth, *Yahweh enlists human participants*. Yahweh does more than merely divulge intents and purposes to a human partner, as is the case with Abraham. In the contest with Pharaoh, Yahweh selects human agents as representatives and uses them to enact divine decrees. Moses is not just a confidant. He is a "god" to Pharaoh (7:1), initiating cycles of disasters in response to Pharaonic obstinacy and receiving Pharaoh's requests for forgiveness and blessing. Moses sets disasters in motion, but that is the extent of his involvement. Yahweh remains the sole perpetrator of all the violence suffered by Pharaoh, his people, and his land, while distancing Moses from the deaths of the firstborn throughout Egypt (12:23). Instead of sending Moses to Pharaoh to initiate the disaster, Yahweh sends him to the Israelites to undertake protective measures.

Fifth, *the entire land suffers for the decisions that the king makes*. The reach of Pharaoh's sovereignty and power is comprehensive. All life, including the well-being of animals and the land itself, is affected by the decisions the ruler makes. The whole realm, therefore, either benefits or suffers from pharaonic decrees. There are undoubtedly many in Egypt who do not directly participate in the oppressive policies of the king and are thus undeserving of the calamities that Yahweh brings. Nevertheless, Yahweh's action, although directed toward compelling and humiliating Pharaoh, brings suffering to many human beings who have had no say in what transpires. It is the nature of kingdoms that those ruled by kings suffer or benefit undeservedly because of the decisions kings make—a harsh reality that Israel also experiences when it lives under its own kings.

5

A Covenant Made and Remade

> Let them be ready on the third day, because on the third day Yahweh will descend on Mount Sinai in the sight of the entire nation.
>
> EXODUS 19:11

Yahweh delivers Israel from Egypt and the oppressive world Egypt represents in order to establish a new people that lives in subservience to Yahweh and embodies Yahweh's order on the earth. Salvation leads to covenant making. Mount Sinai, where Yahweh had announced the divine descent into Egypt, now becomes the site where Yahweh descends to bring into being a nation unlike all other nations. Abraham's descendants will not be defined or organized by the systems that configure the affairs of other nations. Rather, they will be defined by choosing the God who has chosen them. In Egypt, Yahweh referred to the descendants of Abraham and Sarah as "my people" (Exod 3:7) and demonstrated divine commitment to Israel through signs and wonders. Now, at Sinai, Yahweh forms the people into a nation that reflects Yahweh's restorative work in creation—a nation defined by devotion, dependence, and obedience to Yahweh. At Sinai, Yahweh in turn devotes the divine self to Israel and fully identifies with the nation. Yahweh intends to carry out the work of restoration through the nation established by covenant at Sinai and as a consequence will become enmeshed in the affairs and challenges that beset the nation in a violent world.

What identification with a nation will mean for Yahweh is reflected by the fact that Yahweh descends upon Sinai twice. In the first instance, Yahweh lays out the contours of the relationship and Israel accepts it through the medium of covenant-making (Exod 19:1–24:18). The covenant at Sinai renders the vision that founds and grounds Israel's identity as a nation and represents the restoration of the divine-human relationship on its original footing, with Yahweh as sovereign and provider and Israel as the obedient agent that carries out Yahweh's will for creation. The second Sinai descent (Exod 34:1-2) takes place within the context of another, scaled-back covenant-making event that reflects adjustments Yahweh has made in light of Israel's shocking worship of a golden calf (Exod 32:1-35). The debacle marks the first instance in which Yahweh's killing emanates from Yahweh's anger. Viewed within the context of the covenant-making events, the episode invites reflection on the association of divine anger with divine violence.

The Covenant as Ideal Vision

At Sinai Yahweh reestablishes the human-divine relationship on its original foundation. Israel emerges from a human system in Egypt that Yahweh has thrown into chaos. Now at the mountain, Yahweh sets the divine order in place on the earth, through a people who, by living within that order, will be a kingdom of priests and a holy nation. In the unbounded wild place between Egypt and Canaan—two lands that reflect the world that men have made—Yahweh forms a people birthed by divine deliverance and defined by devotion and obedience.

> You have seen what I did to Egypt and how I lifted you up on eagle's wings and brought you to me. Now, if you will diligently obey my voice and observe my covenant, you will become my treasured possession among all the nations. The whole earth belongs to me, but you will belong to me as a kingdom of priests and a holy nation. (Exod 19:4-6a)

The invitation to the covenant makes clear, first, Yahweh's status as Creator, demonstrated by the wonders in Egypt, and second, Israel's unique mission as a nation that embodies a restored relationship between God and humanity. The new people, Yahweh's treasured possession, will undertake a mediatory role within the world ("a kingdom of priests") and reveal Yahweh's unique character ("a holy nation").

Yahweh then dictates a series of protocols that must be observed prior to and during the covenant-making between God and people. The protocols likely draw from Israel's recent experience in Egypt, where strict ritual codes governed audiences before Pharaoh. Egyptian documents make references to purification and washing, a period of preparation in a waiting area, and the maintenance of silence before being ushered into Pharaoh's throne room to await the ruler's appearance. Entrance to the throne room was rigidly choreographed so as to enhance Pharaoh's splendor, and infractions—especially physical contact with Pharaoh or speaking without being addressed—could have disastrous consequences.[1]

As the first item of business, Yahweh thus conveys in unmistakable terms the awe and honor befitting the Creator and the kind of relationship Israel will adopt in becoming God's people. Yahweh, Creator and Sovereign, requires the people to undergo a three-day period of preparation and to appear before God in clean clothes. Yahweh sets a boundary around the mountain that differentiates the holy space from the people's space, and warns that under penalty of death no one may enter the holy space until they hear the signal (a long trumpet blast [v. 13]). Moses plays the role of usher, instructing the people in the protocols and helping them navigate the King's space. When the trumpet sounds, Moses brings the people to the mountain, where they stand awaiting further directions. Yahweh is the last to enter (v. 20). The whole scene—complete with fire, cloud, and thunder—creates a sense of awesome majesty and splendor, and the people tremble (v. 18).

The distinctly political cast of the ceremony is further enhanced by the incorporation of elements widely attested in treaty-making in the ancient world, particularly treaties made between a high king, or suzerain, and a subject king, or vassal. The covenant ceremony itself does not strictly follow covenant protocol but suggestively evokes the procedures of treaty-making. Elements of the treaty form in the Sinai ceremony include the suzerain's invitation to make a covenant, an elaboration of the good things the suzerain has done for the vassal, the dictation of stipulations required by the suzerain, a list of blessings and curses that will come to the vassal as a result of obedience or disobedience, agreement by the vassal, ratification of the treaty, sacrifice, and a covenant meal. The covenant at Sinai is a unique event, but it invites the reader by way of allusion to consider the covenant in political as well as religious terms. This kingdom of priests has a king.

The political ambience of the covenant constructs a frame of reference by which Israel may understand what is about to transpire between the nation and its God. The nation is to show all the deference and respect that a

---

1. Garry J. Shaw, *The Pharaoh: Life at Court and on Campaign* (London: Thames & Hudson, 2012), 79–85.

vassal shows to a suzerain and is to live obediently according to the dictates of the high king. These expressions of fidelity will ensure that Israel will stay in the good graces of the cosmic Sovereign and enjoy the benefits that the high king has the power to bestow. Alternatively, if Israel treats the Sovereign with disrespect, curries relationships with other monarchs, or refuses to observe what the king has decreed, it can expect the kind of response from Yahweh that rebellious vassals commonly receive from their suzerain.

Moses serves as the intermediary between the Sovereign and the people, just as he did in Egypt. He relays Yahweh's words to the elders of the nation and relays the nation's commitment to obey everything Yahweh has set before them (vv. 7-8). He brings the nation to the foot of the mountain to meet God (v. 17), warns them again not to encroach upon Yahweh's space uninvited or unprepared (vv. 21-24a), and brings Aaron up with him to receive Yahweh's commandments (v. 24b).

The commandments that Yahweh sets before the nation reinforce the association between who Yahweh is, what Yahweh has done for Israel, and what Israel must do to actualize and maintain the relationship. Following Yahweh's self-identification—"I am Yahweh your God who brought you out of the land of Egypt, out of the house of slavery" (20:2)—is a set of ten commandments, the first three of which have to do with the disposition Israel must maintain toward Yahweh: no other gods before Yahweh, no representations or worship of the divine in the form of created things, no empty use of the divine name (vv. 3-7).

The second and third commandments are noteworthy for the way Yahweh expands on them. Elaborating on the prohibition of idolatry, Yahweh declares that he is a "passionate" deity who visits the "guilt" of the parents to their descendants to the fourth generation of those who "hate" him, but who displays devotion to the thousandth generation of those who "love" him. The meanings of the four words in quotation marks are notoriously difficult to pin down, let alone translate. We note the declaration here because it is a remarkable disclosure of divine identity, uttered in the context of an unequivocal command for respect and obedience. The root of the word here translated "passionate"—traditionally rendered "jealous"—signifies raw, intense, and focused emotion, of which jealousy is but one expression (cf. Num 25:11; Deut 29:20; 1 Kgs 14:22; 19:10; 2 Kgs 10:16; 19:31; Ps 69:10; Isa 42:13; 63:15; Joel 2:18; Zech 8:2).

Yahweh's self-identification as a passionate deity would seem to associate Yahweh with the other deities of the ancient world, who like their human counterparts were susceptible to caprice and impulsiveness. The declaration as whole, however, distances Yahweh from other deities by situating Yahweh's passion as a response to human dispositions toward him, that is, through differing responses to those who hate versus those who love him. "Hating" and "loving" also have a wide sphere of meaning and can refer to rejecting and choosing, respectively (cf. Deut 21:15-16; Prov 8:6; Ezek 16:37; Amos 5:15; Mic 3:2; Mal 1:2-3). The declaration as a whole makes a rhetorical point. Yahweh's response to those who relate with hate pales in comparison to Yahweh's disposition to show mercy to those who relate with love. Thus, in this self-identifying declaration, Yahweh self-discloses as a deity of intense emotion but situates divine passion within the context of relationship and an overwhelming inclination to bless.

It is noteworthy that Yahweh's anger is mentioned in the laws themselves only in the singular instance of oppressing widows and orphans, discussed in the previous chapter.

> You shall not oppress a widow or orphan. If you actually oppress them, and if they cry fervently to me, I will certainly hear. My anger will burn and I will kill you with the sword. So your wives shall become widows and your children orphans. (22:22-24)

The declaration underscores the intensity of Yahweh's commitment to justice. Oppression of the powerless is the one instance, among all the laws, that is said to provoke Yahweh's anger. The elaboration attached to the law emphasizes that Yahweh's passionate involvement with Israel extends to a concern for the way Israelites treat each other. Radical disrespect, whether toward Yahweh or toward others in the nation, will stir Yahweh to forceful action to set things right.

After the people assent to the covenant stipulations, the ceremony concludes with a portrait of unity and communion. Moses leads a group of men up the mountain where, we are told, they see the God of Israel.

> Then Moses, Aaron, Nadab, and Abihu, along with seventy Israelite elders, ascended and saw the God of Israel. Under his feet there was something like sapphire tile and like the sky itself in purity. God did not lay a hand on the Israelite leaders. They saw God and ate and drank. (24:9-11)

The scene relates an amazing event with surprising brevity and mystery. The main point—that the men saw God—is emphasized by repetition at the beginning and end. But what did the Israelites see? The reference to God's feet and the sapphire tile suggests the image of God in regal splendor and seated above the firmament (cf. Ps 11:4; Isa 66:1). Perhaps the Israelites find themselves in the throne room of the cosmic king, where they enjoy a feast in communion with God. Sinai and the sky, the earthly and the heavenly spheres, the material space and the Creator's space all converge in this one moment. The identification of Yahweh with Israel, and vice versa, is now completed. For the first time since the beginning of the exodus narrative (5:1), Yahweh is identified as "the God of Israel."

The brief scenario represents the inverse of the story of Babel (Gen 11:1-9). The latter depicts the human race bent on asserting its own identity and objectives apart from any relationship to the Creator. Unified humanity attempts to make a name for themselves so that they will not be dispersed. They operationalize their objective by building a tower, a sort of artificial mountain, with its top in the sky. Yahweh, however, descends to the site, confuses their language, and scatters them over the face of the earth. Now at Sinai, men again ascend to Yahweh's domain. The difference of course is that the ascent follows the establishment of a right relationship, founded on Israel's acknowledgement of the supremacy of the Creator and their agreement to obey the ordinances that the Creator has set in place. Humanity at Babel attempted to makes its own way to heaven and was rebuffed. Humanity at Sinai enters Yahweh's space at Yahweh's invitation and following protocols that Yahweh has set in place (vv. 1-2). The narrator's comment that Yahweh did not lay a hand on the Israelites accentuates the wonder of the moment. Human beings are with Yahweh in Yahweh's space but find themselves in no peril. Whatever we make of the particulars, the overall scenario is of a human community now established on the foundation of reverence and obedience necessary for the restoration of humanity and creation as a whole.

The Covenant Violated

If the covenant ceremony depicts the ideal of the divine-human relationship as properly constituted, the debacle surrounding the golden calf constitutes a dramatic reality check (Exod 32:1-35). With Moses absent for forty days, the people run amok. The scene, both in content and narration, conveys a sense of unbridled chaos. It is a cacophony of reversals. The people do not mention the name of Yahweh and credit "this man Moses" with bringing them out of Egypt (v. 1). Aaron the priest does nothing to stop the affront, but rather directs the collection of gold earrings, makes them into a calf, builds an altar when the calf is presented, and proclaims a festival for Yahweh (vv. 2-5). The suddenness and extremity of the reversal is incomprehensible. Aaron and the leaders of the throng had only forty days earlier ascended Sinai and seen the God of Israel. Now they are party to sacrifices offered to a calf that the people celebrate as the god(s) who brought them out of Egypt!

The scenario presents Yahweh with a dilemma. What to do now? Yahweh has identified completely with Israel. Yahweh's purposes are to be carried out through a people exclusively devoted to Yahweh. Yahweh's identity and reputation in the eyes of the world are now tied inextricably to the nation that Yahweh has constituted through deliverance and covenant. And now that nation has descended into chaos.

As with Abraham before Sodom, Yahweh discloses divine intentions to Moses. Using the same verb that characterized the pre-flood creation and Sodom and Gomorrah, Yahweh tells Moses that Israel is "ruined" (v. 7). Given the state of affairs, coupled with the realization that the nation is "stiff-necked," Yahweh contemplates dealing with ruined Israel along the same lines as in the two previous instances—Yahweh will wipe the people out and start over again with Moses.

> Now let me alone. Let my anger burn against them. Let me consume them. Let me make you into a great nation. (v. 10)

One thing, however, distinguishes Yahweh's deliberations here from those before the flood and at Sodom. The annihilation Yahweh contemplates emanates from anger. It is the first time that Yahweh's anger and Yahweh's involvement in mass killing, potential or actual, occur in the same episode. The anger indicates that Yahweh has much more of the divine self invested in the relationship than had been the case before the flood or with the cities of the plain. Yahweh has expressed wholehearted commitment to Israel. The blatant disrespect and disregard expressed by the people hits Yahweh hard.

Yahweh has had ample opportunity to know how "stiff-necked" the Israelites can be. Scarcely out of Egypt, the people had complained that they were about to die from hunger. Yahweh responded by sending manna and quails (Exod 16:1-36). Immediately thereafter they complained again about not having water, provoking a quarrel with an exasperated Moses who appealed to Yahweh for help (17:1-7). Even then, Yahweh responded with forbearance at the people's protests (vv. 2, 7), and directed Moses to bring water out of a rock. Now, however, the enormity of the affront is magnified by the fact that Yahweh and Israel have entered an agreement of reciprocal choosing, wherein Yahweh is devoted solely to Israel and Israel is to devote itself solely to Yahweh.

Moses, for his part, has come to know Yahweh and Yahweh's plans and purposes. He has evidently taken note of the many occasions in Egypt where Yahweh declared that he had done his signs and wonders "so that the Egyptians will know that I am Yahweh." Yahweh has established a reputation by pummeling Pharaoh. Much depends on enhancing that spectacular beginning and the notoriety that has come to Yahweh . This is the point Moses seizes on in order dissuade Yahweh from the planned annihilation.

> Why should the Egyptians say, "With malicious intent Yahweh brought them out, to slaughter them on the mountains and make an end to them on the face of the earth"? Turn from your burning anger and relent from bringing calamity on your people. (32:12)

Moses also brings up the matter of Yahweh's faithfulness. Yahweh made promises to Israel's forebears that Yahweh has not yet brought to fruition. What about them?

> Remember Abraham, Isaac, and Israel your servants, to whom you swore by your own self. You promised them, "I will multiply your descendants like the stars of the sky, and all this land, which I said I would give to your descendants, and they will possess it forever." (32:13)

Moses's words strike at the heart of Yahweh's plan to restore humanity through the agency of Israel. How does Yahweh want to be regarded?

Yahweh does not argue. Although walking back the decision to destroy the ruined nation, Yahweh says nothing more, leaving Moses to take matters into his own hands. This Moses does. He descends the mountain as Yahweh has directed. When Moses sees the golden calf for himself, however, he also becomes enraged (v. 19). His first action is to destroy the calf, grind it to powder, put it in water, and make the people drink it (v. 20)—perhaps as an object lesson on idolatry, predicated on the gastronomic principle of "what goes in must come out."

Aaron then steps into the same role in relation to Moses's anger that Moses earlier adopted in response to Yahweh's anger (v. 22-24). He implores

Moses not to be angry, echoing Yahweh's declaration about Israel by telling him the people are inclined toward the bad (v. 22; cf. v. 9). Then his intercession shifts into self-defense mode: "I threw (the gold rings) into the fire and out popped this calf!" (v. 24).

As Moses watches the continuing mayhem, he suddenly takes a more drastic step. Overlooking Aaron's extraordinary defense, Moses calls all those "on Yahweh's side" to stand with him at the gate of the camp. Moses's tribal kinsmen, the Levites, rally to his side, whereupon Moses issues a prophetic oracle:

> Thus says Yahweh, the God of Israel: "Let each man put his sword at his side. Go back and forth through the camp from gate to gate. Everyone is to kill his brother, his friend, and his associate." (32:27)

Oracles are to be understood as messages from Yahweh delivered through the prophet. But we have not been told that Yahweh gave Moses any such message. Did the narrator simply omit that part of the earlier conversation? Or does Moses, in hot anger, now presume to speak for Yahweh? Is he addressing the situation as he thinks Yahweh would or in a way Yahweh would approve of? Whatever the case, the result is the slaughter of three thousand kinsmen, friends, and associates at his direction. Moses declares, furthermore, that the Levites' murderous zeal "has filled your hands"—pointedly evoking an idiom that elsewhere denotes the ordination of priests (e.g., Exod 28:41; 29:9, 20; Lev 16:32; 21:10; Num 3:3)—and even declares that their zealous violence has brought a blessing upon themselves (v. 29).

The next day, Moses attempts to close the matter by stepping into a mediatory role. He tells the people that they have committed a great sin and offers to settle things with Yahweh (vv. 30–34). Moses then pleads with Yahweh to forgive the people, going so far as to ask that his name be erased from Yahweh's book, a vivid image that says that Moses wants to have no part in going forward if Yahweh doesn't agree. Yahweh, however, calls Moses's bluff and turns the image on its head, declaring that the offenders will be the ones erased. Then Yahweh instructs Moses to lead the people on to the next destination, informing him that an angel will go ahead of them and that Yahweh will deal with the offenders at the appropriate time. The interchange reveals a deep ambivalence on Yahweh's part—a determination, on the one hand, to respond directly to Israel's rebellion and a commitment, on the other, to persevere with the nation nevertheless.

The episode concludes with a terse report of Yahweh's eventual response: "Yahweh struck the people, because of what they did with the calf that Aaron made" (v. 35). The blow that Yahweh strikes in retribution sends a message. The people know all too well how Yahweh struck the Egyptians; the noun form corresponding to the Hebrew verb used in this verse (*nagaph*) signifies the "strike" Yahweh leveled against the firstborn of Egypt (Exod 12:13, 23, 27). The terse report of the blow, however, sets Yahweh's response to Israel's sin in sharp relief when compared to that which relates Moses's response. Yahweh's human partner acts in the heat of the moment, immediately calls for the deaths of offenders, and enlists others to carry out the work. Yahweh, while initially enraged and pondering an even more violent response, heeds Moses's plea for mercy and responds later in an unspecified manner.

Yahweh's Presence

Ensuing events signal a distancing and restraint on Yahweh's part. Yahweh tells Moses that it is time to depart for the land promised to the ancestors and reiterates the promise that Yahweh's angel will go ahead of the people (33:1-6). Yahweh, however, will not accompany them, "or I would consume you on the way, for you are a stiff-necked people" (v. 3). The declaration suggests that Yahweh is reconsidering just how to continue with the people. Yahweh intends to remain faithful to the ancestral promise and to continue to employ Israel as an agent of divine blessing. Yet, at this point, Yahweh will do so from a distance, through Yahweh's angel. The declaration that the people are "stiff-necked" and would be "consumed" echoes Yahweh's initial words to Moses when the golden calf was made (cf. 32:10, 12; 33:5). Yahweh, who has responded with graciousness to multiple episodes of complaining on the way to Sinai (15:22-25; 16:1-21; 17:1-7), has come to a conclusion about Israel. Israel is an inveterate, intransigent people; the covenant has not changed them. This realization, in the aftermath of Israel's recent waywardness, now prompts Yahweh to a reassessment of the relationship. Yahweh has decided that the relational bond cannot be as close as originally intended, because Israel's incorrigibility will keep the nation continually under threat and Yahweh in perpetual vexation. Whether for Israel's own good or Yahweh's, Yahweh has determined that distance is necessary for the sake of the relationship.

This, however, is not the end of the matter. Yahweh's announcement provokes dismay and expressions of grief. The people mourn and refuse to wear jewelry. This display evidently impresses Yahweh, who repeats the charge that they are a stiff-necked people and declares that if Yahweh were to travel with the Israelites even for a moment, Yahweh would "make an end" of them. Then Yahweh instructs the people to remove their jewelry, a strange command given that the people have already done so. Thomas Dozeman offers an intriguing explanation. Jewelry is associated with marriage in many biblical texts (Isa 49:18; Ezek 16:8-14) but also with attracting illicit lovers (Ezek 23:40). In this sense, the command that the Israelites take off their jewelry may convey that Yahweh is pondering divorce.[2] If this is the case, Yahweh's comment, "Let me know what I should do with you" (v. 5), implicitly asks whether the Israelites are committed to staying in the relationship. In any case, the people readily comply; they take off all their ornaments and do not wear them from that time on.

Israel's expressions of grief and obedience appear to influence Yahweh to take up residence within the nation again, though at a distance. This is confirmed by a short account of Yahweh's presence with the people (vv. 7-11). The account emphasizes both Yahweh's presence and Yahweh's distance. We are told that Moses would pitch the tent of meeting "outside the camp, at a distance" and that those who sought Yahweh would have to "go out" to the tent, which was "outside the camp" (v. 7). The people, for their part, observe due reverence whenever the pillar of cloud descends on the tent and Moses goes in to speak to Yahweh; the whole nation rises and bows down as they stand at the entrance of their own tents.

Moses, however, appears to have some questions about whether Yahweh will indeed remain with Israel (vv. 11-16), even though Yahweh remains close to Moses and speaks with him "face to face, as one speaks to a friend" (v. 11). Moses wants to bind Yahweh more closely to the nation and seeks assurance that he remains in Yahweh's good graces. He reminds Yahweh of the unique relationship that Yahweh has entered into with Israel, and he argues that Yahweh's presence with Israel is the definitive factor that sets the nation apart from all others. Moses goes on to press Yahweh to confirm divine favor and presence by showing him Yahweh's glory. Yahweh agrees to an extent, and on Yahweh's own terms:

> I will bring the full measure of my goodness right in front of you and proclaim the name "Yahweh" before you. I will be gracious to

---

2. Thomas D. Dozeman, *Exodus*, Eerdmans Critical Commentary (Grand Rapids: Eerdmans, 2009), 722-23.

whom I will be gracious, and I will show kindness to those I show kindness. (33:19)

The response is noteworthy for its association of Yahweh's name, the preeminent symbol of Yahweh's supremacy as Creator, with Yahweh's goodness, graciousness, and kindness. The name that Yahweh speaks as Moses is sheltered in a cleft of a rock is the name that is to be honored throughout the earth. The declaration reaffirms, after Yahweh's anger has erupted, Yahweh's beneficence with respect to Israel and, at the same time, Yahweh's freedom to bestow that beneficence (and, by implication, to withhold it) as circumstances and relationships warrant.

The disclosure also intimates Yahweh's willing vulnerability. Yahweh allows a part of the divine self to be seen by Moses and demonstrates care to ensure that the disclosure does not result in Moses's demise. Does Yahweh's openness signal a softening of the divine attitude toward Israel as well?

The Covenant Restored

Before the nation departs from Sinai, Yahweh instructs Moses to cut two tablets of stone, on which Yahweh will write the words that were written on the previous tablets. Moses ascends the mountain and cuts the tablets, whereupon Yahweh descends upon the mountain a second time and stands with him. Yahweh proclaims the divine name to Moses and then mentions salient attributes that touch on the events that have transpired at Sinai:

> Yahweh descended in a cloud and stood with him there. He proclaimed the name "Yahweh." Yahweh passed in front of him and proclaimed "Yahweh, Yahweh: A God compassionate and gracious; slow to anger and abundant in devotion and faithfulness; who maintains devotion to the thousandth generation; who bears with iniquity, transgression, and sin; not acquitting those not innocent; who brings the iniquity of the fathers onto the children and grandchildren, to the third and fourth generation. (34:5-7)

The repetition of the divine name calls attention to Yahweh's intention to define those attributes that will promote Yahweh's reputation to the nations of the world; self-identification articulates the attributes by which the God of Israel seeks to be known by the rest of the world.

The declaration establishes an interpretive context within which to view the divine anger that erupted when the Israelites made the golden calf. Yahweh here repeats and expands on the earlier self-identification at the time of the first covenant. In that initial self-disclosure, Yahweh was presented as a passionate God who visits the iniquity of parents upon their descendants to the third and fourth generations but displays steadfast devotion to thousands of those who love God and observe God's commandments. Now, in the aftermath of Yahweh's angry outburst, Yahweh prefaces the same declaration by associating the divine name with compassion, graciousness, forbearance, and effusive devotion. These attributes define Yahweh and explain the complementary yet unequal relationship between divine love and anger. Yahweh here acknowledges divine anger but does not identify anger as a divine attribute per se. Rather, the mention of Yahweh's anger points to Yahweh's patience and forbearance. The declaration that Yahweh is "slow to anger" conveys self-restraint; Yahweh is willing to put up with a great deal of rejection, breaking out in anger only after a long accumulation of offenses. Yahweh's anger, as the following comparison between those who reject and love Yahweh emphasizes, pales in comparison to Yahweh's devotion, as illustrated by the "third and fourth" to "thousands" calculus of Yahweh's generational response. In short, the proclamation of the divine name, in tandem with the articulation of divine attributes and generational calculus, overwhelms divine anger with divine love. Anger does not define Yahweh. Yahweh's anger is not impulsive or capricious but breaks out only after long provocation and egregious rejection. Yahweh's disposition inclines toward patience and mercy; anger is the consequence of relentless provocation, not an attribute of the divine.

Moses understands the disclosure as an invitation to restore the relationship. He now takes the initiative, acknowledging Israel's stubbornness, asking for pardon, and requesting that Yahweh once again take Israel as an inheritance (v. 10). Yahweh responds by making a covenant that is predicated on what Yahweh will do *through* Israel rather than what Yahweh has done *for* Israel.

> He said, "Look, I am making a covenant in the presence of the entire nation. I will do wonders that have never been done in the whole world or among all the nations. Every people on earth among which you are located will see the awe-inspiring work of Yahweh that I do along with you." (34:10; cf. 20:5–6)

Walter Brueggemann has drawn attention to the wider sphere of creative activity evoked by Yahweh's words, particularly with respect to the flood narrative. Yahweh's promise to "do wonders" utilizes the Hebrew verb *bara'*, which signifies Yahweh's creative work when the world began (Gen 1:1, 21, 27; 2:3, 4). The events at Sinai reflect a pattern of initial goodness, sin that brings destruction, and a new divine initiative, paralleling the pattern of creation, flood, and renewal of creation that configures Genesis 1-9. The ruination of a good creation, generated by human sin, leads first to destruction and then to a renewal of the relationship through a covenant.[3] The replication of the pattern at Sinai thus indicates that Yahweh has decided to make a new beginning, now with the recognition that the human partners cannot be depended on to carry through on their end of the relationship. So, God here, as after the flood, makes a unilateral covenant that binds God to humanity while at the same time modifying the relationship. Yahweh realizes that Israel is stiff-necked and yet, perhaps encouraged that Moses has affirmed the same, decides to continue the relationship, knowing full well that Israel will be unfaithful in the future. Thus, "the newness is possible because YHWH wills a relationship of fidelity that is not precluded by the recalcitrance of the object of YHWH's fidelity."[4]

Yahweh then presents what interpreters commonly perceive as another ten commandments, although the list is not as well-defined and is more diverse in content and form than the formulaic list in the Decalogue. The content and thrust of the new list indicate that Yahweh realizes that Israel will fail to grasp what is expected in the relationship. The terms will need to be spelled out more concretely. The first two commandments in the list are the same ones that begin the Decalogue—so confirming their priority—but the first (v. 14) is embedded within an elaboration of the practices that Israel must observe to ensure compliance with the commandment (no covenants with the peoples of Canaan, the destruction of Canaanite worship centers and paraphernalia) and the consequences that will ensue if they do not do so (ensnarement by the Canaanites, participation in sacrificial rituals, and intermarriage [vv. 12-16]).

The section concludes with Yahweh's direction that Moses record that "I have made a covenant with you and Israel" (v. 27). Declarations of Yahweh's devotion to Israel thus frame a list of Yahweh's requirements. The structure reinforces Yahweh's commitment to Israel and expresses divine expectations, which, after the golden calf debacle, Yahweh nonetheless rec-

---

3. Walter Brueggemann, *Old Testament Theology: An Introduction* (Nashville: Abingdon, 2008), 67.

4. Brueggemann, *Old Testament Theology*, 67.

ognizes that Israel will not keep. Moses, for his part, merely summons the leaders and the people and relays the commandments that Yahweh gave him on Sinai (vv. 31-32).

Yahweh's Anger

As noted above, the incident of the golden calf marks the first time in the overall narrative that Yahweh's anger and Yahweh's violence have come together, and it is only the second instance in which Yahweh has been angry at all.[5] Yahweh has engaged in mass killing many times previously—in the flood, at Sodom and Gomorrah, in Egypt—but none of these situations is presented as an expression of Yahweh's anger.

It is true that Yahweh has been angry before, specifically when Moses persisted in protesting Yahweh's assignment and implored Yahweh to choose someone else. Yahweh's anger on that occasion, however, resulted in a concession to Moses: Yahweh designated Aaron to be Moses's "mouth" (Exod 4:13-16). The first report of divine anger, in other words, results not in the punishment of the offender but in making accommodations to the offender's vacillation. Israel likewise provokes Yahweh with protests and complaints on the way to Sinai. Yet in these cases as well, Yahweh responds not with anger but with concessions; that is, Yahweh receives the complaints and gives the people what they want (Exod 16:1-17:7). Taken together, these two instances reveal that the divine anger and violence that break out with the making of the golden calf are not essentially connected. Yahweh has been angry and has accommodated. Yahweh has been provoked and has responded with concessions. Human rejection does not inevitably provoke divine anger. Divine anger does not inevitably find expression in violence. Even in the present case, where rejection, anger, and violence converge at the foot of Sinai, the narrator emphasizes the violence taken at human initiative and with human agency; the report that Yahweh sent a plague constitutes little more than a tagline at the end.

5. An exception of sorts is the reference to Yahweh's "fury" (*kharon*) in Exodus 15:7. The Hebrew noun almost always occurs in association with another word for anger (*'aph*). It stands alone in this verse, however, and as something "sent" by Yahweh, which consumes his enemies like stubble. "Fury" in this instance should therefore be understood as a weapon hurled by the Divine Warrior against the Warrior's enemies, as opposed to a reference to Yahweh's emotional disposition towards the Egyptians.

The factor that precipitates Yahweh's anger in this instance is Israel's rejection of the reciprocal choosing and honoring of Yahweh that constitute the basis of the relationship. If Yahweh is to renew creation through Israel, this relationship must be maintained without compromise. The Sinai covenant has bound Yahweh with Israel, Yahweh's reputation with Israel's behavior, and Yahweh's purposes with Israel's fidelity. Yahweh's anger, along with that which results from it, must be contextualized within Yahweh's decision to identify with Israel and to invest the divine self in the relationship formalized at Sinai. Anger, as with love and compassion, conveys the intensity and completeness of Yahweh's commitment to Israel, as well as Yahweh's vulnerability with respect to Israel. Because Yahweh has so completely committed to Israel, Yahweh is vulnerable to Israel's provocations.

The golden calf narrative does not shy away from the emotional intensity that Yahweh experiences while witnessing Israel's sudden descent into chaos. Seething anger appears to muddle Yahweh's ability to think and respond clearly. Yet anger does not overcome Yahweh, nor does it push Yahweh to a destructive action. The fact that Yahweh summons Moses but then tells Moses to leave him alone discloses both the intensity of emotion that presses Yahweh and Yahweh's self-restraint. As in the case of Sodom and Gomorrah, Yahweh confides in a friend. Yahweh tells Moses to go and see for himself what Israel is doing, as if seeking confirmation that the divine anger and intended response are warranted. Yahweh distances himself from Israel and what Yahweh has done for Israel by telling Moses that Israel is "your people, whom you brought up from the land of Egypt" (32:7). Yet Yahweh does not act immediately or impulsively. In the presence of Yahweh's human partner, Yahweh expresses outrage, as if hoping that Moses might respond with a more rational, objective perspective on what has happened. And Moses does not disappoint; he appeals to reason, helps Yahweh think through the consequences of giving full vent to divine wrath, and ultimately changes Yahweh's mind.

Yahweh's anger is intense, but it is not uncontrollable. The intensity of Yahweh's anger flows out of the intensity of Yahweh's love for Israel. Yahweh has shown this love by delivering the nation from bondage, guiding it through the wilderness, and identifying with this nation above all the nations of the world. Yahweh sought and secured Israel's ready willingness to enter the relationship and obey divine commandments, both to be expressed by exclusive devotion. At Sinai, Yahweh freely binds the divine self to Israel—a bond expressed through love, compassion, and devotion, that is, the language of emotion and vulnerability. Anger occupies the same sphere and communicates an intensity commensurate to the damage done to relationship. "If we want to believe in a God who is emotionally engaged," writes John Barton, "then we have to accept that this will mean a God who knows anger and vengeance as well as forgiveness and love." The biblical God "is not an impersonal force policing cosmic order, but an interventionist God who has a highly personal concern with what happens to people."[6]

The manifestation of divine anger also serves as an object lesson that reinforces the character of covenant relationship. In the aftermath of the golden calf debacle and the reconstituted covenant, Yahweh acts the part of the Near Eastern suzerain and, in three paradigmatic episodes, demonstrates that the divine sovereign will not be trifled with. Soon after their departure from Sinai, the Israelites complain again in ways that correspond to their protests on the way to Sinai (Num 11:1-35). This time, however, Yahweh responds not with accommodation but anger, a point accentuated by references to Yahweh's smoldering anger at the beginning and end of the unit (vv. 1, 33). As a result, the "fire of Yahweh" consumes outlying parts of the camp (vv. 1-2), and a plague strikes as the people are eating the quail that Yahweh has sent (v. 33). Immediately thereafter, Yahweh again becomes angry when Aaron and Miriam challenge Moses's privileged position as Yahweh's spokesman (Num 12:1-9). Yahweh calls the three to the tent and confirms Moses's unique status and role, punctuating the speech with a rebuke: "Why were you not afraid to speak against my servant Moses?" When Yahweh withdraws, Miriam is leprous. She is healed only after Moses appeals on her behalf, and Yahweh makes a point by banishing her from the camp for seven days.

The third instance of divine anger, at Baal Peor (Num 25:1-18), follows the thread of the golden calf incident and underscores that Israel is indeed a "stiff-necked" people. Yahweh grows angry when Israel forms an attachment to Baal Peor. In response to this affront, Yahweh tells Moses to impale the leaders of the nation in order to assuage divine anger. As the people are weeping, an Israelite man brings a Midianite woman "to his brothers, before the very eyes of Moses and the entire congregation of the Israelites" (v. 6). The narrative accentuates the egregious character of the offense, which remains unspecified but is somehow connected to the problem of foreign women seducing Israelite males to worship other gods. As at the foot of Sinai, Yahweh strikes a blow and a Levite responds to the offense with a dramatic act

---

6. John Barton, "The Dark Side of God in the Old Testament," in *Ethical and Unethical in the Old Testament: Gods and Humans in Dialogue*, ed. Katherine J. Dell, LHBOTS 528 (New York: T&T Clark, 2010), 126.

of violence. Phinehas, the grandson of Aaron, takes a spear and runs both of them through. Yahweh thereupon commends Phinehas for his zeal, in much the same way that Moses commended the Levites for bringing a blessing on themselves by slaughtering their kinsmen. Here as well, Yahweh makes a covenant—in this instance a covenant of peace for Phinehas and his descendants (vv. 7-13; cf. Exod 32:25-29).

Divine Anger and Divine Violence

The covenant-making and remaking at Sinai establish three trajectories for associating divine anger and violence that are significant for interpreting subsequent instances where Yahweh's violence is explained in terms of divine anger. First, *divine anger must be viewed with reference to Yahweh's devotion to Israel*. Love, devotion, and mercy are attributes of God that express the intensity of Yahweh's commitment to Israel. Anger is an expression of that intensity in the negative, but it is not a divine attribute. Yahweh is a loving God and a devoted God—even a passionate God—but Yahweh is not an *angry* God. Yahweh's anger is not an uncontrollable impulse that erupts in destructive rage. Rather, outbursts of Yahweh's anger are episodic and focused, the culmination of a long period of offenses. In the apt words of Abraham Heschel, "Anger prompted by love is an interlude."[7] Yahweh's disposition leans heavily toward forbearance. The intensity of Yahweh's devotion to Israel, however, corresponds to the intensity of Yahweh's anger when Israel blatantly and egregiously turns from covenant fidelity to other gods and disrespects, in various ways, Yahweh as the lord of creation. With the decision to identify with Israel, to bind Yahweh's self and work to Israel, Yahweh commits to Israel with the totality of the divine being and so becomes vulnerable to provocation.

Second, *divine anger may be regarded as an accommodation to Israel's world* in that Yahweh, as Israel's suzerain, responds to Israelite infidelity in light of what might be expected from an offended king. The nature of the covenant prompts Israel to think of Yahweh as a majestic emperor and itself as a subordinate entity who enjoys a favored status. Within the context of this understanding, the expression of divine anger in response to disloyalty and insubordination has a didactic function, connecting what Israel knows about kings to how it should view itself in covenant relationship with Yahweh. Yahweh as Israel's suzerain must be accorded the highest respect and

---

7. Abraham J. Heschel, *The Prophets*, vol. 2 (New York: Harper & Row, 1962), 75.

the most diligent obedience, a point that divine anger makes in the negative. Yahweh assumes the role of suzerain as a platform for defining for Israel, and in a way that it understands, its role in the relationship and what is expected of it. Israel is to be a people delivered from bondage for the purpose of becoming a nation that reflects Yahweh's holy character to the world, a people who reflect a restored humanity that acknowledges the Creator's supremacy and lives within the order that the Creator establishes.

Finally, *divine anger results in divine violence when Yahweh must act to maintain or restore the divine mission through Israel for the sake of the world.* Outbreaks of divine violence in the narrative literature that follows occur in response to one of three fundamental threats to these purposes, namely when: 1) Israel no longer acknowledges Yahweh as the sole and supreme deity who defines the nation's identity and practice; 2) Israel dishonors Yahweh by trivializing the relationship or disregarding the ordinances that Yahweh has given; and 3) Israel unravels and descends into chaos and confusion.

At Sinai, Yahweh fully identifies with a nation torn between fidelity to the God who brought it into being and an impulse to act in ways that are characteristic of nations in a world saturated by violence. Through the divine identification with Israel, Yahweh is now fully present and directly involved in "worldly affairs." The ensuing narrative will see more divine adjustments and entanglements in the systems of the world that humans have made. Yahweh, however, now has a sense of whom he is dealing with and what he is up against. Yahweh will nevertheless struggle to maintain sovereignty over Israel so that the nations of the world will see and know the majesty of the world's creator.

6

God and Kings

Listen to their voice and set a king over them.

1 SAMUEL 12:22A

The repercussions of Yahweh's decision to identify with and work through the nation of Israel ripple through Israel's entrance into the land and its exile from it. Yahweh's decision at Sinai to be bound to Israel entails assuming responsibility for the welfare of the nation, including the protection of the nation from its enemies. Israel is a nation created by Yahweh through deliverance and covenant and whose identity and practices are defined by its sovereign. In Israel, Yahweh establishes a nation that embodies and manifests the created order to the whole world. The events in Egypt and Sinai have demonstrated that Yahweh is utterly and irrevocably committed to the nation, as the agents of Yahweh's renewal of the world.

Yahweh struggles to restore the world through Israel, which is inclined to mimic the violent systems of the world. We will leave aside, for the moment, Israel's invasion of Canaan, an instance of divine and human violence so massive and troubling that it requires more than a summary treatment. Here, our interest is drawn to how the narrative relates how Yahweh's decision to identify with Israel pulls Yahweh into the violent affairs of nations and how that decision results ultimately from Yahweh stepping back from the nation altogether.

From the time Israel leaves Sinai, Yahweh's plans for the nation are frustrated by external and internal complications. Shortly after leaving Egypt, the Amalekites attack Israel (Exod 17:8-16). Moses directs Joshua to choose men and fight the attackers, while Moses and two others climb to the top of a hill. Moses's staff evidently still has the power to defeat Israel's foes, but it is wielded at Moses's initiative, not at Yahweh's direction. Yahweh does not make a direct appearance in the account until victory has been achieved, at which time Yahweh declares that the memory of Amalek will be erased. The ostensible absence of Yahweh from the battle may indicate divine reluctance to participate in the violence, but Yahweh's declaration makes clear that Yahweh regards Israel's enemies as Yahweh's enemies. Moses confirms as much from the human side by erecting an altar to commemorate the victory and declaring that Yahweh will henceforth be perpetually at war with the Amalekites. Moses adds that the battle with Amalek will persist over the course of generations. The comments of both Yahweh and Moses thus envision a future for Israel defined by perpetual violence.

A corresponding internal complication—Israel's inveterate refusal to trust its divine sovereign and follow divine commandments—erupts as the nation stands at the brink of entering the land that represents the fulfillment of Yahweh's promises (Num 14:1-25). At a discouraging report from ten of the twelve men dispatched to reconnoiter the land, the people vehemently protest and, worse, declare that death in Egypt would have been better than the deaths they foresee if they attempt to enter the land. The protest directly challenges Yahweh's power to defeat Israel's adversaries and insinuates that Yahweh intends death rather than life for the people. When the people decide to choose a new leader to take them back to Egypt, Joshua and Caleb step in to plead with the people and uphold Yahweh's reputation. "The protective covering of the people of the land has been removed!" they declare. "And Yahweh is with us!" (14:9).

When the people threaten to stone Caleb and Joshua in response, the glory of Yahweh appears at the tent of meeting in view of the entire nation, whereupon Yahweh expresses a sense of exasperation to Moses: "How long will this people disrespect me? How long will they continue not to trust me, despite all the signs I have done among them?" (v. 11a). In a reprise of the golden calf incident, Yahweh discloses a plan to strike the people with a pestilence, disinherit them, and start over with a new people descended from Moses.

In response, Moses expands his previous argument to articulate clearly what is at stake for Yahweh at this point and in all that is to come. The situation, he tells Yahweh, impacts Yahweh's reputation. If Yahweh follows through, Moses argues, the Egyptians and "all the nations who have heard about you" (v. 15) are sure to hear of it. They will conclude that Yahweh killed the Israelites because Yahweh was unable to bring them into the land promised to their ancestors. The plea confirms, first of all, that Yahweh intends that Israel will be a vehicle for making Yahweh known to all the nations of the world and, second, that Yahweh's defeat of the peoples of Canaan will play an essential role in impressing Yahweh's faithfulness and power upon the nations.

Moses then exhorts Yahweh to consider how divine power will be wielded in response to Israel's protests. Moses argues that Yahweh has an opportunity to confirm what Yahweh has said about being a God who refrains from anger whenever possible. Moses, in short, reminds Yahweh of Yahweh's own words—uttered at the second covenant-making event at Sinai—and exhorts Yahweh to put the words into action:

> And now, let the power of my Lord be great as you have spoken, "Yahweh is long in anger but abundant in faithfulness, who bears with the iniquity and transgression but in no way acquits the guilty, but who visits the iniquity of parents upon the children to the third and fourth generation." (Num 14:17–18; cf. Exod 34:6)

Yahweh's greatness, Moses contends, is displayed by Yahweh's faithfulness, which Yahweh has displayed through acts of forgiveness from the moment that Israel left Egypt to the present (v. 19).

The appeal succeeds, but not completely. The people are forgiven as Moses has requested. Yet Yahweh refuses to dismiss the affront.

> Nevertheless, as I live and Yahweh's glory fills the whole earth, none of those who have seen the glory and miracles I did in Egypt and the desert—and who have tested me these ten times and did not obey my voice—will ever see the land I swore to their ancestors. None of those who disrespected me will see it. (14:21–22)

Yahweh's response suggests two reasons for the offense. The first focuses on Yahweh's glory, which Yahweh declares fills the entire earth and which the people now see on display in front of the tent of meeting. The reference to glory underscores the privilege that Yahweh has given to Israel, who out of all the people of the earth have seen Yahweh's glory and experienced powerful signs in Egypt and in the wilderness. Their refusal to enter, therefore, expresses disrespect, ingratitude, and faithlessness. Second, Yahweh declares that Israel has stretched divine patience to the breaking point: they "have tested me these ten times and did not obey my voice" (v. 22b). The reference to "ten" does not indicate that Yahweh has been keeping score but rather emphasizes that this incident is the last of a long series of challenges that manifest Israel's disobedient attitude toward Yahweh. This disposition cannot abide with Yahweh's intention to establish Israel as a nation that bears witness to Yahweh's supremacy and establishes Yahweh's order in the world. Such people belong in the trackless expanse of the wilderness, not in a land that will establish Yahweh as the sole and supreme authority.

Yahweh as National Deity

Divine violence follows two trajectories throughout the narrative from wilderness to exile. First, Yahweh, in the role of divine protector, defends the nation and delivers it from its enemies. Second, Yahweh responds forcefully to flagrant challenges to divine supremacy, specifically as these involve the pursuit of other deities and powers in defiance of Yahweh's place as Israel's sole sovereign. It is worth noting that divine anger is commonly part of the mix in the latter instances but is never implicated in the former. In other words, divine violence emanates from divine anger as a consequence of Israel's rejection of the reciprocal choosing that defines the covenant, but it is never said to be a factor in the violence that Yahweh metes out against Israel's enemies.

The book of Judges develops these trajectories by setting divine violence in counterpoint to human violence. Unlike in the book of Joshua, where Yahweh makes war on Israel's behalf, here Yahweh manages and directs violence through human agents. In Judges, Yahweh's violence assumes a patterned and predictable expression, which comes in response to Israel's persistent proclivity to abandon Yahweh in favor of other deities. A programmatic introduction defines the pattern (Judg 2:11–23). It begins when Israel "does evil in Yahweh's eyes" by forsaking Yahweh for the Baals and Astartes. This provokes Yahweh, and, as a consequence, Yahweh leaves Israel to face its enemies without the benefit of divine protection (vv. 14–15).

> The anger of Yahweh simmered against Israel. He handed them over to plunderers who plundered them and sold them into the hands of their enemies around them. They were never able to resist their enemies. Everything that went out from Yahweh's power brought calamity, as Yahweh had said and Yahweh had sworn to them. So they were in a lot of trouble. (Judg 2:14–15)

When the Israelites cry out, Yahweh is moved to compassion and sends a deliverer to free them from oppression and restore order. When the judge dies, however, the people return to the practice of worshiping other deities, which in turn provokes Yahweh to anger, initiating a new cycle of the pattern.

Yahweh thus takes an indirect approach to Israelite waywardness in the land. Divine anger in response to Israelite idolatry results in divine abandonment rather than devastating punishment. Yahweh hands Israel over (2:14; 6:1; 13:1) or sells them into the hands of oppressors (2:14; 3:8; 4:2; 10:7). Yahweh's acts of deliverance are related in similar terms. Yahweh hands over the Canaanites to Judah (1:4), Cushan-Rishathaim to Othniel (3:10), and the Ammonites to Jephthah (11:32). A brief note that Yahweh threw the army of Sisera into a panic (4:15) is the only instance in which Yahweh is said to be involved directly in combat. In all other instances, Yahweh metes out violent deliverance principally through human agents, remaining discreetly in the background while the judges attribute victory to Yahweh's involvement. Thus Ehud proclaims that Yahweh has handed over the Moabites (3:28), and Deborah and Gideon declare the same with reference to the Canaanites and Midianites respectively (4:14; 6:15; 8:3, 7).

As the stories of the judges progress, however, Yahweh takes an increasingly active role in directing the judge's activity. Aside from the aforementioned reference to sending Sisera's army into panic, Yahweh does not act directly in the cases of Othniel, Ehud, and Deborah. The angel of Yahweh, however, makes an appearance to Gideon and divulges a winning military strategy. More directly, Yahweh's spirit comes upon Jephthah, whom the leaders of the tribes had already enlisted as a deliverer (11:29). An angelic appearance and the empowerment of Yahweh's spirit then come together in the story of Samson. The angel of Yahweh appears to Samson's mother and instructs her about the child. The spirit stirs in the boy, and when he has grown Yahweh directs Samson's affection toward a Philistine woman in order to pick a fight with the Philistines (14:4). The spirit of Yahweh subsequently rushes upon Samson, transforming him into a one-man wrecking crew (14:6, 19; 15:14).

The measured, almost detached exertion of divine violence contrasts significantly with the violence generated by the human agents whom Yahweh chooses. As the narrative runs its course, the level and scope of violence intensifies. The gruesome assassinations of Eglon and Sisera, and the associated battles, lead into the beheading of Oreb and Zeeb, the execution of Zebah and Zalmunna, two more battles, and ultimately to the slaughter of Gideon's children by Abimelech and the ignominious death of the latter. The slaughter of progeny extends into the story of Jephthah, who sacrifices his daughter to fulfill a vow and, unlike Gideon, fails to prevent an intertribal war instigated by the Ephraimites. Samson kills thirty men for their clothing, burns Philistine crops, strikes a large number of Philistines "hip and thigh" (15:8), kills another thousand at Ramath-lehi, and kills even more when he brings the temple down on the crowd that has come to mock him.

Divine violence in Judges is controlled, focused, and managed. Yahweh primarily acts from a distance, allowing other nations to oppress Israel and raising deliverers when Israel cries out for relief. By contrast, the violence generated by human beings is excessive, unpredictable, and often uncontrollable. Whereas Yahweh repeatedly hands Israel over to violence, brings deliverance through human agents, and then brings peace, human violence grows and intensifies with the activity of each new judge so that, after the end of Samson's story, violence continues with a force all its own. The final, judge-less section of the book relates a descent into social chaos, manifested by the inexorable unraveling of human bonds and paroxysms of violence. A son steals from his mother, who makes an idol from the silver when it is returned to her (17:1–13). A Levite and his concubine are threatened at Gibeah in Benjamin, and the concubine is raped and killed (19:22–30). An intertribal war engulfs the entire nation and almost wipes out the tribe of Benjamin (20:1–48). The entire town of Jabesh-Gilead is put to the sword—men, women, and children—with the exception of four hundred virgins. Women are abducted while dancing in a religious festival (21:1–24). Epitomizing the no-holds-barred maelstrom, the tribe of Dan decides to leave the territory that Yahweh allotted to it and attack the prosperous and unsuspecting town of Laish, burning it down and slaughtering its inhabitants.

Like the Other Nations

The disintegration of Israel continues into the books of Samuel, which begin by transposing images of decay at the heart of the nation (in the persons of the corrupt priest Eli and his sons) with anticipations of a new, reconfigured Israel (through the prophetic song of Hannah). Eli and his sons represent the old, tribal order of the judges that has descended into chaos. The nation looks to the priests to maintain order and stability through ritual and instruction, and Yahweh looks to the priests to honor Yahweh's sovereignty, holiness, and reputation by the same means. Eli's sons Hophni and Phinehas, however, care nothing for such things and treat Yahweh with blatant disrespect (1 Sam 2:12). Eli communicates the same by his passivity when he hears that his sons have dishonored Yahweh and the boundaries Yahweh has set, in striking contrast to the zeal for holiness that ought to shape priestly disposition and practice (Exod 32:25-29; Num 25:6-13). The dissolution of these boundaries at the center of Israel's life signals the utter disordering of the nation and evokes Yahweh's intervention. The priestly house that oversees and exemplifies tribal Israel's death spiral itself disappears and gives way to a new order of priests (1 Sam 2:27-36). As if bearing the chaos away from the nation, Yahweh—represented by the ark—departs Israel as a captive to the Philistines, to begin anew by demonstrating Yahweh's power over pretending deities. Yahweh humbles Dagon in his own house and then humbles the Philistines with plagues of rats and tumors, until the longsuffering and bewildered captors send the ark back to Israel with gifts.

First and Second Samuel, in short, relate the undoing and remaking of Israel. As 1 Samuel opens, Israel is a tribal society led by judges whom Yahweh empowers as circumstances dictate. Loyalty to kin holds the nation's social system together. Yahweh is a mobile deity whose shrine is a tent. As 2 Samuel closes, the nation is a monarchy, ostensibly united under the rule of a king. Yahweh has signed onto the new system by promising to establish a royal dynasty and agreeing, grudgingly, to upgrade the divine residence to a temple.

The remaking of Israel pivots on a significant set of conversations between Yahweh and Israel (1 Sam 8:1-22; 12:1-25). They are facilitated by Samuel who, by virtue of his role as judge, prophet, and kingmaker, mediates the transition from kinship society to monarchy. The two conversations arise from Israel's demand that they be given a king "to govern us like other nations" (1 Sam 8:5; 8:4-22; 12:6-25), and the implications and consequences of that demand. Israel's petition confronts Yahweh with a significant, although apparently not unforeseen challenge. Acquiescing to the demand will erase much of what has made Israel a unique manifestation of Yahweh's ordering presence, so that Israel will indeed resemble the surrounding nations. Yahweh delivered Israel from the oppressive structures of monarchy in Egypt and reconstituted the nation along different lines in the wilderness. Yahweh delivered Israel from a monarch in Egypt and conquered kings in the Transjordan and Canaan so that Israel could be established as a nation under the rule of Yahweh, not a human monarch. The nation's demand for a king calls for a radical reconfiguration of society that will transform the nation to conform with the very system that Israel has been defined over and against.

Yahweh lays out the implications of this transformation in no uncertain terms (8:10-17). A king will require a standing army and conscript young men to populate it. A king will redefine who people are and where they will work. He will confiscate land and property, take the produce of the land to give it those who work for him, levy taxes, and ultimately enslave the populace. In the end, the people will cry out under the oppression of the king who rules over them, just as they cried out under Pharaoh (Exod 2:23) and during the period of the judges (Judg 3:14-15; 4:2-3). A society that kings rule reflects the oppressive ordering of human life that the people of God have been defined over and against.

One may detect a note of exasperation, and perhaps resignation, in the way that Yahweh responds to the demand. When Samuel voices to Yahweh his displeasure about the demand, Yahweh responds:

Heed the voice of the people, everything they've said to you. It's not you they've rejected from being king over them, but me—just as they've done in everything they've done since I brought them up from Egypt and up till now. They've abandoned me and served other gods. That's what they're doing to you. (1 Sam 8:7-8)

Samuel expands on these comments by recounting Israel's stubbornness and waywardness, from the exodus up to the present day (1 Sam 12:7-12). Israel has rejected Yahweh's rule from the moment of its liberation, so that the present petition represents only the latest instance of a persistent, resolute waywardness (8:7-8). Israel has rejected Yahweh's divine kingship and rejected Yahweh's vision for the nation. Israel wants a human king and wants to be like all other nations (8:4; 12:19-20). This demand, Samuel declares, is an egregious act of wickedness, and it is catastrophic (12:17; cf. v. 19).

Given this scenario, we may understand why Yahweh gives in and tells Samuel in so many words, "Give them what they want" (8:7, 22). Yahweh has had sufficient experience with this people to know that they will not be dissuaded, even when Yahweh spells out for them what it will mean to have a king (8:10-28). There is no reasoning with them. Yahweh therefore makes the best of the situation and once again adapts to the demands of the human partner.

Yahweh may have been rejected as king, but Yahweh will not step aside as Israel's Sovereign. Samuel makes this clear in two ways. First, Yahweh, not the people, will choose the king. Yahweh's choice, in the person of Saul, conforms to everything the people could ask for in a king (9:1-11:15). Saul is an impressive physical specimen from a family of considerable means (9:1-2), and Yahweh empowers him, as Yahweh did the judges before him, to lead the Israelites in battle against the Ammonites (10:1, 10-12; 11:6-11; cf. 8:20). His name ("Asked For"), furthermore, suggests that Yahweh may well have selected Saul as an ideal object lesson on kingship and the nation's expectations of kings.

Second, Yahweh dramatically confirms Samuel's admonitions that the people are still obligated to serve and obey Yahweh (12:13-19). Although the relationship has been redefined once again, its essential character remains the same. Yahweh remains the divine overlord, and Israel remains a nation bound by covenant to honor and obey. Samuel reiterates this continuity by rehearsing again, with slight modification, the consequences that face Israel for obedience and rebellion. If the nation *and its king* follow Yahweh, all will be well; but if the nation rebels and disobeys, Yahweh's power will work against the nation *and its king* (12:14-15; cf. Deut 6:24-25; 7:9-14; 8:1-6; 10:12-13). To punctuate the admonition, Samuel calls on Yahweh to bring thunder and rain to confirm the people's wickedness. Yahweh obliges and terrorizes the congregation with a display of power (vv. 17-19).

The decision to give Israel a king has profound implications for how Yahweh will continue to order and renew the world through Israel. The concession pulls Yahweh directly into the very system that Yahweh has resisted since first descending into the world. For one thing, Yahweh will, from now on, deal with the nation primarily by dealing with its king. This means that Yahweh's objectives will often have to work in tandem with national objectives, which is to say *royal* objectives. This complicates Yahweh's work considerably. Now fully entangled within the oppressive structures of monarchy, Yahweh will have to work with and through the very kinds of human beings that Yahweh has opposed.

The fortunes of the king will reflect on Yahweh's standing in the world of nations and deities. The king will be the most visible representative of Yahweh's rule, supremacy, and character in the world. Yahweh will, therefore, have to adapt the divine mission through Israel to the mechanisms and realities of kingship, which operates under its own rules and principles. By agreeing to Israel's demand for a king, Yahweh is drawn into the contests of power and violence that define the ends and means of monarchies. Although Yahweh will retain veto power over royal policies, the monarchical system will establish, evaluate, and evict kings through its own structures and processes. This means Yahweh will have to put up with a great deal more mess and will have fewer options available to advance divine purposes.

Yahweh also becomes enmeshed within the oppressive use of power that drives and upholds monarchies and is thus implicated in the material effects the system has on human lives. Identifying with the nation by identifying with the king means that Yahweh will have to abide with a measure of the injustice and violence that Yahweh deplores. Furthermore, Yahweh will have to deal with kings who act according to political expediency as opposed to divine counsel and dictates, bringing the constant vexation of apostasy, foreign entanglements, injustice, militarism, and social policies that enhance the stature of the king but do not glorify God.

To be sure, Yahweh will not be a silent partner. The God of Israel remains an active, unwelcome, contentious, challenging, chastising presence in the face of the kings. Through the prophets, Yahweh will continue to call kings to account, judge their practices, announce the failure of their policies and the ends of their reigns. At all times Yahweh will confront both king and nation with unwelcome reminders that their aims are not ultimate and their power derivative. Amidst all the trials and travail, Yahweh will remain true to character, not given to caprice but remaining slow to anger, enduring all manner of affronts and insults, and abounding in steadfast love. Yet, when the situation demands, Yahweh will not be reluctant to take up violence in order to bring down a king.

Yahweh's booming confirmation of Samuel's warning to the assembly of Israel, through thunder and hail, underscores that Yahweh could and still may react less graciously to Israel's inveterate obstinacy. The thunder and hail make the point, and the people respond accordingly by asking Samuel to pray for them "so we won't die" (v. 19). Samuel, however, assures the nation that Yahweh will not discard the nation. The reason is telling—"on account of Yahweh's great name, because Yahweh decided to make you his very own people" (v. 22). Yahweh's international reputation still governs Yahweh's decision-making with reference to Israel. Having identified with Israel as the vehicle and manifestation of Yahweh's ordering, restoring work in the world, Yahweh has decided to continue with Israel, knowing well where the course of monarchy will eventually take the nation and the relationship.

Yahweh Goes All In

Yahweh's experiment with monarchy proceeds in fits and starts. Saul, the king who epitomizes what the people want, does not work out. After a promising beginning, Saul fails twice to acknowledge Yahweh's superiority by failing to carry out what Yahweh directs him to do. The particulars in the first instance (1 Sam 13:8–15) are obscure but have to do with Saul's apparent disobedience through a transgression of sacrificial decorum. The second instance (1 Sam 15:1-33) presents a clearer, though not entirely unambiguous, scenario of disobedience. The case involves Yahweh's command that Saul settle the blood feud with the Amalekites by wiping them out—men, women, children, and livestock (v. 3). Saul, however, spares the best of the livestock, along with Agag the Amalekite king, and brings them to the sanctuary at Gilgal.

The situation prompts a rare moment of divine self-disclosure to Samuel: "I am sorry that I made Saul king, because he has turned from following me and has not fulfilled my words" (v. 11a). The comment is reminiscent of the prior occasion when Yahweh expressed sorrow, also in connection with the obliteration of people and animals: "I will erase humanity, whom I have created, from the surface of the earth—people together with beasts, creeping things, and the birds of the sky, because I am sorry I made them" (Gen 6:7). When confronted, Saul claims that he has brought the livestock and king back to Gilgal to slaughter them as a sacrifice (1 Sam 15:20-21). Whether Saul has misinterpreted Yahweh's commandment or openly defied it makes no difference. Yahweh throws the book at Saul, indicting him via association with the crimes of divination and idolatry (v. 23) and rejecting him from the kingship. Saul's seeming confusion on sacrificial matters associates him with Eli and his sons and so underscores his removal from the new system that is emerging. When Saul pleads with Samuel for forgiveness, the prophet retorts that Yahweh does not have second thoughts as a human being does (vv. 28-29); Yahweh has decided that Saul will not do as king, and that is that.

Yahweh then turns immediately to select a king who reflects Yahweh's own choosing, rather than one who embodies the kind of king the people requested (see 1 Sam 13:13-14). Yahweh's selection is a brash youth who distinguishes himself by defending Yahweh's reputation, even though Israel's king and the Philistine Goliath believe he is incapable of doing so on the field of battle. When the giant calls out to the Israelites—including the king who stands head and shoulders above others—and openly defies them (and thus their God), the Israelites cower in fear. David, however, asks indignantly, "What shall be done for the man who kills this Philistine and removes the insult from Israel? And who does this Philistine think he is that he derides the ranks of the living God?" (17:26). David realizes that Yahweh's reputation is at stake in the challenge of the Philistine. When he confronts Goliath in the field, David elaborates:

> You come to me with a sword and spear, but I come to you in the name of Yahweh of Hosts, the God of the ranks of Israel, whom you have

insulted today. Yahweh will release you into my hand, and I will kill
you and remove your head. I will give the corpses of the Philistine
camp today to the birds of the sky and beasts of the land. The entire
land will know that there is a God in Israel, and everyone gathered
here will know that Yahweh's victory does not come by means of a
sword or spear, because this is Yahweh's battle. He will give you into
my hand. (17:45-47)

David gets it. This is the kind of person Yahweh can work with. David has been quick to stand up to a brazen challenge to Yahweh's people in defense of Yahweh's honor. He understands that Yahweh will answer the challenge if someone is courageous enough to represent the deity on the field of battle. And in contrast to Saul, David is regarded by those around him as the least likely candidate to fight the people's battles in the way battles are conducted (cf. 8:20).

Yahweh henceforth works vigorously to promote David and undermine Saul. David's stock rises rapidly, while Yahweh keeps Saul off-balance by harassing him with an evil spirit (1 Sam 18:6-10). David gains experience and acclaim as a military leader under Saul's command and wins the hand of Saul's daughter because, we are told, "Yahweh was with him" (18:14; cf. vv. 2, 28). He exploits his friendship with Jonathan, the heir apparent, to keep tabs on what Saul is planning in response to the increasing threat to his power that David represents (19:1-7; 20:1-42) and so is able to stay one step ahead of Saul in the political sweepstakes. Yahweh makes sure, moreover, that Saul cannot exercise the self-control and discretion required of a monarch faced with a popular challenger. Yahweh twice sends an evil spirit to force his hand with David by driving him to throw a spear, first at David (18:10-11) and later at Jonathan when the latter is exposed as David's accomplice (20:33). In the main, however, Yahweh appears content to let David acquire power through his own efforts and abilities.

The young man turns out to be a savvy political operator. He parlays his status as an outlaw into that of a tribal warlord by rescuing villagers from Philistine marauders (23:1-14), running a protection racket in the vicinity of Carmel (25:1-13), and parceling out booty from a successful raid on the Amalekites to tribal elders (30:26-31). Yahweh intervenes infrequently, mainly to direct or confirm David's plans to strike Israel's enemies or determine whether a village is loyal to him or Saul (1 Sam 23:2-4, 10-21; 30:8). In one notable instance, Yahweh strikes dead an influential landowner who had resisted David, making his widow—and presumably the influence she wields as his widow—available to David (25:37-42). Other than these instances, Yahweh appears to regard David as fully capable of playing the political game and getting the best of Saul by his own devices (1 Sam 24:1-22; 26:6-25). This entails quite a bit of violence as David consolidates power. David thereupon builds a reputation as the commander of Saul's army and is celebrated for the number of enemies he has killed: "Saul has killed his thousands, but David his ten thousands!" (1 Sam 18:7).

Violence swirls around David after Saul and his sons are killed on the battlefield and David assumes the kingship. In quick succession, David executes the Amalekite who brings news of Saul's death (2 Sam 1:1-16), his forces engage in a bloody battle with the forces of Saul's son Ishbosheth (2:12-32), his general Joab assassinates Ishbosheth's general Abner (3:26-30), assassins kill Ishbosheth and bring his head to David (4:1-8), and David orders the execution and mutilation of the assassins (4:9-12). The trajectory of violence continues once the tribes of Israel gather to make him the uncontested king. Thereafter David captures the city of Jerusalem (5:6-10) and wins two decisive battles against the Philistines (5:17-25). After taking a break to establish Jerusalem as his royal city, David continues to campaign against the Philistines (8:1) and to expand his military operations. He defeats the Moabites and executes Moabite prisoners (8:2), defeats the king of Zobah and a relief force of Arameans from Damascus, plundering their cities as well (8:3-8). He kills eighteen thousand Edomites (8:13-14) and attacks a rebellious Ammonite vassal and the coalition of Arameans who have come to support the rebel (10:1-19).

Yahweh, for the most part, remains discreetly in the background, directing rather than fighting the two battles against the Philistines and assuring the young king of victory (5:18-25). The reports are the only two episodes that recount Yahweh's direct participation in David's battles. Both instances are defensive operations against the Philistines. The narrator sets Yahweh at even more of a distance from those battles that David initiates and that expand David's power and renown (8:1-14), stating only that "Yahweh gave David victory everywhere he went" (2 Sam 8:6b; cf. 1 Sam 18:14). Yahweh utilizes violence to assist Israel's leader in defense of threats by enemies, but Yahweh does not appear to initiate any of David's aggressive maneuvers. Rather, Yahweh only participates when David asks for direction against an enemy force or as a means to enhance David's reputation (and thus Yahweh's) among the nations of the region.

Yahweh is nevertheless drawn deeper into the monarchical matrix. This happens during the two windows that interrupt the accounts of David's conflicts. The first entanglement occurs when David decides to move Yahweh's shrine to Jerusalem and build a proper temple for Yahweh's residence. David cloaks the decision in religious language, but the motivation is at least partly political. The intent behind his declaration to Nathan the prophet—"Look, I'm sitting in a house of cedar, but the ark of God is sitting under the curtains" (2 Sam 7:2b)—could be read either as "It's not right for me to live in a beautiful house while God's ark remains in a tent" or "Now that I'm a king with a reputation, it doesn't look good to worship my patron deity in a tent," or both. Notably, building Yahweh a nice house doesn't seem to have occurred to David until he had finished building his palace and gotten settled in (2 Sam 7:1).

The idea does not appeal to Yahweh, who responds with a retort that implicitly puts David in his place: "Is it you who should build me a house in which to live?" (7:5). Yahweh then implicitly chastises David for his presumption by reminding him that Yahweh has always chosen a tent as a shrine and never once asked any of the judges who preceded David to build a temple. Another reminder follows: Yahweh is the one who elevated David from humble beginnings to his ruling position over Israel. Yahweh has always been with David. Yahweh is responsible for the fact that David's reputation equals that of the great kings of the world. Yahweh has brought about the peace that David now enjoys (7:6-11a).

Then Yahweh reverses the tables on David, declaring, "Yahweh will build you a house" (v. 11b). The house that Yahweh will build, however, will be of a different kind. Yahweh speaks of building a dynasty for David and decrees that one of David's sons will build the temple that David envisions: "I will establish your offspring, someone who comes out of your own body, after you, and I will establish his kingdom. . . . He is the one who will build a house for my name, and I will permanently secure his royal throne" (v. 12b). The decree is remarkable. In response to David's presumption, Yahweh not only agrees to David's plan but affirms the political impulse that stands behind it. Yahweh will not remove David as had been the case with his predecessor and instead will establish David's dynasty forever (vv. 15-16).

By doing so, Yahweh cedes more power to the human partner but does so on Yahweh's terms. The implications are far-reaching. The tent shrine exemplifies Yahweh's freedom and initiative. Yahweh chooses where to be worshiped and how Yahweh will stay there. The tent stands apart from and outside of the structures of power. It is a vestige of the old Israelite system in which Yahweh raises up leaders and brings deliverance as occasion warrants. A mobile deity, moreover, is difficult to pin down and therefore troublesome to kings. A mobile deity is an unpredictable deity. Better for the purposes of a monarchy is a house where God takes up permanent residence. The arrangement ensures that the king will always know where to find Yahweh and can control access to God. Even better is the assurance of permanence. In return for agreeing to the temple, Yahweh retains the king's acknowledgement and acclamation of Yahweh's supremacy, not only over the nation but throughout the whole world.

David is positively giddy about the restructured arrangement. "Who am I, my Lord Yahweh, that you would take me this far?" (v. 18). "Therefore, you are great, my Lord Yahweh! There is really no one like you! There is no God besides you!" (v. 22). "Your name will be magnified forever, saying, 'Yahweh of Hosts is God over Israel,' and David your servant will be secure before you!" (v. 26). Best of all, where David is concerned, is that Yahweh has agreed to support David and his descendants. And so David ends: "And now, be willing to bless the house of your servant, to be forever before you. Because you, my Lord Yahweh, have so spoken, and your blessing will bless the house of your servant forever" (v. 29).

If this first instance brings a surprisingly gracious response from Yahweh, the second window provokes the opposite. Yahweh's response on this occasion arises from a singular act of violence that David perpetrates against a trusted associate and his wife, namely Uriah the Hittite and Bathsheba (2 Sam 11:1-25). In this case, David's presumption takes the form of an unbridled abuse of royal power. When David's violence violates the trust and well-being of his subjects, Yahweh steps in. Yahweh addresses the matter, as Yahweh has done with David's plan to build Yahweh's house, through the agency of the prophet Nathan. After the prophet skillfully exposes David's crimes, Yahweh speaks through the prophet and issues a scathing indictment (2 Sam 12:7-10). Yahweh repeats the themes of the prior, gracious response to David's presumption, but turns them on their heads. Once again Yahweh opens by reminding David that he is king because Yahweh has made it so; Yahweh rescued David from Saul and gave Saul's kingdom and wives to David (vv. 7-8). In return, Nathan charges, David has despised Yahweh and the word of Yahweh (vv. 9, 10). What David has done is a direct affront to Yahweh, and this is where Yahweh draws the line.

Yahweh then issues a verdict. The target is, as it was in the first instance, David's house. Yahweh tells David that violence will always plague David's dynasty (12:10). And whereas Yahweh had earlier promised to bring relief from David's enemies (2 Sam 7:11), Yahweh now intends to establish trouble from within David's own house (2 Sam 12:11). When David offers a terse confession, Nathan assures him that Yahweh will not kill him, but also informs David that the child that he has fathered through Bathsheba will die "because you have shown such blatant disrespect" (v. 14).

When the child is born and sickens, David publicly entreats God with prayer, fasting, and prostration, refusing to be dissuaded by the nation's elders. We do not know whether the outward expression of piety is genuine or not. We cannot doubt, however, that it arises out of deep dismay. By striking the dynasty Yahweh has promised to uphold, Yahweh sends the unmistakable message that David should not take Yahweh's blessing for granted; that is, to presume that Yahweh's promise provides a warrant for David to do as he pleases. It would be one thing for Yahweh to deliver this message to David in private. But for Yahweh to do so in such a public fashion does not enhance David's reputation and weakens the political leverage he has undoubtedly held as Yahweh's beloved.

Confirmation comes when David learns of the child's death. David's display of grief has been so pronounced that David's courtiers are afraid to relay the news for fear that he will harm himself. David surprises them, however, by taking a bath, changing his clothes, worshiping, and getting something to eat, responding to their baffled questions by saying, in effect, "I thought maybe God would listen to me and heal the child. What good will all this fasting and praying do me now?" (vv. 21–23).

The two situations elaborate, in complementary ways, the implications of Yahweh's decision to work within the monarchical systems that configure ancient civilizations. By assenting to David's decision to build a temple and promising to establish his dynasty, Yahweh fuses Yahweh's reputation and work in the world with the king's reputation and business. This becomes clear during the interchange between David and Yahweh about the temple building, in the form of two statements each by David and Yahweh. After a brief narration of their interaction with each other, Yahweh declares, "I have been with you everywhere you have walked, and I cut off all the enemies that faced you. I will make you a great name, the equal of the great names that are in the world" (2 Sam 7:9). Yahweh then goes on to connect the dynasty and the temple in a decree about Solomon: "He is the one who will build a house for my name, and I will establish the throne of his kingship forever" (2 Sam 7:13). David responds in the same way. First, he recounts how Yahweh gained a reputation by the great and awesome deeds he did to redeem Israel and bring them into their land (2 Sam 7:23). Next he calls upon Yahweh to fulfill what Yahweh has promised.

And now, Yahweh God, fulfill forever the promise you have given to your servant and his house. Do as you have promised, and let your name be great forever, in that it will be said, "Yahweh of Hosts is God over Jerusalem!" And the house of your servant David will be established forever. (2 Sam 7:25-26)

The fact that David presses Yahweh to fulfill what Yahweh has just said reveals that David wants to seal the deal. Even David realizes the import of what Yahweh has just done. The promotion of Yahweh's name will come about through Yahweh's promotion of the king's name.

The import is far-reaching. Yahweh now identifies fully with the king and the king's city and so steps into the role and expectations that define what it means to be a deity in the ancient Near East. Yahweh lives in a house that contains a representation of the divine presence (the ark of the covenant). Yahweh guarantees the stability of the cosmic order by securing the king's rule and reign. Yahweh brings justice to the world through the agency of the king. Yahweh exalts the king as a means of establishing Yahweh's preeminence in the world. In these ways Yahweh becomes like the other deities of the ancient world and works within the monarchical system to reveal Yahweh's character and purposes. Yahweh will henceforth be expected to see to the welfare and well-being of the nation and will be called upon to protect the nation from its enemies. Yahweh's means and ends therefore merge with the nation's means and ends, which is to say, with *royal* means and ends. Yahweh's identification with Israel through identification with the king, therefore, further restricts what Yahweh wants to do in the world and how Yahweh will do it.

As we have noted above, this means that Yahweh has resolved to put up with a great deal of ungodly activity. The story of David illustrates that an excess of violence saturates the arena of kingship in the ways that kings secure and maintain their power, in the ways that kings deal with enemies, in the propensity of kings to expand their power and influence at the expense of other nations, and in the ways that kings suppress dissent and rebellion. Yahweh appears to take all of this in stride, along with the manipulation and maneuvering, the public posturing, and the exploitation of others that accompany the violence. In the face of it all, Yahweh maintains a detached stance, acting with measured force, by providing direction and assent when required in order to deliver the nation and king from the violence inflicted by Israel's enemies.

The Uriah/Bathsheba affair, however, reveals that this relationship is fraught with tension and turmoil. To overreach, to consider oneself above or outside the obligations of the covenant that bind the nation—and even above the God who supports them—constitutes an occupational hazard that few kings will be able to avoid. Yahweh will not countenance arrogance and presumption of the kind displayed by Pharaoh. David's presumption has not taken the form of direct defiance, but Yahweh has made it clear that the affair is a flagrant affront (2 Sam 12:9, 10). Yahweh thereupon asserts divine power and sovereignty by striking the house that Yahweh has promised to uphold. David has taken the wife of a trusted ally; Yahweh will give David's wives to one of David's companions. David killed Uriah by the sword of the Ammonites; the sword will never turn away from David's house. David took and impregnated the wife of someone in his service; Yahweh will strike the child (2 Sam 12:8-14). To punctuate the gravity of the offense, the narrator reports that "Yahweh struck the child that the wife of Uriah bore to David" (v. 15). It is the first instance, since the case of the evil spirit sent to harass Saul, that the narrator reports a direct act of violence on the part of Yahweh.

The extent of Yahweh's involvement in the calamities that beset David thereafter is difficult to ascertain. Although Yahweh announces that the offended deity will bring calamity against David's house (using the same verb employed to establish David's kingdom), the events that ensue arise from human connivance and intrigue. The crown prince Amnon concocts a plan to rape Tamar (13:1-19). Absalom devises a ruse to murder Amnon (13:23-29). Joab develops a strategy to get Absalom back in David's good graces (14:1-21). Absalom plots to turn David's subjects against him (15:1-14). Joab commands the execution of Absalom against the express orders of David (18:10-17). Strangely, we are told only once of Yahweh's involvement in the entire mess, and in that instance Yahweh again works from a distance to deliver David from an enemy, in this case Absalom. When Absalom listens to the counsel of Hushai, whom David has planted among Absalom's advisors, over that of Ahithophel, the narrator remarks that "Yahweh directed that the good advice of Ahithophel be frustrated, so that Yahweh might bring calamity to Absalom" (17:14).

To sum up, Yahweh's agreement to give Israel a king results in Yahweh's identification with the king and consequent entanglement within the royal project of making a name for oneself. Yahweh, therefore, colludes with the very entities of arrogance and destruction that Yahweh opposed and defeated in Egypt (Exod 3:1-15:21). Yahweh appears to accept this arrangement as the way things must be and directs it toward bringing the recognition of Yahweh. In making a name for David, Yahweh will also make a name. This means that Yahweh will have to deal with the violent operations of kingship and work within them. The situation also places Yahweh directly and persistently in conflict with the arrogance of kings.

The trade-off for all of this is that kingship offers a vehicle for the continued enhancement and visibility of Yahweh's supremacy in the world. Say what one will about David, David is fiercely loyal to Yahweh. The young man who defended Yahweh's reputation against the jibes of a giant remains cognizant that he owes his power and position to Yahweh's work on his behalf (2 Sam 5:12). At the high point of his reign, he aspires to build a house where Yahweh's name may be magnified forever (2 Sam 7:26) and at his lowest point—when fleeing Jerusalem—he acknowledges that he can return only if Yahweh so ordains (2 Sam 15:25; 16:12). David may represent all the unsavory aspects of kingship, but he is Yahweh's man all the way.

Kings and Kingdoms

With the accession of Solomon, Yahweh assumes the role of tutelary deity of Jerusalem and takes a place among the other deities and cities throughout the ancient Near East. Yahweh now has a house and a city, as well as a king and people, to uphold and defend. Following the conventions of ancient Near Eastern theology and statecraft, Yahweh's work and reputation will henceforth be connected to the welfare of the city and the well-being of the king. That is, Yahweh will make a name among the nations and carry on the divine agenda of renewal from a particular location and within a particular system.

Solomon's reign demonstrates how this works in practice and illustrates Yahweh's ambivalent relationship with the human king. The process by which Solomon becomes king follows that by which David gained the throne, replete with intrigue, maneuvering, deal-making, and violent deaths. Solomon's rival, Adonijah, along with those who supported him and the previous regime (Abiathar the priest and Joab the general), all meet violent ends. Their roles are filled by new leaders (Zadok the priest and Benaiah son of Jehoiada) who owe their positions to the new monarch (1 Kgs 1:1–2:35). Solomon also is quick to dispense with a potential troublemaker and promote himself as the recipient of divine blessing and support (1 Kgs 2:36–46). All takes place apart from Yahweh's ostensible participation.

The narrator introduces Solomon's reign by alluding to the tension that will define Yahweh's relationship with even the most faithful of kings. The account opens with the report of a political act—Solomon's marriage to the daughter of Pharaoh—reflecting the making of alliances that constitutes a component of statecraft (1 Kgs 3:1). The narrator then informs us that Solomon loved Yahweh, as evidenced by walking in the statutes of his father David, but with one exception: that is, Solomon sacrificed and offered incense at the high places (3:3). The note links Solomon with the people, who are said to do the same thing (3:2) but more significantly foreshadows the charge by which Solomon and future kings will be judged (2 Kgs 16:4; 17:9-11). The introduction leads into the first episode of Solomon's narrative, in which Solomon presents offerings at "the great high place" at Gibeon (1 Kgs 3:1-15).

At that location, Yahweh appears to the new king with a magnanimous offer: "Ask what I should give you" (3:5). Solomon responds with due deference to Yahweh. He first acknowledges Yahweh's faithfulness to David in return for David's faithfulness to Yahweh, now confirmed by his accession to his father's throne. He then acknowledges his lowliness by referring to himself as a little child who lacks the ability to govern the nation. Three times he refers to himself as Yahweh's servant before asking that Yahweh give him the acumen necessary to discern right and wrong for the benefit of the people. The request, along with the self-deprecating language, pleases Yahweh, so much so that Yahweh promises Solomon wealth and honor in addition, so that no king on earth will be his equal. Finally, Yahweh promises a long life if Solomon will follow the course of his father David and observe Yahweh's statutes and commandments.

This promising beginning, in which Solomon voices his subservience to Yahweh, portends well. Yahweh endows Solomon with wisdom, and as a result Solomon achieves international notoriety and influence. The scope and breadth of his wisdom elevates Solomon to such heights that people all over the world come to Jerusalem to hear what he has to say (4:29-34). Solomon's fame enhances Yahweh's reputation as well. The point is underscored by a visit from the Queen of Sheba, who hears about the fame of Solomon "due to the name of Yahweh" and comes to Jerusalem to examine the king (10:1-13). The magnitude of Solomon's acumen, achievement, and opulence overwhelms her, prompting her to acclaim the good fortune of Solomon's subjects and then to praise Yahweh, whom she acknowledges as the power behind Solomon's throne.

Imbued with divine wisdom, Solomon becomes a powerful ruler. Under his reign, Israel becomes a force to be reckoned with. Supported by a system of taxation and a powerful military, Solomon's rule and influence extend to the Euphrates River (4:1-28). Most important for the narrator, however, is the construction of the temple and Yahweh's descent to take up residence within it, signified by the transferal of the Ark of the Covenant into the Holy of Holies and the cloud that fills the place (8:4-11). Yahweh's presence in the temple binds the deity and the king within a tight web of expectations. The king is expected to honor and serve the deity who dwells in the temple. Building a temple for his God and installing the cult object that represents the presence of his God casts Solomon in the eyes of the public as a pious king, as do his sacrifices and prayers. Augmenting his authority is Yahweh's support for his kingship, an endorsement that Solomon is not reluctant to reiterate (5:5; 8:20, 25-26). As he dedicates the temple, Solomon points out the temple's potential for expanding Yahweh's reputation and influence. The temple will be a place where people from around the world who have heard of Yahweh's "great name, powerful hand, and outstretched arm" may gather to encounter the God of Israel, and so "all the peoples of the earth may recognize your name, to fear you as does your people Israel and to recognize your name that is proclaimed over this house that I have built" (8:43).

For his part, Yahweh will be expected to defend the city against all enemies (see Pss 2, 46, 48), ensure the city's prosperity, and uphold the king. Now, as tutelary deity of Jerusalem as well as the God of Israel, Yahweh's reputation will henceforth be attached to a city as well as a people. The king and the deity thus maintain a mutually beneficial relationship that advances the welfare of the city and nation. The king honors and obeys the will of the resident deity, and the deity ensures the welfare of the city and secures the king's reign.

Yahweh, however, declares that the arrangement is conditional rather than a unilateral expression of the divine promise to David. Both at the onset and the completion of construction Yahweh accentuates the conditional character of the promise to David, making Yahweh's dwelling in Jerusalem and the continuity of the dynasty contingent on Solomon's devotion and obedience (6:11-13; 9:1-5). In the latter instance, Yahweh elaborates what will happen if Solomon or his children disobey Yahweh or worship other gods (9:6-9). The scenario Yahweh paints is catastrophic: the exile and humiliation of the people and the reduction of the house to a heap of ruins, all at the hands of Yahweh. If this happens, Yahweh insinuates, Israel's reputation will be destroyed, but Yahweh's will remain intact. Although now tightly bound to Jerusalem and its king by promise and residence, Yahweh will break free of them if the king abandons the exclusive devotion that defines the covenant relationship with Israel. The declaration suggests that something in Solomon's kingly practice has not inspired Yahweh's full confidence.

Circumstances confirm Yahweh's concern. Over the course of his reign, Solomon acquires many wives, a large number of which are not Israelites and therefore not devotees of Yahweh (11:1-8). The harem is an instrument of statecraft, as political alliances in Solomon's world are commonly cemented by an exchange of daughters. As such, the treatment of the daughters, now wives, likely has repercussions for relationships with their families or peoples. Political expediency dictates that the foreign wives, and by extension their people, are treated with respect. On this basis, prohibiting any of the wives from practicing ceremonies of worship to their people's deities may be perceived as an affront to the people and an insult to their gods. Conversely, building places for worship and rituals would be perceived as an appropriate practice of respect.

The narrator reports that Solomon loved many foreign women and that Yahweh had warned the Israelites not to marry them, as the women would draw Israelite men toward their gods. While the specific warning is not related in the Torah, Moses did warn kings that acquiring many wives would turn their hearts away (Deut 17:17), while Joshua warned that intermarriage with the surviving peoples of the land would entrap and torment the Israelites until they vanished from the land (Josh 23:12-13). At the least then, Solomon's acquisition of wives, and particularly foreign ones, oversteps his prerogatives and manifests a disposition to make compromises even if they clash with divine priorities. The end of the matter is a foregone conclusion. We do not know if Solomon participates in the worship of the deities or if he justifies and limits the practices. The worship of other gods in the vicinity of Yahweh's city in and of itself is evil in God's sight. Yahweh is furious. While David was Yahweh's man all the way, the narrator comments that the same could not be said of Solomon (1 Kgs 11:6).

The situation puts Yahweh in a difficult position. Yahweh has clearly warned Solomon that worshiping other gods is a deal-breaker. Solomon's turning toward other gods is therefore completely unacceptable. Yet Yahweh is also bound by a promise to David, specifically Yahweh's assurance that while David's temple-builder son would be punished for his iniquity, he would never be rejected by Yahweh as Saul was (2 Sam 7:12-16). To complicate matters further, the optics do not look good. Yahweh chose one king (Saul), and that king didn't work out. Yahweh then chose a second king, and now that king's son is not working out. A worrisome pattern may be emerging that calls into question the entire monarchical arrangement. How will Yahweh's participation in a failed project impact Yahweh's reputation, and how will it inform the divine plan for Israel?

Yahweh's solution is to honor the promise to keep David's son on David's throne but to restrict the throne's purview to David's city and tribe and choose yet another king for the rest of the nation (11:11-13). The account is related with a sense of detachment. When telling the story of Saul, the narrator relates Yahweh's direct involvement in the rejection of the king, going so far as to reveal Yahweh's regret for making Saul king (1 Sam 15:11a) and the prophet's anger and grief at Yahweh's decision (1 Sam 15:11b; 16:1). Saul's rejection takes the form of a direct and public confrontation at Gilgal (1 Sam 15:10-22), at which the prophet Samuel charges the king with insubordination and iniquity, and by association with divination and idolatry. Faced with a humiliating denunciation of his kingship, Saul pleads for forgiveness. When Samuel turns to leave, Saul tears his robe. The prophet transforms the torn robe into a metaphor for the king's rejection, declaring that "Yahweh has ripped the kingdom of Israel away from you this very day and has given it to an associate of yours, who is better than you" (15:28). The selection of Saul's replacement likewise incorporates high drama, as the sons of Jesse are paraded before the prophet, and Yahweh explicitly discloses that he will make his selection on the basis of internal rather than external criteria (16:7).

In response to Solomon's apostasy, however, Yahweh utters the message of judgment directly but in an undisclosed context. The message echoes what Samuel said to Saul, that is, that Yahweh will rip the kingdom away from Solomon and his son (1 Kgs 11:11-13; cf. 1 Sam 15:28). Jeroboam, Yahweh's choice to replace Solomon as "king over Israel" (11:37), is introduced without fanfare, as the third in a line of rebel leaders that Yahweh has raised up to destabilize Solomon's reign (11:28-40). We are not told why Yahweh chooses Jeroboam, but the disclosure that Jeroboam was a man of considerable energy and competence suggests that external criteria are back in the mix (11:28). Jeroboam's selection takes place with little ceremony and evidently not in a public arena. The prophet Ahijah simply accosts him as he is on the road out of Jerusalem and speaks to him in the name of Yahweh (11:29). In an ironic nod to the circumstances of Saul's rejection, the prophet tears his own robe into twelve pieces and directs the young official to take ten of them as a sign that Yahweh will make him king over ten of the tribes (vv. 29-35). Yahweh concludes by setting the terms of the relationship along similar lines as those set before Solomon. Jeroboam may rule over all he desires. Yahweh will be with him, give Israel to him, and establish a dynasty through him, provided that he emulate David by doing what Yahweh declares is right and by walking in Yahweh's ways and commandments (vv. 37-38). We read, however, of no response from Jeroboam, no reciprocity or expression of gratitude, no sense of relationship. There is only silence, as if the matter between God and kings is now all business.

The decision, however, only doubles the trouble for Yahweh. After the death of Solomon and the rending of the kingdom, the rival kings continue in the ways of Solomon rather than David. Yahweh successfully prevents the outbreak of hostilities between Rehoboam and Jeroboam, allowing the latter to consolidate power and establish his kingdom (12:21-24). Jeroboam's first order of business, however, is not to give due honor and gratitude to Yahweh but, on the contrary, to redirect religious sentiment toward political ends. Concerned that the sacrificial cult in Jerusalem may turn his subjects back toward Rehoboam, Jeroboam constructs alternate altars at Bethel and Dan, casts golden calves in place of the Ark of the Covenant, installs non-Levitical priests at high places throughout his kingdom, and inaugurates the new system by offering sacrifices at a fall festival (12:25-33).

By taking the initiative to organize worship and sacrifice without consulting Yahweh, Jeroboam usurps a divine prerogative and signals that Yahweh is to serve his objectives. Yahweh responds decisively to this egregious affront by sending a prophet to proclaim the future desecration of the altar at Bethel (13:1-6). When Jeroboam strikes back at Yahweh by ordering the arrest of the prophet, Yahweh paralyzes Jeroboam's hand, forcing the king to acknowledge Yahweh's superiority. The confrontation, however, does not change Jeroboam's ways (13:33-34), eliciting another prophetic message from Ahijah to Jeroboam's wife (14:6-14). After reminding Jeroboam that he is king because of Yahweh's efforts, the outraged deity accuses the king of going beyond the wickedness of his predecessors, making his own gods, and provoking Yahweh to action. With a striking rhetorical flourish, Yahweh declares that the king has "thrown me behind your back" and that Yahweh will obliterate his descendants. Finally, the prophet announces that Yahweh will strike Israel and scatter the nation for provoking its God.

> Yahweh will strike Israel like a reed that sways in the water. Yahweh will pluck Israel from this good land, which he gave to their ancestors, and he will scatter them beyond the Euphrates. For they made their sacred poles, provoking Yahweh. (1 Kgs 14:15-16)

Yahweh evidently has sized up the monarchy and knows where it will end. Turning to other deities, in any way, will provoke Yahweh to drastic action. Coupled with the report that Rehoboam undertook a similar program that also provoked Yahweh (14:22-24), Yahweh's words are a striking admission that the whole project is heading toward failure.

Yahweh and the Violence of Kings

The rest of the story underscores, on the one hand, Yahweh's commitment to Israel and Judah in the face of repeated provocation and against the backdrop of how things will end. The precedents set by Solomon and Jeroboam ripple throughout the reigns of succeeding kings, making it possible to discern patterns in Yahweh's involvement in the affairs of kings and nations, particularly as these relate to Yahweh's participation in the violence that swirls around kings. The Israelite monarchy, when all is said and done, does not prove to be a vehicle by which Israel can bless the nations.

In the international arena, Yahweh defends the kingdoms of Israel and Judah and brings victory in battle for kings in those instances when the kings recognize Yahweh's status as Israel's God. Yahweh, for example, responds to devoted kings who ask for divine assistance. When the Israelite king Jehoram despairs during a campaign to subdue a rebellious Moabite king, the pious Judahite king Jehoshaphat seeks a prophet who can inquire of Yahweh on their behalf (2 Kgs 3:1-27). A long march into desolate country has exhausted the troops' supply of food and water, leaving them in a helpless situation. When the prophet Elisha is summoned, he makes it clear that he will make the inquiry only because he holds Jehoshaphat in high esteem. Yahweh then speaks through the prophet, promising that the wadi will be filled with pools and, for good measure, declaring that Yahweh will hand over Moab as well. The pools of water that appear the next day not only revive the troops and their animals but also trick the Moabites into making a disastrous attack on the superior Israelite force.

Two paradigmatic accounts suggest that Yahweh defends kings when doing so enhances the divine reputation. Yahweh's intervention against a besieging Aramean force at Samaria, during a time when Aram and Israel are struggling for dominance, appears calculated to send a message both to Israel and the Arameans (1 Kgs 20:1-34). In the two battles that ensue, prophets deliver messages punctuated by the so-called recognition formula ("you will know that I am Yahweh," vv. 13, 28), thus presenting divine intervention in the battles as manifestations of Yahweh's supremacy. After the first battle, the Arameans explain their defeat by holding that Yahweh prevailed because Israel's God is a god of the highlands rather than the plains (20:23). When the Arameans threaten Israel the following spring, a prophet announces that Yahweh will defeat them again:

> A man of God approached and spoke to the king of Israel, "Thus says Yahweh. Because the Arameans have said, 'Yahweh is a god of the high country and not a god of the lowlands,' I will deliver this great multitude entirely into your hand. So you will know that I am Yahweh." (1 Kgs 20:28)

By besting a superior force on a field of the Arameans' own choosing, Yahweh once again displays sovereign power and upholds the divine reputation before both peoples.

The second account reports an even more striking demonstration of Yahweh's power. This takes place when the Assyrian emperor Sennacherib's forces besiege Jerusalem. The episode occurs during the reign of Hezekiah, one of the few kings of Jerusalem who practices the devotion and obedience Yahweh looks for in a king. In this case, the Assyrian Rabshakeh attempts to undercut the people's confidence in Yahweh's protection, first by insinuating that Hezekiah's policy of closing high places has displeased Yahweh (2 Kgs 18:22), and second by claiming that Yahweh directly commanded the Assyrians to assault Jerusalem (18:25). A third tactic directly challenges Yahweh's supremacy:

> Don't listen to Hezekiah, because he's fooling you when he says, "Yahweh will deliver us!" Have any of the gods of any of the nations succeeded in delivering their lands from the hand of the king of Assyria? Where were the gods of Hamath and Arpad? Where were the gods of Sepharvaim, Hena, and Ivvah? Did they deliver Samaria from my hand? Who among all the gods of the land has delivered their lands from my hand? Will Yahweh really deliver Jerusalem from my hand? (2 Kgs 18:32–35)

Hezekiah bucks royal precedent and sets the matter directly before Yahweh, first by reporting the words to the prophet Isaiah and then directly through prayer. In both cases, Hezekiah points to the utter hopelessness of the situation and emphasizes that Yahweh's reputation has been sullied. The messengers he sends to the prophet Isaiah discreetly raise the question of whether Yahweh has heard the mocking words (19:1–4). Hezekiah's prayer then emphasizes what is at stake for Yahweh (19:14–19): Yahweh is the one true God and Sovereign over all the nations of the earth; the Assyrian king has mocked Yahweh; the gods the Assyrians claim to have overthrown are no gods at all (19:14-19). Presenting the Rabshakeh's challenge as a dramatic opportunity to display Yahweh's power to all nations, Hezekiah appeals to Yahweh to save his people, "so that all the kingdoms of the earth may know that you, Yahweh, you alone, are God" (19:19). Yahweh responds with a terse comment that confirms Hezekiah's words: "I will defend this city in order to save it, for my own sake and the sake of David my servant" (19:34). The dramatic nature of the challenge then leads Yahweh to strike the Assyrian hosts directly, in a manner reminiscent of Yahweh's slaughter of the Egyptian firstborn (Exod 12:29-30). It is the singular instance, during the time of the kings, when Yahweh strikes down an enemy force without employing human agents (19:32-36).

On the domestic front, Yahweh brings down kings and dynasties that emulate Jeroboam and Rehoboam, that is, kings who violate the reciprocal covenant bond that forms the foundation of Yahweh's relationship with Israel. These kings, like Jeroboam, provoke Yahweh to action. The Hebrew verb *ka'as*, often translated "provoke to anger," signifies in these instances an egregious disrespect of Yahweh that disqualifies the king and moves Yahweh to intervene. The conventional translation, "provoke *to anger*," is somewhat misleading, as the vocabulary of anger does not explicitly occur in association with the verb and the corresponding noun. In fact, Yahweh's anger is rarely mentioned at all with reference to the kings of Israel and Judah, and only at strategic junctures. The narrator reports Yahweh's anger at David (*kharah*; 2 Sam 24:1), Solomon (*'anaph*; 1 Kgs 11:9), Jehoahaz (*kharah*, 2 Kgs 13:3), Manasseh (*kharah*, 2 Kgs 23:26), and in summaries (*'anaph*, 2 Kgs 17:18; *khemah*, 2 Kgs 22:13-17; *'aph*, 2 Kgs 24:20). While Manasseh is said to "provoke" Yahweh as well (2 Kgs 22:53), the verb does not occur in proximity to the report of divine anger. Only in the narrator's explanation of the Northern Kingdom's exile are provocation and anger linked (2 Kgs 17:17-18). Little in the verb signifying provocation, in short, associates the action directly with divine anger. Rather, each occurrence of provocation reports Yahweh's response to idolatrous practices that violate the covenant and move Yahweh to action—revealing a deity who intervenes violently when reciprocal choosing has been violated, but not a persistently angry one.

Yahweh removes kings through the kinds of intrigues, assassinations, coups, and exterminations that are endemic among the kingdoms of the time (cf. 2 Kgs 8:7-15). Baasha, who exterminates Jeroboam's house and carries out Yahweh's judgment, nevertheless follows Jeroboam's ways.

He likewise provokes Yahweh and receives the same prophetic word of condemnation (1 Kgs 15:29-30; 16:1-4, 7). As was the case with his predecessor, Baasha's son meets a violent end after a brief two-year reign, and his successor exterminates his entire house (16:8-10). In the chaos that follows, another general takes the reins of power. Omri makes even greater room for idolatry and so also provokes Yahweh (16:25-26). Ahab his son goes so far as to erect an Asherah, intensifying the provocation (16:33) and soliciting the prophetic judgment leveled against Jeroboam and Baasha (21:21-26). Ahab's unexpected self-humiliation in response to the prophetic word gives Yahweh the opportunity to show a willingness to respond to repentant partners but does little more than prolong the inevitable (21:27-29; 22:53).

The fourth iteration of the pattern, this time when Jehu is anointed on the battlefield, is noteworthy for a number of reasons. Unlike the usurpers before him, Jehu is an ardent Yahwist who eliminates the priests and paraphernalia of Baal worship from the kingdom (2 Kgs 10:16-17, 29). His zeal, however, goes beyond his mandate; he also massacres forty-two Davidic princes whom he meets during the course of his purges (10:12-14). Yahweh commends the general and promises him a dynasty lasting four generations (10:28-30) but says nothing about the excessive killing that Jehu undertakes. The limitation of the dynasty, even for a loyal devotee, intimates that Yahweh has come to the conclusion that the strategy of replacing provocative kings will not produce lasting results. Yahweh also seems to have scaled down expectations for the kings. Jehu's descendants, while not turning Israel to other gods, are nevertheless content to maintain the status quo. This appears to be the best Yahweh can expect at this point, as none of the kings of Jehu's dynasty are said to provoke Yahweh.

Yahweh in effect seems to yield to the inevitable. Jehoahaz, Jehu's son, angers Yahweh by failing to close Jeroboam's shrines at Bethel and Dan and to remove an Asherah pole in Samaria (13:1-6). Yahweh tries the pre-monarchical strategy of delivering Israel into the hand of an enemy and then sending a savior in response to prayer, but Jehoahaz does not close the shrines. From this point on, Yahweh assumes indirect forms of engagement. Yahweh withholds punishment from Israel and allows the conflicts between Israelite and Aramaean kings to take their course (13:22-25). Yahweh also lends unspecified support to Jeroboam II (14:27). By the time the fourth descendant, Zechariah, is assassinated, Yahweh is no longer in the picture, leaving the nation to fend for itself while internal strife and external threats propel the kingdom toward defeat and exile. A summary explanation for the destruction of the kingdom highlights Israel's persistent and intransigent apostasy despite repeated prophetic warnings, the sum of which provokes Yahweh to remove the nation from the land (2 Kgs 17:11, 17-18).

The kings of Judah do not turn their kingdom to other gods during this period and so do not provoke Yahweh. Although many of the kings do things that are evil in Yahweh's sight, they hold to the bond that unites Yahweh to Jerusalem and the people. That changes however with the long reign of Manasseh. Manasseh adopts the practices of the indigenous peoples, erects altars for Baal, and worst of all, builds altars for astral deities and installs an Asherah in the temple precinct (2 Kgs 21:1-8). The narrator accentuates the sense of outrage these practices provoke by recalling Yahweh's declaration to David and Solomon, that is, that Yahweh had chosen Jerusalem to be the place where "I will set my name forever," provided the people obey the law of Moses. The blatant acts of disrespect and disobedience not only break the exclusive covenantal bond but also, as the narrator's reminder indicates, irreparably damage Yahweh's reputation. Yahweh cannot let this stand. No doubt remembering the futility of a long experience with the kings of Israel, Yahweh deals with the affront immediately and drastically. Through the prophets, Yahweh declares an end to the divine arrangement with kings, due to the provocations Yahweh has had to put up with since delivering the nation from Egypt: "I will leave what is left of my inheritance and deliver it into the hands of their enemies. They will be plunder and booty for all their enemies, because they have done evil in my sight and have provoked me from the time their ancestors left Egypt to this very day" (vv. 14-15).

Yahweh is no longer of a mind to deal with Israel's persistent intransigence, not even when Manasseh's son Josiah leads the people in repentance, covenant renewal, and the destruction of every vestige of idolatrous worship (2 Kgs 22:1–23:25). Even though Josiah turns to Yahweh with all his heart, and although he eradicates the places and practitioners of idolatry in Samaria as well as Judah, Yahweh is unmoved. The God of Israel has already decided to bring an end to the kingdom; Yahweh wants nothing more to do with Judah and Jerusalem (23:26-27; cf. 22:15-17; 24:3-4). As Yahweh had done earlier with Israel, Yahweh stirs up conflict with nations and leaves the kings of Jerusalem and Judah to suffer the consequences of their rebelliousness.

The End of the Matter

Yahweh's decision to restore humanity from the inside out begins when Yahweh identifies with a family, then with a people, and finally with a kingdom. The decision to let Israel have a king pulls Yahweh inexorably into the system Yahweh has opposed since delivering Israel from Pharaoh. The transition to kingship brings about significant modifications to Yahweh's relationship with Israel. Yahweh cedes more power and initiative to kings and adapts to their objectives. With the singular exception of the Rabshakeh's challenge, Yahweh does not fight for Israel directly or through spirit-empowered agents. Rather, Yahweh assumes an advisory role on issues of war or indirectly delivers Israel's enemies into the power of the king—thus allowing the king also to receive the accolades that kings require to maintain their status and authority.

The decision to identify with kings also means that Yahweh's reputation and work in the world is attached to the aims of kings and tangled up with what is expected of deities within the monarchical systems of the ancient Near East. Yahweh's standing in the world, and thus Yahweh's influence and work, is associated with the king's standing among his royal peers. The relationship is mutually beneficial to the extent that kings keep up their end. Yahweh promises to ensure the security of the Davidic kings in Jerusalem and the continuity of the dynasty, and to reside permanently in the temple. Divine promises are contingent on the kings emulating the devotion of David and demonstrating submission by walking in Yahweh's ordinances. Yahweh continues the program with Jeroboam, although apparently rethinking the decision after Jeroboam shows no inclination to respond in good faith. In all cases the kings are required, at a minimum, to maintain the exclusive devotion to Yahweh that Yahweh gives to the nation.

Yahweh's use of or implication in violence in a monarchical mode is targeted, strategic, and for the most part limited to aiding and abetting the normative violence associated with kingship. Yahweh defends faithful kings under threat from other powers, as well as unfaithful kings when they appeal for help, by delivering the enemy forces into the king's power. Yahweh removes and replaces kings who violate the exclusive devotion required by the covenant by stirring up trouble from without and within, announcing the removal of the wicked king, and letting political processes take their course. In only two instances does Yahweh directly participate in royal battles, in one case miraculously providing water to a stranded army and in the other case decimating an Assyrian army. In both of these cases, Yahweh's reputation is on the line.

It remains to review the connection between divine violence and divine anger. First, *the language of anger is rarely associated with the violence that Yahweh perpetrates or instigates with reference to kings.* Yahweh's anger is said to burn in response to the sins of Jehoahaz and the total disregard of Manasseh (2 Kgs 13:3; 2 Kgs 23:26), and in the latter case is associated with Yahweh's decision to abandon Judah and Jerusalem. Likewise, Yahweh's prophet Huldah declares that Manasseh has kindled Yahweh's wrath (2 Kgs 22:17). Yahweh is said to be furious at Solomon's turning away and at the many idolatrous practices that the people of the northern kingdom persistently practice (1 Kgs 11:9; 2 Kgs 17:18).

For the most part, however, Yahweh's judgments on the kingdoms are explained with reference to Israel's and Judah's provocations, which, as noted above, signify the outrageous turning to other gods that destroys the core of the relationship between Yahweh and the kingdom. As noted at many previous points, Yahweh's judgments are not impulsive or capricious outbreaks of rage. Yahweh is "provoked" by many kings, endures repeated affronts, and acts only when the relationship—whether with the kings or the nation as a whole—has been irretrievably broken. The testimony of Yahweh's relationship with kings confirms that Yahweh is indeed "compassionate and gracious, slow to anger and abounding in steadfast devotion" (Exod 34:6). However expressed or conceived, *Yahweh's anger in the narrative literature is directed toward Israel only, and only when Israel persistently refuses to reciprocate Yahweh's exclusive choosing of the nation,* the honoring of which is essential if Yahweh's restorative purposes are to be accomplished through Israel.

The destruction of Jerusalem and the exile of the population to Babylon brings the story to a dismal end. Yahweh's decision to enter a world of violence in order to rescue it has not succeeded and has drawn Yahweh into the very systems and practices of violence that Yahweh intended to overcome. What began as a friendship and identification with a family has generated a series of adaptations that, over the course of time, has ensnared Yahweh in a violent world. Despite points of hope and faithfulness, the overall project lies in ruins. Yahweh has stepped away, and Yahweh's people once again find themselves slaves to a foreign king. Yet Yahweh is not completely done with the people, nor has Yahweh abandoned the work of rescuing the world in partnership with faithful human agents. The break in the trajectory of the narrative at this point, however, reveals that Yahweh will have to find another way.

7

The Land Promised and Taken

> Joshua attacked the entire land: the highlands, the Negev, the lowland, and the slopes, along with their kings. No one survived. He wiped out everyone who drew breath, as Yahweh the God of Israel commanded.
>
> JOSHUA 10:40

The book of Joshua presents arguably the most troublesome episode of divine violence in the Bible. Following the command of Yahweh, the Israelites invade a land whose peoples have not threatened or attacked them and proceed to slaughter men, women, and children as an expression of divine obedience. Yahweh initiates the battles, fights for Israel, and wins victories, while Israel follows through, occupies the land, and massacres the population, showing no mercy. The account of these conquests in Joshua 2-12 is communicated with an air of triumphalism and little sense of regret save for the fact that the Israelites did not finish the job.

The scope and scale of the violence, and the fact that Yahweh and Israel work in tandem to perpetrate it, has been a problem for Christian interpreters throughout history. I have noted previously that the early Christian teacher Origen deflected the violence by allegorizing the book.[1] John Calvin waited until the end of his life to write his commentary on the book and counseled against holding God to the same moral commands and principles that God had instituted to regulate human

---

1. Origen, *Homilies on Joshua*, ed. Cynthia White, trans. Barbara J. Bruce, Fathers of the Church Patristic Series 105 (Washington, DC: The Catholic University of America, 2002).

behavior.[2] The ripple effects of a century of genocide, now promoted by extremist ideologies that legitimize mass slaughter in the name of God, have brought Joshua front and center in the church's ethical and theological vision. These factors, along with the fact that Israel's invasion of Canaan completes the story of the Pentateuch in important ways, require that we devote particular attention to both the story and the way it is narrated within the context of the larger narrative complex we have elaborated in the last few chapters. The issue of divine violence in Joshua must be addressed through careful reading of the book, with attention to the ways that Joshua fits within the larger story of Yahweh's identification with and working through Israel.

The Promised Land

The invasion and settlement of Canaan is the culminating act of a drama that begins with the expulsion of Adam and Eve from the garden. Eden was the place on earth where Yahweh God first called humanity to care for the creation (Gen 2:8). Eden signifies the importance of an abode where Yahweh, humanity, and creatures are united under Yahweh's beneficent authority. The breaking of the original relationship with Yahweh also broke the human relationship with creation, resulting in a loss of place. If, therefore, Yahweh is to restore the original harmony with humanity and creation, Yahweh will have to establish a place to do it within the unholy mess that creation has become. That is, for Yahweh to renew the creation from the inside out, Yahweh will have to carve out a place where a reconstituted human community can live under Yahweh's reign and the order that Yahweh establishes.

This is in part why Yahweh's calling of Abraham begins with references to land: "Depart from your land, your family, and your father's house to the land I will show you" (Gen 12:1). As noted in an earlier chapter, the series of blessings that follows the land promise elaborates what Yahweh will do for and through Abram: Yahweh will make Abram into a great nation with a great reputation for the purpose of blessing the nations of the earth through him. But it all begins with a land. At the beginning of Abram's story Yahweh makes a promise that drives the whole of the Pentateuch, one that is fulfilled only when Abram's descendants take possession of the land of Canaan. From

---

2. See Ronald G. Goetz, "Joshua, Calvin, and Genocide," *Theology Today* 32 (1975): 263-74.

this point on, references to Yahweh's promise of the land weave the events of the narrative together (e.g., Gen 24:7; 26:3; Exod 33:1; Num 14:16, 23; Deut 6:10, 18; 11:9, 21; 26:3; Josh 1:6). With the land promise to Abram, "creation begins anew, as a history of anticipation of the land."[3]

The promise of land speaks of Yahweh's working in space just as the promise of descendants speaks of Yahweh's working through time. Yahweh calls Abram to "go to the land I will show you." The land is chosen as Abram is chosen. The land called Canaan will become the land called Israel, the place that the chosen nation will inhabit and on which Yahweh will establish an ordering presence in the world. The identification of people with land forges a deep bond with a particular terrain. Anthony Smith, who has written on the ways that ethnic groups and nations construct their identities, has elaborated the profound attachment to a territory that stands at the core of ethnic identity. He describes a nation's identification with its homeland as "an alleged and felt symbiosis between a certain piece of earth and 'its' community."[4] The features of the land are held to shape and nurture the essence of the nation. The land is the arena for the formative events that configure collective memory. The land is where national heroes exemplify national virtues and the place where the people's ancestors are buried.

The sentiment finds expression in Israel's ancestral narrative in two ways. First, Canaan is the location in which Yahweh's relationship with the ancestors begins and matures, marked on Yahweh's part by appearances to the patriarchs in which Yahweh elaborates the promise, and on the part of the patriarchs by the erection of altars in the land dedicated to Yahweh (Gen 12:7-8; 13:18; 26:25; 33:20; 35:6-7). Second, the land is the place where the ancestors are buried (Gen 23:16; 25:9-10; 35:19-20, 29; 49:31; 50:1-14). The tethering of memory and destiny to the land comes together in the story of Abraham's purchase of a burial plot in Canaan (Gen 23:1-20). The purchase fuses space, time, and relationship—land, descendants, and faith in Yahweh—in embryonic form. The burial plot marks the land as home.

Situating Israel in a land is also necessary for what Yahweh wants to do through Israel. Land gives Yahweh standing among the powerful deities of Israel's world, who are also identified with particular lands. We have noted in the last chapter how an Aramean king explained a humiliating defeat at

---

3. Walter Brueggemann, *The Land: Place as Gift, Promise, and Challenge in Biblical Faith*, OBT (Philadelphia: Fortress, 1977), 17.

4. Anthony D. Smith, *Chosen Peoples: Sacred Sources of National Identity* (Oxford: Oxford University Press, 2003), 44. See also Anthony D. Smith, *Myths and Memories of the Nation* (Oxford: Oxford University Press, 1999).

the hands of the Israelites by claiming that Israel's god was a highland god, giving Israel the advantage on that terrain (1 Kgs 20:23). The Aramean general Naaman, grateful for Yahweh's healing ministry, expresses the sentiment in a more literal way when he requests two-mule loads of Israelite soil to take back to Damascus so that he can devote himself solely to Yahweh (2 Kgs 5:17).

Yahweh accommodates to the identification of deities and lands when it serves a purpose. When the Assyrians resettle Samaria with peoples from other parts of their empire, Yahweh sends lions to kill them because they do not worship Yahweh. As a result, the people appeal to the Assyrian emperor for help, declaring, "The nations you have deported and resettled in the cities of Samaria don't know the ways of the gods of the land. He has sent lions among them and they are killing them since they don't know the ways of the gods of the land" (2 Kgs 17:26). The emperor in turn remedies the situation by sending a Samaritan priest back to the land so that the peoples can be properly instructed in the way they should show reverence to the god of the land. The identification with the land that Yahweh takes by conquest thus elevates Yahweh's status as much as it does Israel's.

Canaan, like Egypt, becomes the arena of the mighty works by which Yahweh demonstrates supremacy and power to all the nations of the world. It is to be the place where Yahweh makes a great nation, renowned throughout the world. By giving Israel the land, Yahweh intends to create a space that recovers the Edenic harmony resulting from a restored relationship of reciprocal choosing. As it was in the garden, humanity will live in dependence and submission to the Creator, and the creation will benefit.

Yahweh communicates this ideal clearly by elaborating the details of the life Israel will enjoy in the land if the nation remains loyal and obedient. Yahweh will send the rains that produce lavish fruitfulness. Yahweh will grant peace and rest in the land and free the nation from fear. Yahweh will remove dangerous beasts from the land and prevent the sword from passing through it. Yahweh will look upon Israel with favor and enable the nation to fulfill the divine mandate to be fruitful and multiply. Yahweh will keep the covenant with the Israelites and dwell among them (Lev 16:1-12).

The association between Israel's covenant relationship, the status it will enjoy among the nations, and Yahweh's blessing on the land and people is made explicit for the generation that prepares to enter the land by reporting a Mosaic exhortation (Deut 28:1-13). The passage begins and ends with declarations that national obedience will bring national eminence: "Yahweh your God will make you preeminent over all the nations of the earth" (v. 1b) and "Yahweh will set you as the head and not the tail; you will be on top and not at the bottom" (v. 13a). As a result, "all the peoples of the earth will see that the name of Yahweh is spoken over you, and they will be afraid of you" (v. 10). Those who live in the land with Yahweh, no matter where they live, will enjoy lavish and unremitting blessing, along with the livestock and crops (vv. 4, 11). Yahweh's blessing will come to Israelite wombs, barns, and storehouses, and the people will experience such abundance that they will lend to other nations (v. 12b).

The Land and the Peoples

The invasion and settlement of Canaan is first and foremost a divine act that demonstrates Yahweh's faithfulness and commitment to Israel. The reiteration of the land promise throughout the narrative of the Pentateuch underscores Yahweh's faithfulness and ability to follow through on divine promises, as well as Yahweh's exclusive devotion to Israel. The narrator of Joshua emphasizes Yahweh's faithfulness with a summary that caps the allotment of lands to the Israelite tribes.

> Yahweh gave Israel the entire land that he swore to give their ancestors. They occupied it and settled it. Yahweh gave them rest on all sides, just as Yahweh swore to their ancestors. None of their enemies could stand up to them. Yahweh delivered all their enemies into their hands. Not one word of any of the good words that Yahweh spoke to the house of Israel failed. Every one came to pass. (Josh 21:43-45)

Divine faithfulness to Israel, however, does not mean divine judgment on the indigenous peoples. The conquest account nowhere presents the invasion of Canaan and the violence that accompanies it as a visitation of judgment; there is no statement of judgment directed toward the peoples of the land anywhere in the book of Joshua. This, however, has not dissuaded many interpreters from claiming that the wars were justified by the heinous sins of the peoples of the land. These interpreters draw support from a few vague references to the peoples of the land, chief among them Yahweh's comment to Abraham that the iniquity of the Amorites had not yet reached the tipping point (Gen 15:16) and Moses's declaration that Yahweh is giving the land to the Israelites because of the wickedness of its peoples, not because of their own righteousness (Deut 9:1-6). So, for example, Christopher Wright takes Yahweh's comment on Amorite iniquity to mean that "the Amorite/Canaanite society of Abraham's day was not yet so wicked as to morally justify God's acting in comprehensive judgment on it."[5] The judgment thesis is attractive because it changes the moral calculus of the violence; the peoples of the land were wiped out because they deserved punishment.

It is important to note, however, that the two declarations are set within reiterations of the land promise. In the Genesis statement, Yahweh explicitly declares that Yahweh will judge the nation that enslaves Abraham's ancestors (Egypt) but does not mention judgment with reference to the Amorites. This would be a strange omission if the sins of the Amorites were worse than all other peoples (Gen 15:13-14). There is likewise no direct pronouncement of judgment on the Canaanites in the Deuteronomic text. In this passage Yahweh undercuts Israelite presumption with a rhetorical contrast between supposed Israelite righteousness and Canaanite wickedness, before clarifying that Yahweh is driving them out "in order to fulfill the promise that Yahweh made to your ancestors, to Abraham, Isaac, and Jacob" (v. 5). The Canaanites are wicked, to be sure, but the connection between their wickedness and their removal is not specified. Deuteronomy, in fact, suggests a reason other than judgment for the reason that Yahweh is driving them out, namely, that if any remain in the land they will draw Israel away from its covenant relationship (Deut 7:1-8; 12:29-31; 20:16-18). Yahweh nowhere directly declares that the peoples of the land are being judged, although Moses pointedly reminds Israel that that they have angered Yahweh since the day the nation left Egypt (Deut 9:7).

The only passage that directly associates the Canaanite sin and expulsion from the land attributes their fate to the land itself rather than Yahweh. While there is no direct statement that the Canaanites have incurred God's wrath, Moses elsewhere declares that Canaanite practices have so defiled the land that the land itself has vomited them out. He warns the Israeiltes not to do "any of these disgusting things. . . . Otherwise the land will vomit you also for defiling it as it vomited the nation that was before you" (Lev 18:27-28; cf. 20:22-24).

Instead of explaining the invasion of Canaan as an act of judgment, Moses instead explicitly situates it within the context of Yahweh's overall work in the affairs of nations. While recapitulating Israel's journey northwards through the Transjordan, Moses digresses to mention nations that had inhabited the region prior to Israel's time. Moses forbids Israel to harass the Edomites and Moabites, because Yahweh has given them their lands as

---

5. Christopher J. H. Wright, *The God I Don't Understand: Reflections on Tough Questions of Faith* (Grand Rapids: Zondervan, 2008), 92.

possessions. Moses notes that the Emim, "a large and numerous people," previously occupied the territory presently inhabited by Moab and that the Horim previously inhabited Edom's territory. Moses also mentions the Zamzummim, the erstwhile inhabitants of Ammon's territory, who were likewise dispossessed. Moses then makes the startling statement that Yahweh destroyed the Zamzummim before the Ammonites and the Horim before the Edomites (Deut 2:1-23).

> (Ammon) is also considered to be the land of the Rephaim. Rephaim lived in it previously, though the Ammonites called them Zamzummim; a great and numerous people as tall as the Anakim. But Yahweh exterminated them before the Ammonites so they could dispossess them and settle there instead of them. (vv. 21-22)

The analogy with the land promise is clear. Yahweh has given lands to other peoples as possessions and enabled those peoples to destroy the indigenous inhabitants, just as in Israel's case. Moses thus presents Yahweh's gift of Canaan to Israel, not to mention Yahweh's slaughter of the indigenous inhabitants, not as a unique occurrence but rather an instance of Yahweh's mysterious involvement in the migration and settlement of peoples (cf. Amos 9:7).

What sets Israel apart, then, is not Yahweh's participation in invasion, slaughter, and dispossession but rather the unique nature of the relationship that binds Israel to Yahweh and the purpose Yahweh has for giving Israel possession of Canaan. The angel of Yahweh reiterates this purpose when speaking to Moses from the burning bush:

> I have come down to deliver them from the power of Egypt and to bring them up from that land to a good and spacious land flowing with milk and honey, to the place of the Canaanites, Hittites, Amorites, Perizzites, Hivites, and Jebusites. (Exod 3:8)

As we noted earlier, Yahweh delivers Israel for the purpose of bringing the nation to the land of Canaan and giving it to Israel as promised to the nation's ancestors. The exodus and the conquest are thus inseparable elements of Yahweh's story. Yahweh delivers Israel from one land to bring it into another. The saving God is also the conquering God.

Creation imagery, specifically the dividing of water, signals that the exodus and conquest are to be taken together as related acts of creation. The imagery, it may be recalled, evokes Near Eastern creation myths that depict creation as a victory over the powers of destruction and the subsequent establishment of order by the victorious deity. Chaos is restrained as long as order prevails but always threatens to break out with uncontrollable force. The image is picked up by Israel's creation narrative as well, but the splitting of the water in the biblical case accentuates the sovereign power of the Creator (Gen 1:6-8). There is no combat or struggle against an opposing and powerful chaos, only the utterance of divine speech that begins the ordering of the cosmos.

It was Yahweh who brought chaos back to the creation when human sin flooded the earth, in the failed attempt at re-creating the world by wiping it out and starting anew (Gen 6:1-9:17). Yahweh then began creating from the inside out, by delivering Israel, the family-turned-nation, from the agony of Egypt by splitting the sea and transferring the people from a warped order into the undifferentiated vastness of the wilderness (Exod 14:21-31; cf. Isa 51:9-10). Within that boundless expanse, Yahweh established anew the relationship upon which the re-creation of the world must be fixed. At Sinai, Israel acknowledged Yahweh's beneficence, authority, and supremacy and agreed to follow the laws that represent the new ordering of human society. In the wilderness, Yahweh ordered Israel's society, systems, customs, and morality. Now, after forty years, Yahweh splits the Jordan to bring this ordered and ordering people into a new land (Josh 3:1-4:24).

The conquest of the land, therefore, is rendered as the last act in a divine drama of creation, begun through deliverance from the death and despair of Egypt and finished by the establishment of a new nation in its own land. The explanation of the stones that memorialize the miraculous crossing of the Jordan succinctly summarizes the meaning of this work of creation:

> You are to give this explanation to your children: Israel crossed the Jordan on dry ground. Yahweh your God dried up the water of the Jordan in front of you until you crossed, just as Yahweh your God did at the Red Sea which he dried up until we had crossed—so that all the peoples of the world will recognize the power of Yahweh, which is mighty, and that you will reverence Yahweh your God forever. (Josh 4:22-24)

Yahweh's contest with kings bookends the formation of the covenant people. Yahweh defeated Pharaoh to bring the nation into being. A generation later, Yahweh defeats a series of kings to give the nation a land of its own. The violence that Yahweh inflicts on the peoples of Canaan, in other words, is an extension of the violence that Yahweh directed toward the Egyptians. In Egypt, Yahweh stepped into a world of established principalities and powers and delivered Israel through a series of plagues that exposed Pharaoh's powerlessness and brought great suffering to the Egyptian people. The contest climaxed when Yahweh sent an agent of death to slaughter sleeping men and children (Exod 12:29-30). Throughout the conflict, Yahweh enlisted the participation of human agents, Moses and Aaron, who initiated the divine acts of suffering through acts and announcements (Exod 7:20-21; 8:5-6, 16-17, etc.).

In Canaan, Yahweh subjugates the powerful kings of the land through a series of battles. In so doing, Yahweh acquires the land of Canaan by right of conquest and, as the victorious ruler, distributes the land to those who have participated in the conquest. Although Yahweh fights and wins the battles, Yahweh enlists human agents here as well, commanding Joshua and the Israelites to carry out and implement divine objectives. In Canaan as in Egypt, untold numbers of people die as a result of the conflict. In both cases, however, Yahweh directs and perpetrates the violence both for Yahweh's own sake and for Israel's. The narrator underscores the point by linking what Yahweh did to the kings of Canaan to what Yahweh did to Pharaoh, "because it was Yahweh's work to harden their hearts to engage Israel in battle, so that they could be wiped out and be shown no mercy but instead be exterminated, as Yahweh commanded Moses" (Josh 11:20). Yahweh, in short, creates in the mode of the ancient Near Eastern gods, bringing a new nation into being by fighting with and defeating the (human) powers of destruction in both Egypt and Canaan.

This does not mean that the indigenous peoples do not constitute a threat to the realization of Yahweh's plan for and through Israel. To the contrary, remnants of the indigenous populations problematize the full identification of Israel with its land and imperil the reciprocal choosing that binds Israel and Yahweh to each other. The indigenous peoples constitute a threat, however, not so much by what they *do* but by who they *are*. That is, the indigenous peoples of the land threaten Israel by their *difference* from Israel and by their *similarity* to the rest of the peoples of the world. As the earthly location where the reciprocal choosing of Israel and Yahweh is to be manifest, the land must be as exclusively Yahweh's as the nation of Israel is to be.

Yahweh explains, at the beginning and end of the wilderness sojourn, why the peoples of the land must be eliminated. At Sinai, Yahweh concludes a law code by elaborating how Yahweh will fulfill his promise to bring Israel into the land (Exod 23:20-33). Yahweh's angel will be sent before Israel to erase the peoples of the land (v. 23), terrorize and confuse them so thoroughly that they will turn tail and run when Israel enters (v. 27), and inflict them with diseases that will force them to leave (v. 28). Significantly, Yahweh declares that the process will take place gradually and not all at once, until Israel has succeeded in occupying the entire land (vv. 29-30). Israel is to reciprocate by worshiping Yahweh and refusing all associations with the indigenous peoples and their gods. Yahweh concludes with a succinct decree that brings together command and rationale: "They must not live in your land, lest they make you sin against me so that you serve their gods and so be a snare to you" (v. 33).

The terse decree hearkens back to the commandment that begins the law code: "I am Yahweh your God, who brought you out of the land of Egypt, from the house of slavery. You must have no other gods besides me" (20:3). Together, the decrees bracket the law code by reinforcing reciprocal choosing, the first decree by looking back at Yahweh's act of deliverance and the second by looking forward to Yahweh's work to bring Israel into Canaan. The indigenous peoples have an attachment to the land that must be broken if the land is to become fully identified with Israel and Yahweh. As long as they remain in the land, their presence impedes and threatens the covenant relationship.

Yahweh reiterates this explanation for Canaanite expulsion when Israel prepares to enter the land after defeating two Amorite kings (Num 33:51-56). In this case Yahweh emphasizes what Israel is to do, that is, expel the indigenous peoples and occupy the land. Yahweh concludes with a warning that echoes the concluding decree of the Sinai law code. Here Moses accentuates the exclusive character of the covenant relationship in negative terms:

> But if you do not expel the inhabitants of the land from your presence, then those who remain will become splinters in your eyes and thorns in your sides. They will pressure you in the land on which you live and I will do to you what I intended to do to them. (Num 33:55-56)

Moses later expands Yahweh's Sinai declaration and elaborates the rationale (Deut 7:1-26). Moses commands the Israelites to wipe out the indigenous peoples, showing no mercy, when Yahweh clears them away and then forbids any association with them, whether by agreement or intermarriage. He specifically warns the Israelites against intermarriage, explaining that the practice will turn their descendants from Yahweh and so kindle Yahweh's anger (vv. 1-4). The commands lead in turn to an elaborate reiteration of the covenant relationship that binds Israel to Yahweh and that will bind Israel to the land. The rest of the speech begins and ends with commands that Israel destroy Canaanite altars and every piece of indigenous religious paraphernalia (vv. 5, 25-26).

In between the commands, Moses emphasizes the reciprocal choosing that is at the heart of the covenant relationship. Israel is holy, chosen, and the treasured possession of Yahweh (vv. 6-10). If Israel responds by walking in Yahweh's ways, Israel will be blessed (vv. 11-15). Israel is to trust Yahweh to clear the land of its peoples and to destroy them and everything associated with them (vv. 16-28). The declarations make clear that the land must be purged of indigenous deities along with indigenous peoples. There can be only one god in this land. The Canaanites' attachment to the land goes hand in hand with deep attachments to the deities who reside in the territory. Both bonds must be completely severed if exclusive worship of Yahweh is to take place in the land (Deut 6:1-15; 20:15-18).

Summing Up the Background Material

To sum up: The conquest and occupation of Canaan, first of all, represent the last act in the drama that began with Yahweh's promise to Abram. Yahweh's intention to bless all the nations on the earth through Abraham and his descendants requires a land where the restored relationship between Yahweh and human subjects can be lived out fully for the sake of the world. Land and relationship are tightly bound as Yahweh acts to renew the original blessing.

Second, Moses sets the dispossession of the indigenous peoples within the context of Yahweh's superintending activity over the movements of peoples and the possession of territories. Other nations besides Israel have stories about the invasion of lands and the dispossession of indigenous peoples, and behind them all is the mysterious working of Yahweh.

Third, the dispossession of the Canaanites is not rendered as an act of judgment. Although Yahweh finds the practices of the indigenous peoples repulsive, Yahweh makes no direct declaration of judgment. The book of Joshua nowhere casts the wars in Canaan as divine punishment for Canaanite sinfulness. Nor is there any report of divine anger with reference to Canaan. Rather, scant biblical references suggest that the dispossession of the peoples is a consequence of the cumulative impact of their defiling and wicked practices over time.

Fourth, the exodus from Egypt and invasion of Canaan constitute the beginning and end of a creative work in which Yahweh brings a new people into being through deliverance, covenant, and inheritance. The violence Yahweh inflicts in Canaan is an extension of the violence inflicted in Egypt and serves the same end, that is, to demonstrate Yahweh's faithfulness and to announce Yahweh's entrance into the world by devastating victories over human kings. As Yahweh demonstrated in Egypt, a new deity gets attention most quickly and effectively through dramatic demonstrations of power over the human powers in the land. By defeating the power of the Canaanite kings, both severally and in coalition, Yahweh claims a land and displays divine power to the nations of the world. In both Egypt and Canaan, Yahweh employs human agents in programs of mass killing, but it is Yahweh who fights and wins the victories. The difference between human involvement in the violence in Egypt and Canaan is a matter of scope. In Egypt, Moses and Aaron announce and initiate violence under Yahweh's direction. In Canaan, Joshua and Israel perpetrate it.

Finally, life in the land must reflect the reciprocal choosing that characterizes Israel's relationship with Yahweh. The presence of other peoples, gods, and practices obstructs the transformation of the land of Canaan into the land of Israel. Yahweh and Israel alone must inhabit the land. For its part, Israel must take all necessary measures to eliminate the threatening presence of the indigenous peoples. To follow other gods is to betray the exclusive relationship that binds Yahweh and Israel to each other. To follow the ways of other gods is to reject Yahweh as the author of life and goodness. To adopt practices connected to other deities is to reject the order that Yahweh imposes on the land and people to enable both to flourish.

Yahweh the Conqueror

Joshua is one of the most confused and confusing narratives in the Old Testament. The main line of narration asserts that the Israelites swept through Canaan as a single irresistible force and in complete obedience to Yahweh, winning victory after victory and annihilating entire populations. A series of summaries supports this impression: Joshua defeated all the kings in the south of Canaan, wiped out every living being, and took all the land (10:40-42); Joshua defeated all the kings in the north and captured all their towns (11:12); Joshua took the whole land, from the Negeb to Mount Halak (11:16-17, 23); Joshua and the Israelites defeated the kings who ruled the

Transjordan and Canaan (12:1-24); Yahweh gave the entire land to Israel and all Israel's enemies into their hands (21:43-45).

The first section of Joshua (chs. 2-12) presents Israel acting in unity with each other and in complete obedience to Yahweh. Yahweh directs Israel how and when to cross the Jordan and how to assault Jericho, and Israel does exactly what Yahweh says (3:1-4:18; 6:1-21). The Israelites demonstrate covenantal obedience through circumcision, through the celebration of Passover and the Feast of Unleavened Bread (5:1-12), and by renewing the covenant in compliance with the command of Moses (8:30-35; cf. Deut 11:29; 27:1-13). Joshua and Israel act as a unit; the narrator refers to the entire community over thirty times.

Yet immediately following an impressive catalogue of defeated kings (12:1-24), the second section of Joshua opens with Yahweh's declaration to an aged Joshua that "a good deal of the land remains to be possessed." Yahweh then describes the vast swaths of territory that remain in the hands of other peoples and promises to drive them out (13:1-6). Delineations of tribal boundaries subsequently contain reports of residual indigenous populations in the Transjordan (13:13), Ephraim (16:10), and Manasseh (17:12-13)—the last of these including a comment that the tribe could not take possession until they had grown stronger. An associated anecdote tells of the Joseph tribes' request for more territory but their reluctance to take on the Canaanites and their iron chariots (17:14-18). We might also note Joshua's rebuke of the tribes for their procrastination in taking possession of the land (18:3).

On a different note, Israel's decision to spare the Gibeonites leaves an entire Hivite enclave in indigenous hands, in direct violation of Moses's command that no such agreement be enacted (9:1-27; 11:19; cf. Deut 7:2). Israelite spies violate the commandment in the same way when they promise to spare Rahab, leaving a smaller enclave "within Israel to the present day" (6:25). An egregious act of disobedience by Achan leads to an ignominious defeat at the hands of an inferior Canaanite force (7:1-5). Israelite unanimity is called into question when the construction of an altar at the Jordan releases simmering resentments between the tribes east and west of the Jordan, bringing the nation to the brink of civil war (22:10-34). In a covenant renewal ceremony at the end of the book, Joshua declares that the nation cannot serve Yahweh and demands the people get rid of the foreign gods among them (24:19-24).

So, which is it? Did the people of Israel, acting as one and in complete obedience to Yahweh's directives, sweep through Canaan as an invincible force and wipe out everyone in their way until they had taken the entire land? Or did Israel win many victories and take much of the land, but not all, and obey Yahweh, but not in all instances, so that much of the land remained in indigenous hands well after the time of Joshua?

Although numerous attempts have been made to harmonize the conflicting perspectives, I prefer to take the narrative as it stands. This leads me to view the seemingly disjointed narration as an intentional strategy distinctively suited to telling the fullness of Yahweh's story about this, the most extended and extreme instance of divine violence in the biblical story. What Yahweh and Israel say and do in the process of taking possession of the land is so complex and conflicted that telling the story from a single perspective cannot fully capture the import of the drama. The narration of this story, in other words, speaks with multiple voices. There is a narrative and a counternarrative, and fragments of other narratives, each of which vies to give a perspective that must be told. In a sense, then, the extremity of violence in Joshua sets before the reader the contradictions that Yahweh has had to deal with by deciding to identify with the nation of Israel.

The main thread of the conquest narrative (Josh 1-12) is schematic in form and unusually stylized. Overall, the account follows the pattern of Moses's narration of Israel's conquests in the Transjordan (Deut 2:24-3:11). Moses begins the Deuteronomic account by quoting Yahweh's command that Israel cross a river (the Arnon) and take possession of the king's land (2:24). Yahweh also promises to terrorize the inhabitants, who will tremble when they hear about the Israelites (2:25). Moses then sends emissaries to King Sihon, who rejects their message (2:26-30). As a result, Yahweh tells Moses that Yahweh has given Sihon into Israel's hands (2:21). The Israelites defeat Sihon, take all his towns, and wipe out his people (2:31-37). A second battle with King Og of Bashan follows the same sequence (3:1-7). Moses concludes with a summary description of all the land the Israelites took and the narrator ends the account with a comment that Og was one of the last remaining Rephaim (3:8-12).

The story of Israel's conquests in Canaan follows the same pattern. The account begins with Yahweh's command that Israel cross a river (the Jordan) and take possession of the land (Josh 1:2, 11). Joshua then sends spies to Jericho, where we learn that Yahweh has terrorized the people and has delivered the people into Israel's hands (2:9-11, 24). There follows a series of battle accounts, each of which reports that the Israelites defeated the kings, took their towns, and wiped out their people. As in Deuteronomy, the account ends with a summary description of all the land that Joshua took (Josh 11:16-20), including a comment that Yahweh hardened the kings' hearts that corresponds to a similar report with reference to Sihon (Deut 2:30). The summary then concludes with a reference to giants who remained in the land (the Anakim; Josh 11:21-22).

The individual battle accounts in Joshua also follow the pattern laid out in Deuteronomy. Moses recounts the victories over Sihon (Deut 2:31-35) and Og (Deut 3:1-7) with the same scheme. The king attacks the Israelites. Yahweh declares that the king has been delivered into Israel's hands. Moses reports that the victorious Israelites struck the king, captured his town, and wiped out all his people. Moving to Joshua, the accounts of battles at Ai and Hazor incorporate the same elements (8:1-27; 11:1-11), while the account at Jericho omits only the report that the indigenous people attacked the Israelites. After the first three paradigmatic campaigns at Jericho, Ai, and Gibeon, subsequent accounts are pared down to a formulaic repetition of the pattern itself, minus (in most cases) the report that Yahweh gave the city and king into Joshua's hands (10:28-39). The reports of battles, to sum up, are highly stylized. Each is related by a common framework that affirms, in part and in whole, that Yahweh delivered the indigenous peoples to Israel and that Israel prevailed over the kings, took their towns, and wiped out their people.

As we have observed above, however, there are other reports in Joshua that suggest that the rhetorical formula contains more style than substance. We have already noted the jarring description of land outside of Israelite possession that introduces the allotment of tribal lands, as well as reports of resistant indigenous populations and of Israelite diffidence. That is to say nothing about the alternative summary of the story that opens the book of Judges (1:1-36), which undercuts the "all Israel" scenario by rendering the story as a process undertaken by individual tribes and groups, with varying degrees of success or failure.

There is also the matter of Rahab's family and the Gibeonites, indigenous populations who have been spared the fate meted out to the other peoples of the land. Might there have been others? Israel's covenant renewal ceremonies in the vicinity of Shechem (Josh 8:30-35) and at Shechem itself (Josh 24:1-28) suggest as much. Shechem was likely another Hivite enclave (Gen 34:2). There is no account that the town was attacked or taken by the Israelites, nor that its population was wiped out. Yet all Israel assembles at Shechem to reaffirm their covenantal relationship with Yahweh. The first instance pointedly describes "all Israel" in terms of "both foreigner and native" (Josh 8:33). How then did Shechem come into Israelite hands, and what happened to the people of Shechem?

The language of annihilation may be similarly contrived. At the center of the formulaic language of the battle accounts stands the claim that the Israelites wiped out the entire population of the conquered cities, sometimes appended by comments that the Israelites left no survivors or killed everything that drew breath. The Hebrew verb here translated as "wiped out" (*kharam*) elsewhere signifies items that have been transferred to Yahweh as property, which, in the case of human beings, means that the individuals are put to death (Lev 27:28-29). Cognates of the verb occur in a couple of instances outside the Bible to signify a king's slaughter of a population as a dedication to a deity. In both biblical and non-biblical cases, the devotion of human lives takes place at human initiative; people devote other people for slaughter. As this effectively means the massacre of populations in cities so devoted, the term sometimes assumes the broader meaning, as in "to wipe out." Two aspects of the verb's use in Joshua are noteworthy: first, the commandment takes place at *Yahweh's* initiative, rendering the reports that Israel wiped out populations as confirmations that Israel obeyed the divine command in Deuteronomy; and second, the verb occurs only in the first section of Joshua.

A careful reading of Moses's command to annihilate the peoples of the land reveals a striking incongruity. The full commandment reads:

> When Yahweh your God brings you into the land that is your destination, to possess it and clear many nations away from you—the Hittites, Girgashites, the Amorites, the Canaanites, the Perizzites, the Hivites, and the Jebusites—seven nations more numerous and powerful than you, and when Yahweh your God hands them over to you, you must strike them. You must wipe them out completely. Do not make a covenant with them. Show them no favor. Do not intermarry with them. Do not give your daughters to their sons nor take their daughters for your sons. For that will turn your sons away from me and they will serve other gods. Then the anger of Yahweh will burn against you, and he will make a quick end of you. But you are to do this to them instead: you are to tear down their altars, shatter their pillars, cut down their Asherim, and burn their idols in the fire. For you are a people holy to Yahweh your God. Yahweh your God chose you for himself, out of all the peoples on the face of the earth, to be a treasure. (Deut 7:1-6)

The problem is this. Moses commands the Israelites to wipe out the indigenous peoples but then goes on to prohibit interaction with the peoples, as if the command is irrelevant or the people will not comply; the command to wipe out the peoples seems superfluous in light of what follows. Why specify a series of actions designed to keep the Israelites at a distance from the peoples if Israel is to annihilate those people when it enters the land?

The command to wipe out the peoples, in other words, does not appear to be concerned with eliminating them so much as keeping Israel at a distance from them. The passage centers on the distinct practices required to safeguard Israel's identity, detach the indigenous people from the land, and transform the land into a space where only Yahweh is worshipped. The structure of the unit reinforces the point. Moses begins by enumerating the many peoples of the land (Deut 7:1), relates what must be done to transform the land to create a proper arena for Israel to live in covenant relationship with Yahweh (Deut 7:2-5), and concludes with a declaration that Israel is holy because Yahweh has chosen it out of all the nations on earth as Yahweh's treasured possession (Deut 7:6). The practices that Moses elaborates define the boundaries that must be maintained in order for Israel to live out and embody Yahweh's restorative purpose in the world. The unit's focus on separation and transformation, in other words, reveals the command to annihilate the Canaanites as a rhetorical device that emphasizes the ethic of separation in the most extreme way possible.

The Deuteronomic command, then, gives cues that its meaning is to be directed elsewhere. John Goldingay puts the matter succinctly:

> Israel knew how to read the Torah. It knew it was not to assume a literalistic understanding of the Deuteronomic command to devote the Canaanites. Moses did not mean the instruction, and Joshua did not feel bound by it; or rather, Moses absolutely meant it, but also meant it was not to be taken literally. Literally, Israel was to dispossess the Canaanites and destroy their forms of religion and have nothing to do with them; metaphorically or hyperbolically, it was to give them over to Yhwh. Israel knew that the Torah comprises theology, religion and ethic in the form of regulations, and not merely laws for implementing. The commission to devote the Canaanites is chiefly an expression of how radically Israel must avoid being influenced by Canaanite religion.[6]

---

6. John Goldingay, *Israel's Life*, vol. 3 of *Old Testament Theology* (Downers Grove, IL: InterVarsity, 2009), 571.

Recognizing the rhetorical character of the command to annihilate the Canaanites clarifies another incongruity. We have noted above that the command to wipe out the peoples is a Deuteronomic revision of Yahweh's earlier commands, which speak instead of removing the peoples as the task that Yahweh and Israel will undertake together when they enter the land. Turning to Joshua itself, we observe that after the battles in Canaan are summarized by a list of defeated kings (Josh 12:1-24), there is no report that Yahweh directed Israel to wipe out any of the remnant populations, nor any report that Israel did so. Instead, *removing* rather than *wiping out* signifies what Yahweh will do and what Israel does (or fails to do) with reference to the peoples of the land (13:1; 14:12; 15:63; 17:12, 13, 18). The occupation of the land thus takes place in two phases: the conquest of kings and cities in Joshua 2-12 and the removal of remnant populations in Joshua 13-21. This second stage, that of removal, brings the narrative of Joshua back to the earlier Exodus declaration, affirming that the command to wipe out is a rhetorical flourish. Expelling the peoples rather than exterminating them becomes the means of clearing the land as Israel looks to the future.

Yahweh, furthermore, expresses no displeasure that the Deuteronomic commandment ceases to be executed. To the contrary, Yahweh promises to expel the peoples (as opposed to giving them over to Israel) after the kings have been defeated (13:1). Joshua, for his part, confirms the program of expulsion. In a noteworthy exhortation toward the end of his life, Joshua calls Israel to recognize what Yahweh has done to the nations and declares that Yahweh will continue to drive them out so that Israel can occupy their lands (23:3, 5, 9-10). By doing so, Joshua reminds Israel of Yahweh's original declaration, whereby Yahweh and Israel would work together to take possession of the land (Exod 23:20-33; Num 33:51-56). Joshua's reference to the Deuteronomic commandment, via his reference to intermarriage and in the context of an exhortation to drive out the peoples, further confirms the rhetorical character of the commandment.

All this leads to the conclusion that the reports that Joshua and Israel wiped out entire populations serve a rhetorical agenda, which must be understood with reference to the Deuteronomic commandment and in the context of the book of Joshua as a whole. They underscore Israel's commitment to maintaining its radical separation from the indigenous peoples and announce the subjugation of the powers in the land—a necessary first step to establish the land as the arena of covenant living. Although the battle accounts and summaries point to the kind of mass killing that occurs during wars, the accounts employ hyperbole and a fixed scheme of reporting. They confirm in no uncertain terms that Yahweh and Israel defeated the opposing powers of the land and so established the basis for the transformation of Canaan into the Israelite homeland.

The stylized and exaggerated rhetoric of the battle accounts in Joshua 2–12 is attested in the military literature of the great powers of Israel's world. Kings of the time trumpeted their victories with quite a bit of chest-thumping. Hyperbole and figurative language commonly configured reports of battles and military campaigns throughout the ancient Near East. Kings customarily described their victories in grandiose and exaggerated terms. An instructive example can be drawn from the Merneptah Stela, which recounts an Egyptian pharaoh's subjugation of various lands and peoples in the late thirteenth century BCE. The account describes Merneptah's invincibility and recounts how the god Amon delivered a powerful enemy into his hands.[7] It concludes with a list that contains the earliest reference to Israel outside the Bible:

> Carried off is Ashkelon; seized upon is Gezer;
> Yanoam is made as that which does not exist;
> Israel is laid waste; his seed is not;
> Hurru has become a widow for Egypt!
> All land together, they are pacified;
> Everyone who was restless, he has been bound. (*ANET*, 378)

Despite his claim, however, Merneptah did not actually consign Israel to oblivion! On the contrary, Israel's "seed" continued to grow and gain power in the land. The exaggerated rhetoric underscores the point of the whole report: Merneptah effectively subdued the peoples and the land. The account thus refers to conflicts that actually happened but puffs them up to enhance the prestige of the pharaoh. Merneptah did not annihilate Israel any more than Israel likely annihilated the peoples of the land.

The voice that acclaims Yahweh's and Joshua's victories thus seeks to praise Yahweh's victories in a manner befitting the deeds of a great king in Israel's time. Israel's invincibility and the claims of wiping out entire populations are coded devices conventionally employed to report the conquest and subjugation of the land and its peoples. In Joshua, Yahweh is the invincible

---

7. Ancient conquest accounts also contain reports of a deity fighting the king's enemies directly. For more information, see K. Lawson Younger, Jr., *Ancient Conquest Accounts: A Study in Ancient Near Eastern and Biblical History Writing*, JSOTSup 98 (Sheffield: JSOT Press, 1990).

warrior who collapses walls and summons the powers of heaven to defeat the opposing powers of the land. Yahweh is the wise and powerful God who terrorizes adversaries, delivers Israel's enemies into their hands, and gives the strategies that bring victory for his people. This is Yahweh, the warrior God, who claims a land by right of conquest and parcels it out to his loyal subjects, as do the great potentates of Israel's world. To tell the tale in any other way but in the manner of great kings would be to diminish who Yahweh is and what Yahweh has done in the land.

Yahweh, the Kings, and the Peoples

What then of the command to wipe out the peoples of the land? Is that an exaggeration as well? Does subjugation of the peoples and the land necessarily require their extermination? As if to respond to such questions, the narration of Joshua diverges from literary convention to give the story two important twists. The first entails a subtle but ingenious narrative strategy that redefines the enemies who threaten Yahweh and his people in the land. The command in Deuteronomy points to the peoples of the land as the enemies whose difference threatens the exclusive and reciprocal covenant life that Yahweh will establish with Israel in the land. It views Israel as a single unified people, called to complete devotion to the one God (Deut 6:4-5). This devotion is to be expressed by unswerving and total obedience to the commands of Moses in "this book of the law," that is, the book of Deuteronomy (Josh 1:8-10; cf. Deut 28:61; 31:26).[8] In contrast to the unity that characterizes Israel, the peoples of the land are consistently rendered in plural terms. They are listed as separate peoples. They serve many gods and follow different ways. They are led by many kings. The Deuteronomic commandment thus presents the peoples as an *existential* threat to Yahweh's purpose through Israel in the land, but not necessarily as a *military* threat.

The narration of the conquest account, on the other hand, progressively shifts the sense of the threat Israel faces away from the peoples toward the kings of the land. It does so by presenting the kings as an increasingly hostile force.[9] A king appears indirectly but aggressively at Jericho when his men

---

8. "This book of the law" is the phrase that Deuteronomy uses to refer to itself (Deut 29:21; 30:10; 31:26).

9. On this, see Lawson G. Stone, "Ethical and Apologetic Tendencies in the Book of Joshua," *CBQ* 53 (1991): 25-35, and the expansion of the scheme in L. Daniel Hawk, "Conquest Reconfigured: Recasting Warfare in the Redaction of Joshua," in *Writing and Reading*

arrive at Rahab's door, demanding that she turn over the Israelite spies who have come to her house. Rahab, however, thwarts the men, and thus the king, when she tells them that the spies have left and that they must hurry if they are to capture them (2:2-7). A Canaanite woman thus assumes the role of protector in contrast to the men sent by the Canaanite king. Yahweh in turn informs Joshua that he has given the king and his warriors into Joshua's hands (6:2).

At Ai, Israelites set an ambush and lure the king into attacking them in an open field (8:1-22). Then, after Israel is duped into making a peace treaty with Gibeon, the narrator reports that five Canaanite kings, who are identified individually by name and city, assemble to launch an attack on Gibeon. The threat prompts Joshua to launch a preemptive Israelite strike (10:1-9) that results in a great victory through Yahweh's hands. That account leads to a formulaic list of seven conquests in the south (10:29-42), all but two of which report victory over a king. Following this, the narrator reports that an even greater coalition of kings assembles in the northern part of Canaan to fight against Israel with "a vast number of people as numerous as the sand at the seashore, and horses, and a huge number of chariots" (11:4). Those kings are also vanquished, as expressed in the narrator's comment that Joshua "captured all the cities of these kings and all their kings" (v. 12).

The narrator concludes the accounts of battles in Canaan by casting them as a series of victories over the kings of the land (as opposed to the peoples; 11:16-17). This leads in turn to a summary of the whole of the conquest that is rendered as a list of kings—the two kings Moses defeated in the Transjordan and the thirty-one Joshua defeated in Canaan (12:1-24). After this point, no mention of a Canaanite king appears, even though we subsequently learn that many cities remain in Canaanite hands. With the listing of the defeated kings, the redirection of threat facing Israel is complete. Although Deuteronomy presents the peoples themselves as the primary threat Israel faces in Canaan, the narration redefines the threat as the kings, by presenting them as an increasingly hostile force.

A complementary literary strategy humanizes the people of the land even as the kings are being demonized. The first three battles in Canaan function as paradigms for all the battles that follow. The accounts of Israel's victories over Jericho, Ai, and Gibeon highlight the reciprocal relationship that will define Israel's life with Yahweh in the land. In each case, Yahweh

---

War: Rhetoric, Gender, and Ethics in Biblical and Modern Contexts, ed. Brad E. Kelle and Frank Ritchel Ames, SBLSS 42 (Atlanta: Society of Biblical Literature, 2008), 147-52.

gives Joshua instructions for the battle and announces that the enemy has been delivered into Joshua's hands. Yahweh then wins the battle over the opposing king, directly at Jericho and Gibeon and through a clever stratagem at Ai. Israel in turn responds with complete obedience to the commands of Yahweh as related by Joshua and prevails over the enemy forces. The lone exception that proves the rule takes place when a contingent of brash Israelites launches an attack on the garrison at Ai, apart from Yahweh's directions, and is unceremoniously defeated by the inferior force (7:2-5).

Preceding each battle account is an anecdote that gives a human face to those involved in the violence. Rahab shelters Israelite spies whom Joshua has sent on a reconnaissance mission to Jericho (2:1-24), Achan steals and conceals plunder that has been dedicated to Yahweh's treasury (7:1, 6-26), and Gibeonite emissaries employ subterfuge to wangle a covenant from Joshua and the Israelite elders (9:1-27). The stories share a common and complex structure, signaling that they are to be read together. Each anecdote appropriates a theme of hiding and discovery and incorporates motifs of interrogation, diversion, doxology, and petition: Rahab hides Israelite spies on her roof and discloses her plans; the Canaanite plunder Achan hides in the ground is exposed and publicly displayed when he confesses; and the Gibeonite emissaries hide their true identities by dressing as though they have arrived from a far-off land, and are only exposed after they have succeeded in securing a pact under oath.[10]

The first and third stories (Rahab and the Gibeonites) relate accounts of peoples of the land who are spared from the fate of annihilation and are subsequently incorporated into Israel (Josh 6:25; 9:27), while the middle account concerns a pedigreed Israelite who is seduced by the plunder of Canaan and consequently suffers, along with his family, the fate meted out to the kings and peoples of the land (Josh 7:24-26; cf. 8:28-30). Taken together, the stories reverse the bad Canaanite / good Israelite typology that implicitly validates the slaughter of the former people by the latter. Wily Canaanites survive and live among Yahweh's covenant people in the land, while a disobedient Israelite's entire family is exterminated.

The focus of these counternarratives can be discerned by looking more closely at the story of Rahab (Josh 2:1-24; 6:22-25). The book of Joshua be-

10. The complete list of plot elements includes an act of concealment, an interrogation, a diversion, a confession (of faith or of sin), a petition and response, a qualification of what has been decreed, an etiological note, and a curse. For more on the scheme see L. Daniel Hawk, *Joshua*, Berit Olam (Collegeville, MN: Liturgical Press, 2000), 19-33; L. Daniel Hawk, "Conquest Reconfigured," 145-60.

gins with a series of speeches that includes Yahweh's exhortation to adhere meticulously to the entire law of Moses as set forth in "this book of the law" as a condition of success (1:6-8), followed by an emphatic declaration of obedience by Israelites (1:16-18). Yet the first thing that Israelites do when entering the land is to transgress precisely the commandment that applies to their mission; two Israelite spies agree to spare a Canaanite prostitute and her family in return for their lives. This is in blatant defiance of Moses's commandment that Israelites are to "make no agreements with them and show them no mercy" (Deut 7:2b). Throughout the episode, the spies are portrayed as passive characters who do what the Canaanite woman tells them to. They aren't even given names.

The Canaanite in the story, however, has a name and thus an identity. Rahab the prostitute displays the qualities of energy, opportunism, and shrewdness prized by the Israelites. What's more, she offers praise to Yahweh, whereas the spies handpicked by Joshua remain silent on matters Yahwistic. As she speaks to the spies hiding on her roof, her words take the form of Israel's confession of faith—an acclamation of the mighty works of Yahweh and a creedal affirmation of Yahweh's singular supremacy.

> For we have heard how Yahweh dried up the water of the Red Sea before you as you departed from Egypt and what you did to the two kings of the Amorites who were across the Jordan—Sihon and Og—how you wiped them out. When we heard it, our resolve melted and no one had any determination to face you, because Yahweh your God, he is God in the sky above and on the earth below. (Josh 2:10-11)

When Rahab asks the spies to spare the lives of her family in return for her protection, the spies immediately agree by exclaiming "Our lives for yours!" (2:14a). Then, when the Israelites take the city, Joshua honors the agreement and spares the family (6:25). Throughout the course of events that ensue, neither Yahweh nor the narrator expresses any concern or consternation about the violation of the Mosaic commandment. In fact, Yahweh gives tacit approval by continuing to direct and fight for Israel at Jericho, as though nothing of consequence has happened.

Rahab confesses the God of Israel, receives mercy forbidden by the law of Moses, and "lives within Israel to the present day." Her inclusion in the covenant community that takes the land is confirmed symbolically by a modification the spies make to the agreement.

Look, we are invading the land. Tie this strand of scarlet cord in the window out of which you've lowered us. Gather your father, mother, brothers and your entire family to you in the house. If any goes outside the door of your house, their blood will be on their own head and we will not be bound. But as for anyone with you in the house, if a hand is laid on any of them, his blood shall be on our heads. (Josh 2:18-19)

The image of a red mark on the portal of a dwelling, protecting those who stay inside from certain death, links the invasion of the land to the exodus from Egypt and, more significantly, signals that Rahab and her family share in the larger Israelite narrative.

The Gibeonites likewise acclaim Yahweh's mighty acts, secure a forbidden covenant with Israel, and remain in the land as Canaanite members of the covenant community. A symbolic allusion also marks them as full participants in the new society Yahweh establishes in the land. After learning their true identity, Joshua honors the covenant he made with them but decrees that they must be wood choppers and water drawers for the community from that day onward (9:18-27). The decree identifies the Hivites with those who renewed the covenant with Yahweh just prior to invading Canaan. At that time, Moses addressed the assembled Israelites who stood before Yahweh as "your tribal leaders, elders, officials, all Israelite men, your children, your women, the resident aliens in your encampments, including those who chop your wood and draw your water" (Deut 27:11). Rahab and the Gibeonites, therefore, represent distinct populations of indigenous peoples who have confessed the God of Israel, experienced deliverance and covenant, and continue to live in the land.

The story of Achan takes the opposite slant. The account introduces Achan by tracing his Israelite pedigree back to the tribal patriarch Judah (7:1). Achan, however, crosses a forbidden boundary and takes plunder from Jericho that has been devoted to Yahweh. (*Kherem*, "devoted," is the noun form of the verb meaning "to wipe out.") He therefore represents those Israelites who are susceptible to the seduction of Canaan and thus transgress covenantal boundaries. His name has no known meaning in Hebrew and may be a cryptogram; a transposition of the Hebrew consonants for the name "Achan" yields the root of the name "Canaan." Is Achan's true identity reflected by the Canaanite plunder he hides under his tent? Whereas Yahweh has been silent when Canaanites are shown mercy, Yahweh is enraged at Achan's sacrilege. Yahweh chastises Joshua, indicts the whole nation for the offense, and tells Joshua to expose the offender. After Achan confesses, Joshua orders that he and his family be stoned to death. Then Joshua directs that they be burned and interred under a pile of rocks. The decree associates Achan with the pile of rubble that later characterizes Ai after it is burned (8:28) and the pile of rocks under which the executed king of Ai is interred (8:29).

The trio of anecdotes make a single point: indigenous peoples who confess Yahweh may be incorporated into the covenant community, while Israelites who step outside the boundaries that define the community must be eliminated. Indigenous people may enter Israel, but transit in the opposite direction is forbidden. The anecdotes push back at a literal interpretation of the Deuteronomic commandment that the peoples of Canaan be slaughtered for the simple fact that they are Canaanites. Rather, the narrative tryptic reinforces our sense that Yahweh's purpose in the Deuteronomic commandment and its execution is not to unleash indiscriminate slaughter upon Canaanites but rather to eliminate Canaanite difference in the land. As we have noted above, Yahweh's intent, expressed respectively in the commands to wipe out and to remove, is to establish a land where Israel can live out a relationship with Yahweh that renews the people and creation; Yahweh, people, and land must be bound by attachments of mutual exclusivity. The anecdotes demonstrate that even indigenous people may remain in the land if they conform to the terms of the covenant relationship.

There are, therefore, at least two voices vying to tell the story and convey what it means. The dominant, militaristic voice uses inflated language and braggadocio to present Israel's invasion in ideal terms, as a glorious campaign in which an invincible God and a roundly obedient people obliterated the peoples of the land and so secured Canaan as a homeland for the people of Israel. A dissenting voice counters the celebratory rhetoric by declaring that things didn't quite happen *that* way, undercutting the voice of militant triumphalism and insinuating that it is perhaps too full of itself.

Conclusions and Implications

How are we to think of the mass violence that Yahweh directs and Israel executes during the invasion and occupation of Canaan? What are we to make of Yahweh's directives to exterminate entire peoples and of the narrator's reports that Israel implemented them completely? Our exploration of the conquest literature provides some ways to think about these questions.

First, *the narratives of exodus and conquest are inseparable components of Israel's origin story.* Yahweh delivers Israel and brings Israel into the land for the purpose of fulfilling the promises to the ancestors. The divine purpose is articulated at the beginning of the narrative, when Yahweh calls Moses to liberate Israel, and is reiterated throughout the ensuing narrative. The exodus looks forward to the conquest, and the conquest assumes the exodus. Both events together manifest Yahweh's power and work as Creator. By delivering the descendants of Jacob from Egypt and bringing them into possession of Canaan, Yahweh creates a new people on earth birthed by salvation, defined by covenant and reciprocal choosing, and established in a place where life with Yahweh can flourish. Yahweh pummels Pharaoh until he releases Israel and then brings the newly liberated people through the water and into the wilderness. After establishing a nation that honors Yahweh's exclusive sovereignty, Yahweh brings the new nation through the waters again and pummels the kings of Canaan into subjection.

Second, massive amounts of blood are shed as Israel is born. The exodus and conquest entail the greatest expressions of divine violence in the Bible between the flood and the apocalypse. Babies die in both Egypt and Canaan. *The exodus and conquest cannot be uncoupled, as if the massive violence in the former is for some reason more acceptable than the violence of the latter.* Yahweh initiates and prosecutes a program of violence in both locations and enlists the participation of human agents to do so. The perpetration of violence in Egypt and Canaan differs in scope and means but serves the same end. The violence, in brief, is a consequence of Yahweh's decision to identify with Israel, honor divine promises, and continue working in and through the chosen nation. The story is unambiguous on this point: Israel would not exist apart from the application of divine power and the execution of divine violence to liberate and conquer. No exodus, no conquest. No violence, no Israel.

Third, *the invasion and occupation of Canaan constitute the final act of the drama that began with Yahweh's decision to step into the world and renew creation by forming a people.* The drama begins with Yahweh's choosing of Abram as an agent of blessing to the world and the promise of a land as the locus of Yahweh's blessing through Abraham's descendants. The decision to initiate an exclusive relationship with Abraham's descendants draws Yahweh increasingly into the violence that configures the affairs of nations in a world gone bad. Yahweh thus takes up violence on Israel's behalf, to advance Yahweh's purpose through Israel and to demonstrate Yahweh's faithfulness and power.

Fourth, *Yahweh's violence is targeted, purposeful, and directed toward divine ends—specifically, the annunciation and demonstration of Yahweh's supremacy in the world and the establishment of a new people in a new land.* In Egypt and Canaan, Yahweh decisively defeats kings, the human agents who wield ultimate power in the warped hierarchies that generate violence. Yahweh does this not only for Israel's benefit but also for Yahweh's own notoriety. The unknown God of slaves enters a world of established deities and powers in a way that a violent world understands. Yahweh defeats the power concentrated in the greatest king and nation of the time and then the cumulative might of Canaan's kings, even overwhelming the kings' capacity to decide and act for themselves by hardening their hearts. The narrative portrays Yahweh's conquest and dispossession of Canaan's kings and peoples as a singular manifestation of Yahweh's sovereignty, set within the context of Yahweh's working through other peoples and other lands.

Fifth, *the violence that Yahweh and Israel visit on the peoples of Canaan does not arise from caprice or judgment.* Nowhere is Yahweh's violence against Pharaoh or the peoples of Canaan associated with Yahweh's anger. Instead, the single outbreak of divine wrath is directed towards the nation of Israel and kindled by Achan's theft of plunder that has been devoted to Yahweh (Josh 7:1, 26). In this instance, divine anger is an immediate and intense response to an act of egregious disrespect and disobedience, foreshadowing the targets of divine anger later on through judges and kings. Likewise, no declaration of judgment is leveled against the indigenous peoples. Neither Yahweh's comment on the iniquity of the Amorites (Gen 15:16) nor Moses's declaration of the Canaanites' wickedness (Deut 9:5) necessarily implies divine judgment. The abominable practices of the nations are lifted up to enumerate practices that Israel must not follow (e.g., Lev 18:1-30), but no direct declaration of judgment is associated with them. Where the connection between the nations' practices and expulsion is made, the demise is explained as the consequence of accumulated corruption (Lev 18:27-28; 20:22). The claim that the massacres of the indigenous peoples constitute an act of divine judgment or wrath, in sum, cannot be supported by the narrative.

Sixth, *the rationale for the erasure of the indigenous peoples from the land, whether through the language of removal or wiping out, is presented as a necessary means to transform Canaan into a land where Yahweh alone, out of all the gods, is worshiped by the nation Yahweh has chosen.* The land must be the exclusive domain of Yahweh's people, as Yahweh's people are the exclusive covenant partners of Yahweh. The peoples of the land represent the multifarious disordering systems and practices that maintain the world made

THE LAND PROMISED AND TAKEN

by humans. In order for Yahweh to undertake a new ordering, with a new system and new practices, the plurality that the peoples represent must be cleared. Only Yahweh may be worshiped by Yahweh's covenant people in Yahweh's land. For this reason, Yahweh's promise to expel the nations, along with Yahweh's command that Israel wipe them out, summon Israel to exclusive devotion. Yahweh makes clear that if Israel refuses to observe and maintain exclusive devotion in the land, thus denying the nation's identity and mission and returning the land to its former state, the bond between land, Yahweh, and the nation will be broken, and Israel will suffer the fate of the former inhabitants.

Seventh, *the Deuteronomic commands to wipe out the indigenous peoples make use of exaggerated language to underscore the imperative of transforming the land into a Yahweh-only space.* The reports that Israel wiped out indigenous populations function in a similar manner to convey the complete defeat and subjugation of the kings of Canaan. The commandments signal their meaning by leading into warnings about practices that will draw Israel from singular devotion to Yahweh (7:1-6; 20:16-18). The individual and summary reports that Joshua and Israel wiped out entire populations are likewise stylized with conventional hyperbole to signify Israel's defeat of the powers. Their exaggerated character is confirmed not only by their conformity to rhetorical conventions in the military literature of other peoples but also by elements within the conquest narrative itself. Reports of Israelite diffidence in the face of Canaanite might and reports of vast territories and various peoples that remain in the land after the conquest caution against a literalistic interpretation of wholesale Israelite victories. Reports that Israel wiped out populations occur only in the first segment of the book. Israel does not continue the practice past the initial campaigns against the kings but turns instead to the task of removing the nations—a strange turn if everyone had already been wiped out. In addition, Yahweh expresses no displeasure at the turn and even promises to participate in the program of expulsion. To view the conquest as a war of extermination, in sum, is to misread the account.

Eighth, *the narrative nonetheless attributes Israel's victories and thus the violence that goes along with them directly to Yahweh.* The trappings of militant triumphalism clothe Yahweh in regal splendor and acclaim Yahweh's supremacy over all opposing powers. Yahweh enters and takes the land like a powerful and invincible emperor. The narrative revels in Yahweh's victories and violence with a celebrative zeal. The tale must be told, and it must be told in this way, for the narrative establishes Israel's claim to its homeland and Yahweh's supremacy over the powers. Although the whole earth belongs to Yahweh, Yahweh nevertheless accommodates to conventions and expectations, assumes the role of a conquering emperor, and claims the land by right of conquest. Yahweh wins the land and thereupon orders it as Yahweh sees fit.

A counternarrative, finally, cautions against viewing the execution and glorification of violence as Yahweh's preferred mode of working in the world. Through subtle means, the narrator presents the kings of the land, rather than its peoples, as the enemies that oppose Yahweh in the land. In defeating the kings, Yahweh does what Yahweh must do to secure a homeland for the covenant people. In counterpoint to the slaughters of anonymous populations, however, the narrator puts human faces on the terrorized peoples, attributing to indigenous people the qualities prized by the covenant people and reporting their praise of Israel's God. *The critique of the conquest begins in the narrative that relates it.* In the stories of Rahab and the Gibeonites we encounter people who are as human as the invaders who have entered their land. In the mercy shown them, in violation of Yahweh's express commands, we see glimpses of what Yahweh ultimately desires and is working toward. Yahweh utters no word of rebuke when peoples of the land are spared, acclaim Yahweh's supremacy, and become members of the covenant people. Their stories confirm that Yahweh is, as Yahweh has said, "a God compassionate and gracious, slow to anger and abundant in love and faithfulness" (Exod 34:5; Num 14:18). The people who live as covenant people in the land Yahweh gives do not inhabit the land because they reflect a single ethnicity but because they practice a singular devotion to the one God through covenantal obedience.

We conclude with a hermeneutical note. In the conquest of Canaan, Yahweh displays a singular aggression for the sake of Israel and the destiny Yahweh intends. The tale that Joshua tells constitutes the final act in Israel's narrative of origins and, at the same time, begins the story of Israel's life in the land. It is a testimony of what God has done, not a template to be replicated by others who assume the identity of God's people. Yahweh strikes and dispossesses peoples for the singular purpose of establishing Israel in the land and within the purview of Yahweh's superintending work in the lives of lands and nations. For this reason, the violence that Yahweh instigates and inflicts in Canaan cannot properly be taken as a model to be imitated. On the contrary, when taken as a whole, the narrative exposes the inflated rhetoric of militant nationalism and critiques the glorification of slaughter, by setting the humanity of victims before the reader's eyes. Joshua therefore cannot, indeed must not, be called upon to imbue the prosecution of any war with a sense of transcendence, especially when such operations take up the conquest narrative to legitimate national means and ends.

8

God Moves to the Outside

> But I say to you who are listening, love your enemies and treat those who hate you well.
> Bless those who curse you and pray for those who mistreat you.
>
> LUKE 6:28-29

Yahweh's grand plan, to heal the world by identifying with a people, ends in disaster. Although the strategy begins well when Yahweh initiates a relationship with Abram, it runs aground when Yahweh establishes a covenant relationship with Abram's descendants. The influence of a violent, broken world proves to have a more powerful effect on Israel than Yahweh's constant expressions of patience, protection, and provision. Yahweh consistently and exclusively identifies with Israel, but Israel just as consistently refuses to respond in kind. Yahweh's attempts to adapt and work within the system, culminating in the endorsement of a monarchy that renders Israel after the fashion of the nations, have done little more than draw Yahweh into the system and the violent practices by which it is sustained. As the story ends, Yahweh's king (Jehoiachin) lives in a foreign land under the power of a greater Babylonian king (2 Kgs 25:27-30). The last episode of the story reports how King Evil-Merodach of Babylon releases Jehoiachin in the thirty-seventh year of exile and gives him an honored seat among the other subject kings who dine at his table. It concludes with the report that Jehoiachin "always dined in his presence his entire life, and his regular allowance was given him each day at the direction of the king, for his entire life" (vv. 29b-30). The whole saga ends, then, with a scenario that depicts the Israelite king as completely dependent on a Babylonian emperor rather than on Yahweh.

The imperial system seems to have the last laugh. Israel's king is swallowed up, and Yahweh is no longer in the picture.

Other narrations of the story, which recount events after the exile (Ezra, Nehemiah, Esther), suggest that Yahweh has largely disengaged. Those who return to the land from exile bring a zeal for Yahweh and a determination to worship Yahweh alone, but we are not told that Yahweh responds. The dedication of the new temple, for example, is reported with remarkable understatement. Whereas the cloud of Yahweh's glory had filled the first temple to such an extent that that priests could not stand (1 Kgs 8:10-11), Yahweh does not make an appearance when the second temple is dedicated. The narrator reports only that the people of Israel, the priests, and the Levites dedicated the house of the Lord with sacrificial offerings and set the priests and Levites in their stations (Ezra 6:16-18). Furthermore, while there are many prayers and references to Yahweh in the books of Ezra and Nehemiah, there are no reports that Yahweh said or did anything in response. And there is no mention at all of Yahweh in the book of Esther, which is set among the Jews living outside the land.

When we resume the story in the Gospel of Luke, there are still kings and emperors. The beginning of God's new work through Jesus Christ takes place "in the days of King Herod of Judea" (1:5) and during the reign of Emperor Augustus (2:1). I follow the story as told by Luke for two reasons. First, Luke's narrative style and scope give the sense of a seamless continuation of the Primary History. Luke explicitly evokes the grand sweep of the narrative through a genealogy that connects Jesus all the way back to Adam (3:23-38) and so invites readers to read his gospel as an account of God's latest and greatest work, against the backdrop of God's dealings with humanity since the creation of the world. At points, Luke even emulates the style of the Septuagint, the version of Israel's scriptures favored by the early church. His decision to do so in the infancy narratives that begin the gospel creates the sense that we are picking up where the Old Testament narrative left off. Luke, in short, writes his gospel in a way that invites us to see it as a continuation of the larger story. Secondly, Luke simply tells more of the story than the other gospel writers. He takes the story past the death and resurrection of Jesus and into the early decades of apostolic preaching, giving us an account of how God continues to work, primarily through the Holy Spirit, through and with God's people, who now are constituted as followers of Jesus Christ rather than members of a nation. We therefore are given a glimpse of how disciples are to live out the new life of God and how God interacts with this new community.

GOD MOVES TO THE OUTSIDE

Luke begins by reminding the reader of the importance of place and of the human systems that dictate the affairs of peoples and lands. The story opens in Jerusalem, with an old priest at the temple. Israel is worshiping God in a new temple, yet still in subjugation to foreign kings. The system has not changed. Yet Yahweh, now known by a title rather than a name ("the Lord"), reengages the world in a new way. Yahweh's name is now so highly regarded that people in the story no longer speak it. Although the title conveys the sense of distance hinted at by the snippets of story set after the exile, Yahweh has not given up on the idea of working with humanity to renew the world. As with Noah and Abram, God begins a new work by reaching out to pious servants. Zechariah and Elizabeth are "righteous in God's sight, observing the Lord's commandments and ordinances without fail" (1:6). The contact this time, however, is made by an intermediary; the Lord sends Gabriel to the temple with words of promise and favor.

The Lord announces a new strategy through Gabriel's proclamation and through three remarkable prophecies associated with a woman living in the village of Nazareth (1:26-38). The move signals a strategic repositioning on God's part. Whereas the story begins in Jerusalem, the center of Israel's life as a nation, and in the temple, where the nation worships God, it swiftly shifts to a small settlement in the heterogeneous, contentious region of Galilee. Here, rather than in Jerusalem, Gabriel announces that God will again establish the reign of a descendant of David:

> He will be great and will be called the Son of the Most High. He will rule over the house of Jacob forever, and his kingdom will have no end. (1:32-33)

The proclamation makes clear that Yahweh has not rejected the idea of working with kings, despite the ultimate collapse of the project. Yet the human partner that the Lord enlists, a young peasant woman, reveals that the Lord will no longer work within that system, but rather opposed to it. God no longer identifies with the monarchical system that exerts power and control through Pharaohs and Caesars but with those most vulnerable to the oppressive machinations of kings. The Lord's pivot to the outside indicates that the failed strategy of working within the system has been rejected. God instead will resume the work of renewal by taking up a position altogether outside the system. The announcement that Mary will conceive a son through the power of the Holy Spirit underscores the point: the child born to Mary will be holy and will be called the Son of God (v. 35).

The king begotten by the Most High and born of a virgin will identify with the lowly.

Mary's song in response to Elizabeth's blessing (1:46-55) further underscores and confirms the new and radical strategy the Lord will initiate through the Son. Mary rejoices because the Lord has now chosen to favor the lowly (v. 48). She speaks of future reversals as though they have already happened: the scattering of those who consider themselves high; the removal of rulers from their thrones; the elevation of the humiliated; and the filling of the hungry with good things while the wealthy are sent away with nothing (vv. 51-53). The song vibrantly announces that the Lord will soon judge—indeed, has already judged—the systems of power that dominate the world and those who benefit by them. The Lord's saving work will no longer be advanced through a king who stands within and is bound by warped human systems but through a king who stands outside of and in judgment of them.

The cadences of Mary's prophetic song echo Hannah's prayer, which also announced Yahweh's intention to subvert the order of things and which looked forward to a divinely anointed king (1 Sam 2:1-10). The reverberations of Hannah's words in the song Mary sings confirm two things. First, the Lord is about to do something completely new and unanticipated, and second, this new work is a continuation of the Lord's work through Israel. Mary punctuates the latter with a concluding flourish that connects what the Lord has begun with the work God initiated through Abraham:

> He has devoted himself to Israel his servant, remembering his mercy, as he promised to our father Abraham and his offspring forever. (Luke 1:54-55)

A second prophecy takes place back at the temple, constituting a second human response, at the center of Israel's faith, to what the Lord has announced at the outskirts. After confirming that the name of his son will be John, Zechariah breaks out in a prophecy that confirms and elaborates the new work that the Lord has announced to a peasant woman in Galilee. His prophecy looks back even as it looks forward, referencing the Davidic monarchy, prophets, covenant, and God's promise to Abraham.

> Then Zechariah, (John's) father, was filled with the Holy Spirit and prophesied this: "Blessed be the God of Israel, because he has visited us and redeemed his people! He has raised a horn of salvation for us within the house of David his servant, as he spoke through the

mouths of his holy prophets—salvation from our enemies and from the power of everyone who hates us—in order to show mercy to our ancestors and to remember his holy covenant, the oath that he swore to our father Abraham to grant that we, having been rescued from the power of our enemies, might serve him in holiness and righteousness all our days. (Luke 1:67-75)

It is important to note that Zechariah, by acclaiming the Lord's deliverance and salvation from Israel's enemies, evokes the many ways that the Lord brought deliverance on Israel's behalf, which would include the violence that Yahweh inflicted and directed in order to rescue Israel from its enemies. Zechariah implicitly affirms what the Lord has done and sets the work of the new Davidic king within the context of all the saving acts God has done on Israel's behalf. What God will do through the new king, in other words, does not mark a divergence or separation from the past, but rather an extension of the past into the present.

Luke reinforces the Lord's decision to work outside the system by recounting two episodes that take place at the beginning of Jesus's messianic mission. After descending on Jesus as he is baptized by John, the Holy Spirit leads Jesus into the desert and into a confrontation with the devil (4:1-13). The appearance of the devil in an adversarial role as Jesus begins his ministry sets God's work through the Son over against the human systems and societies, which are now set within the framework of a cosmic conflict that transcends the human arena. Of the three temptations the devil sets before Jesus, the second expands on the Lord's decision to work *outside of* as opposed to *within* earthly systems of power.

> When (the devil) had led (Jesus) up high, he showed him all the kingdoms of the world at the same time. He said to him, "I will give you all this authority as well as its glory, because it has been handed over to me. And I give it to whomever I want. If then you worship me, I will give you everything." Then Jesus answered him, "It is written, 'you must worship the Lord your God and serve him exclusively.'" (Luke 4:5-8)

The devil's words effectively set the kingdoms of the world in opposition to the kingdom God is setting up through Jesus. Assuming for the sake of argument that the devil is not lying through his teeth, the declaration presents the devil as the power behind the earthly thrones, a power that the devil claims has "been handed over" to him. The phrase recalls the many times that God has handed over or given over enemies into the power of Israel, thus implying that God has stepped out of working within human systems of power altogether, so that they now operate under the devil's power and authority. When this "handing over" took place we are not told. Whatever the case, the move frees God to operate redemptively in a new way. Jesus's rejection of the devil's temptation underscores God's categorical refusal, at this point in time, to work within the system. Jesus punctuates the move by quoting scripture that articulates the only foundation on which the renewal of the world may proceed, namely, exclusive worship of the Lord and obedient service to the one God.

With this scenario in place, Luke takes us from the desert back to Nazareth, where Jesus announces what God will do through him (4:16-30). At the synagogue on the Sabbath, Jesus opens the scroll of Isaiah, reads the prophet's proclamation, and declares that it has now come to pass:

> The Spirit of the Lord is upon me, for he has anointed me to preach good news to the poor. He has sent me to announce freedom for the captives and sight to the blind, to release those who are broken, to proclaim the year of the Lord's favor. (Luke 4:18-19)

With this proclamation, Jesus aligns his messianic mission with the subversive cadences of Mary's song and declares that the beneficiaries of the Lord's work will be the lowly and oppressed, that is, those who have been degraded and cast aside by the wealthy and powerful. The fact that Jesus defines his mission with reference to a prophetic utterance from the Old Testament reinforces the continuity of God's work through Jesus with God's work through Israel, and particularly to the narrative strand that addresses Yahweh's attention to the powerless.

Jesus underscores his stance outside the system, but in continuity with God's historical work, by drawing attention to two instances when God blessed those who stood outside of monarchical Israel (4:24-27). First, he reminds his hearers of a story about the prophet Elijah, whom Yahweh sent outside the boundaries of the kingdom of Israel. When Elijah travelled into Phoenician territory, a widow sheltered and fed him. In response, Elijah alleviated her suffering, first by a miraculous multiplication of her food and then by the resurrection of her son (cf. 1 Kgs 17:8-24). Jesus then reminds the congregation of an incident that occurred during the time of Elisha, when Yahweh sent a leprous Aramean general named Naaman to the prophet and then healed him when he obeyed the prophet's directions (cf. 2 Kgs 5:1-27). In both cases, Jesus makes a point of saying that Yahweh intentionally turned from those on the inside and instead called the prophets to minister to those on the outside, first to a helpless widow and then to an enemy military commander.

Recognizing the theme of a new, subversive move to the outside, which is to be understood as an extension of God's work in and through Israel, is crucial for understanding why the violent God of the Old Testament takes a generally nonviolent stance through Jesus Christ. Yahweh has concluded that the restoration of the world cannot be accomplished by working within the violent, broken systems that configure human societies. Rather than give up, however, Yahweh comes up with a new plan. God now steps outside the systems and refuses to participate in their operations or with their functionaries. In the past, God's work through Israel became entangled in the affairs of kings, in the promotion and protection of faithful kings and the rejection and punishment of rebellious kings. As a consequence, Yahweh became increasingly enmeshed in the endemic violence that dictates the interaction of nations. That program ended in disaster.

In the person of Jesus Christ, God now steps out of the human systems of power altogether. The move effectively frees God from the constraints and compromises that had to be made to continue in meaningful relationship and mission with the nation of Israel and its kings. God is no longer encumbered by the necessity of defending and promoting the welfare of a nation. By identifying with the lowly and oppressed, God is also freed from the operations of violence that capture all who participate and work within the system. God instead experiences the full measure of oppression and violence that maintain human systems of power.

The ministry and teaching of Jesus subsequently fill out the contours of God's stance over against the kingdoms of the world. Jesus's ministry takes place mainly in Galilee and so outside the geographical boundaries of Judea, the Jewish heartland. Jesus also ventures into the country of the Gadarenes (8:26-39) and Samaria (9:51-56), areas that at the time were home to non-Jewish populations. The greater portion of Jesus's parables, in addition, speak of reversals of wealth and power and of those who stand outside conventional social boundaries. One parable speaks of a Samaritan who cares for a victim of violence (10:25-37). Another describes a rich man who finds himself in agony in Hades, while the poor man he has neglected rests in the embrace of Abraham (16:19-31). Jesus also emphasizes God's disengagement from the systems of the world by opposing one to the other and calling his followers to give each its due. When his adversaries try to entrap him with a question about the lawfulness of paying taxes to the emperor, Jesus responds by sharply distinguishing the imperial system from the reign of God, declaring that followers are to give to the emperor those things that are owed to the emperor and give to God those things owed to God (20:20-26).

Does God's disengagement from earthly systems of power mean that Jesus rejects all forms of violence and instructs his followers to do likewise? Jesus indeed models and teaches a nonviolent stance in response to wickedness and violence, but does the witness of Jesus necessarily convey God's categorical rejection of violence as a means of resisting evil in the world and advancing God's restorative purposes? To address these questions, we turn first to four texts—the sermon on the plain, Jesus's statement about those who take up the sword, the cleansing of the temple, and the parable of the wicked tenants—and then to Luke's account of Jesus's passion and death.

The Sermon and the Sword

As we noted in the first chapter, a prominent contemporary approach to dealing with the violence of God takes up Jesus's teachings on nonretaliation and love for one's enemies as the basis for evaluating violent portraits of God. Jesus's pronouncements on the mountain (Matt 5:27-48) and the plain (Luke 6:27-36) are read as straightforward, categorical moral commandments that bind followers of Jesus and that are embodied in the life and crucifixion of Jesus. Read in this way, the teachings are understood to reflect the nonviolent character and disposition of God, and by extension God's interactions with a violent creation. Since, it is argued, violent portraits and declarations of God are incompatible with the nonviolent character of God as reflected in these specific teachings, all texts that speak of God's violence must either be rejected as mistaken presentations of who God really is or interpreted as saying something other than what they plainly say. This approach raises a fundamental question: certainly Jesus's teachings on nonretaliation and enemy love *may* constitute absolute dictates—namely, that Jesus forbids any form of violence for any reason—but *must* they be taken as absolutes? That is, do Jesus's words necessarily signify absolute moral pronouncements? If they do not, then the approach mentioned above reflects one faithful biblical way among many, but not the only faithful way, of interpreting the violence of the biblical God.

GOD MOVES TO THE OUTSIDE

Luke sets the teaching of Jesus on a plain, as opposed to Matthew's setting, where Jesus, like Moses, gathers his followers and teaches them how to live in faithfulness to God. By setting the teaching on a level place, Luke prompts the reader to interpret Jesus's words within the context of God's justice. It evokes the ministry of John the Baptist and the leveling imagery portrayed in the Isaianic prophecy that Luke quotes in full to explain John's ministry.

> As it is written in the book of the words of the prophet Isaiah: "The voice of one shouting in the desert, 'Prepare the way of the Lord. Make straight pathways for him! Every valley will be filled up, and every mountain and hill will be lowered. The crooked will become straight, and the bumpy places smooth roads. And all flesh shall see the salvation of God.'" (Luke 3:4-6)

John's preaching expresses this leveling agenda by calling those with power to lessen inequities, specifying material practices that correlate with what Jesus says to those gathered on the plain: share with those who have less, collect only the taxes required, refuse to extort money from others (3:10-14).

The setting of Jesus's teachings on enemy love reinforces the materialist, justice-enhancing sense of the words he speaks. As in Matthew, Jesus begins his teaching by speaking of those whom God blesses (6:20-23). Yet from the beginning the sermon takes a different trajectory than the one in Matthew. The beatitudes Jesus pronounces in Luke address social rather than spiritual conditions. Whereas, for example, in Matthew Jesus says, "Blessed are the poor in spirit" and "Blessed are those who hunger and thirst for righteousness," in Luke he simply says, "Blessed are the poor" and "Blessed are you who are hungry now." And while Jesus's address in Matthew takes a generalized third-person form, in Luke Jesus addresses the crowd directly, assuring them that "yours is the kingdom of God" and "you will be filled full."

The pronouncements of blessing in Luke are balanced out by a set of woes, absent in Matthew, which proclaim the reverse for those at the center of power and privilege: "Woe to you rich people, because you have received your comfort" (v. 24); "Woe to you who are filled up, because you will get hungry" (v. 25a). The addition of the woes following the blessings, along with the announcements of reversal, hearken back to Mary's prophetic declaration that the Lord "has pulled the powerful from their thrones and has lifted up the lowly" and "has filled up the hungry with good things but sent the rich away with nothing" (1:52-53). The blessings and woes thus identify those to whom Jesus speaks, namely, those who have been victimized by the powers—the poor, the captives, the blind, and the oppressed—whom Jesus identified as the recipients of his ministry when he quoted the Isaiah passage in the synagogue at Nazareth (4:16-21).

Jesus's teachings about enemy love and nonretaliation follow immediately thereafter and so, in Luke's gospel, are addressed specifically to those on the outside of power—an identification that Luke underscores by reporting that the multitude that gathers to hear Jesus includes those who live outside the boundaries of Israel, from "the coast of Tyre and Sidon" (6:17). From Luke's perspective, then, Jesus's teaching on enemy love is to be understood within the context of God's identification with the powerless and outsiders, as a commentary on what God is doing in the world in response to the principalities and powers.

Jesus begins with two pairs of imperatives (vv. 27-28). The first pair enjoins his followers, in parallel terms, to respond to enemies in a way that advances their benefit: "love your enemies; do good to those who hate you." The second pair ("bless those who curse you; pray for those who mistreat you") elaborates the first pair by mandating an other-oriented disposition when dealing with antagonists. A series of examples follow, which illustrate the imperatives with concrete actions: turning the other cheek, giving up one's coat, giving to those who beg, and not seeking the recovery of seized property (vv. 29-30). Jesus then articulates the Golden Rule (v. 31), which parallels the command to love one's enemies and leads, as before, to three elaborations, now framed as challenges. If one loves, does good, or lends only to good people, how is that commendable (vv. 32-34)? Jesus concludes by reiterating the first pair of imperatives ("love your enemies and do good"). Yet this time, Jesus presents them as expressions of God's disposition towards all human beings. Followers are children of the Most High, who is kind to the ungrateful and merciful to all (vv. 35-36).

The open-ended nature of the teaching does not specify the "enemies" to which Jesus refers. A number of candidates have been proposed. Given the tense and brutal character of the Roman occupation, which was maintained by the ruthless suppression of revolts in Galilee, the enemy in mind could be the Romans or, more broadly, gentiles of all kinds. On the other hand, Jesus could be directing his imperative toward the tensions that typically arose in village life, as in the case for instance of a villager who is unable to fulfill his obligation to repay a debt. The traumatic effects of Roman occupation may have contributed to a fraught village life, as waves of rebellions and brutal crackdowns might have set the inhabitants of Galilee perpetually on edge. Finally, it has been argued that the enemies in view here are those who oppose Jesus's mission and persecute Jesus's followers. In short, while the command to love and do good to one's enemies is clearly stated, there is considerable space for identifying the enemies to whom Jesus refers, the situations addressed by his words, and how Jesus's words are to be lived out.

Whatever the case, Luke prompts us to understand Jesus's teaching on enemy love and nonretaliation within the context of a system configured by deep social inequities. Jesus identifies with those harmed by social inequities, while God opposes and delegitimizes those who wield power and privilege within the system. The dispositions and practices that Jesus proclaims actively oppose and reverse the practices that characterize the oppressive human system. Against a system that promotes hatred, cursing, and abuse, Jesus enjoins his followers to do good, bless, and pray. In response to a system that degrades human life through insult and deprivation (the striking of the cheek may refer to an insulting slap in the face),[1] Jesus calls his followers to refuse to defend their honor. Against a system that facilitates the use of power to acquire possessions, Jesus directs his followers to display a radical detachment from possessions, giving to those in need and refusing to cling even to one's clothing. Jesus's words exemplify a new reign, in which the violent ethic of retribution is transformed into an other-oriented determination to treat others as one expects to be treated. The teachings reflect God's primordial ideal of human relationships in opposition to the warped societies that human beings construct. By enacting them, followers display a family likeness to the Creator who makes no distinctions in the kindness and mercy God displays.

The dictates of Jesus, moreover, likely have a pragmatic import. Within the context of village life, the practices would work to restore social equilibrium and maintain harmony. Richard Horsley has drawn attention to the likely devastating effects of brutal Roman repression in Galilee. He proposes that the teachings of Jesus are directed toward restoring village well-being. They convey healthy practices presented to combat the disintegration of village relationships under oppressive rule and harsh crackdowns.[2] The teaching on nonretaliation makes sense with the Ro-

---

1. Darrell L. Bock, *Luke*: 1:1–9:50, Baker Exegetical Commentary on the New Testament 3 (Grand Rapids: Baker, 1994), 592.

2. Richard Horsley, "'By the Finger of God': Jesus and Imperial Violence," in *Violence in the New Testament*, ed. Shelly Matthews and E. Leigh Gibson (New York: T&T Clark, 2005), 51–80.

mans particularly in view. History had shown that villagers were virtually powerless against the might and depredations of Rome. Resistance in the face of humiliation or loss of property at the hands of the Romans or their lackeys was futile. Violence of any kind directed at the instruments of Roman power would lead only to harsher treatment. In short, the words of Jesus in Luke's gospel cannot be detached from the particular hearers of those words and their experience of loss and powerlessness, away from the center of power.

The question remains, however, whether Jesus's words to these traumatized followers should be taken as the articulation of a general principle. Are we to understand Jesus's words and the practices they mention as extending to all human interactions in all contexts? Must Jesus's teachings about nonretaliation and enemy love be understood as a rejection of all violence, even violence that is necessary to preserve life?

Turning to Matthew, we note that Jesus's teachings on enemy love and nonretaliation are situated within a significantly different framework and context (Matt 5:21-48). They occur near the beginning of the first of five blocks of teaching in Matthew (5:1-7:27) and are uttered against a backdrop that depicts Jesus, like Moses, teaching a vast assembly how to live faithfully as God's people. As he does in Luke, Jesus begins with a series of blessings. Yet unlike in Luke, Jesus issues no woes. He instead addresses the character and obligations of his disciples, whom he calls salt and light, and whom he directs to give glory to God through their good works (vv. 12-16). Jesus then makes a pointed declaration that he has come to fulfill the Law and the Prophets, as well as an equally pointed declaration about the Law's enduring authority (vv. 17-19). He then concludes by calling for a righteousness that surpasses the righteousness taught by the scribes and Pharisees (v. 20).

Jesus's teachings on enemy love and nonretaliation follow. They are included within a series of six antitheses that illustrate the righteousness that is lived out by those who are members of the reign of heaven. Thus, while Luke situates Jesus's teachings within the context of God's subversive kingdom, now manifested to and among those standing outside the center of power, Matthew prompts the reader to understand the same teachings as examples of what it means to be God's witnesses in the world and faithfully to fulfill the law of Moses.

In Matthew, the declarations on nonretaliation and love of one's enemy constitute the third of three pairs of antithetical declarations that express the quintessence of Jesus's ethical teaching. The particular form of each pair orients the sayings along a different trajectory than the corresponding declarations in Luke. All are cast as responses to conventional notions of righteousness. Each begins with the citation of a general dictum rendered in absolute terms, after which Jesus responds with a command that articulates the higher righteousness that characterizes his disciples. A series of cases then clarifies Jesus's command.

The first couplet corrects a literal interpretation of the Mosaic dictum mandating "an eye for an eye and a tooth for a tooth" (5:38; cf. Exod 21:24, 27; Lev 24:20; Deut 19:21). Jesus responds with his own command, turning the positive into a negative: "Do not oppose an evil person" (Matt 5:39). Taken at its face, the command appears to call for passivity in response to evil, as if Jesus were telling his followers to step aside when evil arises and let an evil person do whatever he or she wants to. This, however, would be preposterous. Jesus's ministry is itself an act of resistance against a warped world system, and other New Testament writers deal resolutely with evil behavior within the church (e.g., 1 Cor 5:1-13; 2 John 10-11). Hans Dieter Betz, observing that Jesus's words respond to a Mosaic commandment that calls for measured retaliation, has proposed instead that Jesus's command should be understood to prohibit retaliation. He therefore translates the relevant (and slippery) Greek verb, "Do not retaliate."[3] Understood in this sense, Jesus is calling his disciples to go beyond what the letter of the Mosaic law allows and not to take revenge against someone who has harmed them. By refusing to strike back in kind and even displaying an astounding generosity, disciples break the cycle of violence and vendetta that holds the world in bondage and open up the possibility of reconciliation and peace (cf. Rom 12:18-21). Five examples flesh out the thrust of the commandment and illustrate the opposing calculus of reciprocity under the reign of heaven (vv. 39b-42). Rather than giving an evildoer "what they deserve," disciples are to respond to the intended harm or deprivation with generous forbearance.

The second couplet addresses dispositions instead of actions. Jesus begins by citing what may have been the common wisdom, or perhaps a perverse extrapolation from the Golden Rule: "Love your neighbor and hate your enemy" (v. 43). Jesus again responds with a command that recalibrates the sense of what is owed to others. He explains that to observe the law is to acknowledge that God's care extends to the righteous and unrighteous. God's concern and mercy make no distinction, as should be true of those

---

3. Hans Dieter Betz, *The Sermon on the Mount*, Hermeneia (Minneapolis: Fortress, 1995), 280-86.

who aspire to be God's children. Here the issue is a matter of orienting one's dispositions towards those who are potential perpetrators or objects of violence. In conjunction with the practices of nonretaliation he elaborated in the previous antithesis, Jesus now calls for a reorientation of one's thinking toward enemies. He is here concerned with shaping the dispositions of his disciples, without which the practices will not endure.

It is important at this point to note how Luke and Matthew order and combine the sayings on enemy love and nonretaliation. In Luke, the commands to turn the other cheek and give to those who beg are paired together and so serve as examples of what it means to love others. They are, therefore, subversive manifestations of God's reign within the context of an oppressive and violent social context. In Matthew, the commands constitute examples of nonretaliation against an evildoer and thus institute practices that express the core of the Mosaic law. The gospel writers order and combine the sayings to suit their purposes, but in neither case does Jesus's teaching necessarily articulate a comprehensive nonviolent ethic. In Matthew's version, Jesus calls his disciples to a radically new understanding of the enemy, as one worthy of love and care, and to a radical refusal to retaliate when insulted, sued, or forced into service. In Luke's rendering, the commands are viewed as practices and dispositions that contest human regimes of power and that witness to the subversive manifestations of God's reign among those outside these regimes. In both cases, Jesus decisively countermands the myriad violent practices and attitudes that configure a world that has turned in on itself. Yet neither version of Jesus's sayings necessarily constitutes a categorical prohibition of all violence.

The matter of self-defense is left open. The reference to striking the cheek may be interpreted to include striking back in self-defense, but as noted above, a strong case can also be made that the saying refers to the refusal to retaliate for an insult. Jesus's teachings on enemy love and nonretaliation, in other words, provide no unassailable basis for claiming that Jesus prohibited violence in all forms. Jesus's words fundamentally reorient one's dispositions towards enemies and admonish his followers to act accordingly. But taking vengeance is a different matter than defending one's life or the lives of others. On this matter, Jesus's words are not so easy to pin down.

Perhaps more ambiguous in Luke's gospel is Jesus's admonition to his disciples during the evening of his last meal with them (22:35-38). After Peter declares that he will follow Jesus wherever he goes, and Jesus tells Peter that he will betray him before the cock crows three times, the following interchange takes place:

(Jesus) said to them, "When I sent you all without a purse, pouch, or sandal, did any of you lack anything?" They said, "Not a thing." Then he said to them, "But now, let anyone having a purse take it and likewise a pouch. Anyone not having a sword should sell his coat and buy one." For I tell you that what is written must be fulfilled in me: 'He was reckoned among the lawless.' For whatever concerns me is being fulfilled." They said to him, "Look, Lord, here are two swords." And he said to them, "That is enough." (22:35-38)

Luke is the only gospel writer to report this conversation. It seems highly unlikely that Jesus is directing the disciples violently to resist arrest. Two swords would hardly be enough for that task. More importantly, Jesus has come to Jerusalem to fulfill God's purpose through him; a violent response would cast him as a political revolutionary rather than the king who brings in God's reign of peace and righteousness. On this basis, Jesus's comments are symbolic. His reference to a purse, pouch, and sandals recalls his sending of seventy disciples throughout the countryside to preach, heal, and proclaim the reign of God (10:3-4). The phrase "but now" signals the difference between the joy and victory that attended their first mission (10:17-22) and the presently dark time of fulfillment, when the powers will regard Jesus as a criminal. On this view, the sword is a metaphor that conveys a heightened degree of preparation for what lies ahead. The disciples miss the point, but Jesus confirms it by saying "That is enough."

Yet why would Jesus bring up a sword in the first place? If he was speaking symbolically, would he not know that his disciples would take him literally? And why would Jesus, at this time of all times, allow them to carry weapons with them, especially since he knew they did not grasp his intent? Why would Jesus allow his disciples to carry swords into a highly charged situation, when the potential for violence was elevated? Swords were often carried by travelers for defense against bandits. Was this the case with Jesus's disciples when they traveled, so that the presence of swords did not elicit any rebuke from Jesus at this crucial time? If Jesus held to a categorical commitment to nonviolence, why would he have countenanced the presence of swords among his disciples? It seems unlikely that the disciples would have hidden weapons from Jesus, as opposed to carrying them throughout their travels with Jesus's full knowledge. The cryptic interchange, in sum, does not settle the question of Jesus's teaching on nonviolence in one direction or the other.

Temple Cleansing and Wicked Tenants

Compared to the accounts of the event in the other gospels, Luke's report of Jesus's cleansing of the temple is notably brief (19:45-46). Luke downplays the violent elements that other gospel writers report; he does not tell of Jesus overturning the tables of the money changers, scattering their coins, or whipping their sheep and goats (cf. Mark 11:15-17; John 2:13-22). Luke reports only that Jesus threw out those who were selling things, preferring to direct attention instead to the reason that the money changers had provoked Jesus: "He said, 'It is written, "My house is to be a house of prayer," but you have made it a den of thieves!'" This conflation of phrases from Isaiah 56:7 and Jeremiah 7:11 characterizes the state of the temple in Jesus's time. The declaration is significant in light of our overview of what raises God's ire in the Old Testament, namely blatant and egregious disrespect of God's supremacy and holiness. Whereas God intended the temple to be a place devoted to worship, those who inhabit the temple precincts enrich themselves instead. Darrell Bock captures the issue succinctly: "In the very presence of God, as it prepares to worship, the nation dishonors its God."[4] What provokes Yahweh to anger in the Old Testament here provokes Jesus to anger, generating Jesus's forceful action to restore the sanctity of God's house. Jesus, in short, "wishes to uphold God's honor."[5]

Luke next relates a confrontation between Jesus and the chief priests and scribes, which takes place on the grounds of the temple (20:1-8). The group levels a direct challenge at Jesus: "Tell us by what authority you act. Who is the one who gives you this authority?" The challenge encapsulates the core issue that has separated humanity from the Creator since the garden; human leaders here challenge the authority of the Lord's king and thus the authority of God. The first sentence implies that the human agents are in charge and have a right to judge the words and actions of anyone who enters sacred space, the very space devoted to acknowledging and affirming the Creator's supremacy. The next question evokes the issue of recognition ("Who is the one?"), manifesting the leaders' refusal or perhaps inability to recognize the one who holds all authority. Jesus, in turn, implicitly refuses to acknowledge their authority by asking a question of his own: "The baptism of John, was it from heaven or humanity?" (v. 4). The question puts

---

4. Darrell L. Bock, *Luke: 9:51-24:53*, Baker Exegetical Commentary on the New Testament 3 (Grand Rapids: Baker, 1996), 1579.
5. Bock, *Luke: 9:51-24:53*, 1572.

the issue in the plainest terms possible by setting divine authority in opposition to human authority. Each has its sphere. In which sphere was John? The leaders' subsequent refusal to answer the question both validates the dichotomy and ironically reinforces God's authority as manifested through Jesus. They have nothing to say on the topic of authority, so Jesus does not address their challenge.

The encounter, however, gives Jesus the opportunity to recount the entire history of Israel's relationship to God in the form of an allegory (20:9-16). The allegory concerns a man who planted a vineyard, leased it to tenants, and then left the country for a long span of time. When the owner sends a slave to collect the share of the crops owed to him, the tenants beat the man and throw him out. Two other slaves sent in sequence receive similar treatment. The owner then decides to send his beloved son with the hope that the tenants will respect him. The tenants, however, draw the outlandish conclusion that the appearance of the son gives them the opportunity to seize the property for themselves by killing the heir. They therefore throw him out and kill him.

The vineyard alludes to an Isaianic prophecy that excoriates Israel for its disobedience (Isaiah 5:1-7), although in that case Israel plays the part of the vineyard rather than the tenants. It also evokes the divine mandate given to human beings in the beginning, that is, to till and care for the garden that God planted in Eden. The Greek text picks up this nuance by identifying those to whom the vineyard is leased simply as farmers. With this allusion in mind, the image of the vineyard is a recapitulation of God's intention to restore the creation through the agency of Israel. The crops the owner anticipated can likewise be seen as the intended fruit of an ordered life in the world, which reflects the character and mission of the Creator. The sense is underscored by the farmers' reference to killing the son so that "the inheritance can be ours." The idea of an inheritance in the Old Testament focuses on an unassailable and permanent possession that belongs to a particular family or people group. In the book of Joshua, territories were parceled out to the tribes as inheritance, with the Levites being given the "fire offerings" as their unique inheritance (Josh 13:15-19:46). Israel's inheritance, symbolized by the vineyard, entailed living in covenant relationship with God for the sake of the world, a mission clarified by Jesus's declaration that the owner would destroy the farmers and give the vineyard to others.

Jesus tells the parable to the crowd gathered around him at the temple and, as Luke later indicates, has the chief priests and scribes in mind when he speaks of the tenants. The distinction between the nation and its leaders, however, makes little difference in terms of how the matter ends, as the story of Israel reveals that the nation as a whole suffers for the decisions of its leaders. The end that Jesus speaks of is both understandable and violent. Jesus first appeals to a fundamental sense of justice by asking the crowd, "What then will the owner of the vineyard do?" He then answers the question with a terrifying declaration: "He will come and destroy these farmers and give the vineyard to others." The owner's violent response is reasonable, and it is difficult to escape the conclusion that it is in some sense retaliatory.

The temple cleansing and interrogation about John's authority give the reader the necessary framework for decoding the allegorical rendering of Israel's history with God and the violent response from God that it portends. Jesus characterizes the tenants' treatment of the second servant (and presumably the third) as shameful treatment, that is, intentional, egregious acts of disrespect. The owner views the treatment in the same way, as his reasoning for sending his son hinges on his hope that they will respect him whereas they have not respected the previous emissaries (v. 13). The death of the son at the hands of the tenants, therefore, is rendered not only as a despicable act of violence but an outrageous affront to the owner—so outrageous that the act calls for a devastating response on the part of the owner.

The theme of disrespect for God's supremacy and authority is consistent with the issue that provokes a violent response from God throughout the biblical narrative. If there is no respect, if the leaders and the nation go so far as to challenge divine authority directly and blatantly, there exists no basis upon which God may work with Israel to renew creation. God, in the person of the vineyard owner, therefore responds with violence, tearing down and plucking out in order to build up and plant through others.

The allegory also testifies to the forbearance of the God who is slow to anger and lavish in steadfast devotion. It extends the story and the character of God into the present by casting the death of Jesus as both the climax of a series of failed attempts to draw Israel back to covenant faithfulness and the act that provokes God to respond with violence in return. God suffers violence and dishonor far beyond the pale of what any human authority would be expected to endure, sending the beloved son to people who have repeatedly abused those sent previously and hoping against all indications to the contrary that the son might be able to restore the relationship on its proper foundation. The owner of the vineyard becomes both the victim and perpetrator of violence, portraying in symbolic terms the predicament faced by God throughout the Old Testament narrative.

There is no getting around the fact that Jesus explicitly announces God's intention to destroy the nation and give what it possesses to others (that is, to those who live under the reign of God inaugurated by Jesus) and that Jesus justifies the destruction by recounting God's violent history with Israel as it is related in the narratives of the Old Testament. This is the same Jesus who elsewhere tells followers to love their neighbor and turn the other cheek. The allegory and the following declaration clearly attribute the destruction of Jerusalem and its aftermath to the direct action of God. This is not a case of God withdrawing protection and letting matters take their own course. Nor can the allegory be explained as an instance of cultural influence, as if a socially constructed mindset causes Jesus to fit what God wants to say within a cognitive template. Furthermore, Jesus's violent overview of Israel's history and the warning of future destruction cannot be explained as a case of misunderstanding on Jesus's part—at least not without severe ramifications for the church's Christology. Jesus plainly informs the crowd that God will destroy Jerusalem, and the crowd, which knows that God has destroyed Jerusalem before and why God has done it, gets the point and responds immediately with "May it never be!" (v. 16). The allegory itself, along with the passages that precede it, explain both the reason and the inevitability of imminent divine violence with reference to what God has done in the past and why God has done it. Both are consistent with the ways that God is depicted through the course of the biblical narrative.

The eventual interrogation and crucifixion of Jesus manifests the ambiguity and tension that the allegory conveys. Luke again sets the question of authority squarely before the reader by reporting Jesus's interrogation by two representatives of political power: Pilate, the governor representing imperial Rome (23:1-7, 13-25), and Herod (23:8-12), a king who reigns under the aegis of Rome. The confrontation of opposing kingdoms is raised by the assembly of Jewish leaders who bring Jesus before Pilate. They accuse Jesus, among other things, of claiming to be "the Messiah, a king" (23:1). Pilate in turn takes up the accusation and directs it to Jesus in the form of a question, asking him directly if he is the king of the Jews, but receiving only a cryptic "so you say" in response. This is all that Jesus says to either man. Pilate hands Jesus over to Herod after declaring the accusations against Jesus without warrant, and Jesus gives no answer to Herod's questions.

The interchange between Jesus and the rulers displays the complete dissimilarity between earthly and divine systems and accentuates God's disengagement from the former. In Egypt, God pummeled a ruler who stood at the apex of human power, establishing divine supremacy by turning the forces of nature against Pharaoh and manipulating the human king's ability to decide for himself how to respond. That awesome display of power demonstrated God's faithfulness and saving work, while at the same time making Yahweh's reputation known to a world that did not know who Yahweh was. Now facing representatives of the unquestioned hegemonic power of Rome, God's king remains silent, shunning the display of his considerable power. He endures false accusations, humiliation, and abuse with mute passivity, acknowledging the rulers' power over him with no more response than he gave to the chief priests and scribes. In another reversal, it is Pilate, the representative of human power through Rome, who tries to release Jesus, whereas the people, descendants of those whom God released from Pharaoh's power, seek Jesus's death.

The crucifixion of Jesus itself represents the supreme manifestation of God's forbearing character and loving disposition toward humanity. It is the most stunning reversal in the whole sweep of God's story as related by the narrative of the Old Testament. At the cross, God receives the full force and malevolence of human violence without retaliating whatsoever. Unfettered by tethers to human systems of power, the cross displays the love of the Creator in its purest form. At the cross and in the events leading up to it, Jesus categorically rejects violence and the systems that rely on it to maintain power and instead embodies the love of neighbor and refusal to retaliate that he has impressed upon his followers. This same Jesus overcomes the violence by enduring degradation and death through faithful obedience to the will of God. The resurrection then displays God's supremacy over the death-dealing mechanisms of human systems by vanquishing death itself. Through Jesus Christ, God overturns the system. The victim of violence becomes the victor over violence.

The Violence of God in the Shadow of the Cross

Does God's display of self-giving love on the cross mean that God has turned away from violence as a means of dealing with human rebelliousness? A number of instances from the book of Acts suggest otherwise. A relatively mild instance takes place against Saul of Tarsus, who is in the process of "breathing threats and murder against the disciples of the Lord" (9:1). As Saul sets out for Damascus with letters endorsing his plans to imprison followers of Jesus, Jesus appears to him with a flash of light that blinds and floors him. After Paul obeys Jesus's direction that he continue to Damascus and await instruction, Jesus sends a follower named Ananias to restore his sight by the laying on of hands. Although the blindness is temporary and serves the purpose of God's plans for Paul, it is violence nonetheless and signals that God is still not reluctant to utilize harmful force to advance divine purposes.

Paul himself becomes a divine agent of violence when he strikes another man blind. On Cyprus, Paul and his companion Barnabas encounter a magician named Elymas, who attempts to turn the local proconsul against the two men (13:1-12). In response, the Holy Spirit fills Paul, who glares at the magician and vehemently condemns him as a "son of the devil" and an "enemy of righteousness" who "ceaselessly warps the straight ways of the Lord" (v. 10). He then declares that the power of the Lord is directed against the magician and announces that the Lord will strike him blind "for a while," whereupon Elymas is blinded and begins groping around. The dramatic confrontation duly impresses the proconsul, who believes in the Lord when he sees what happens and hears Paul's teaching. Here again, striking a man blind serves God's saving purposes; the blinding of an opponent removes an impediment to Paul's preaching and displays a persuasive demonstration of God's power.

More serious are two instances in which God strikes people dead. The first concerns Ananias and Sapphira, two believers who sell a piece of property and present the proceeds to the apostles (5:1-11). The two keep some of the money for themselves and evidently present the contribution as the entire amount of the sale. In this case, God works through the agency of Peter, who speaks words of indictment and judgment that announce the deaths of the husband and wife when each enters separately. The indictments are telling. The situation is reminiscent of Achan's theft of plunder dedicated to God after the destruction of Jericho, which led the infuriated deity to demand that he and his family be stoned (Josh 7:1-26). Peter brackets his indictment of Ananias with the accusation that Ananias has lied to God, beginning with "Why has Satan filled your heart to lie to the Holy Spirit and withhold the sale price of the property?" and ending with "You have not lied to human beings but to God."

Peter takes a different tack with Sapphira, confronting her with the charge that she has put the Spirit of the Lord to the test. The charge is associated in the Old Testament with the flagrant disobedience and ingratitude Israel displayed at Massah and Meribah, which provoked a fierce divine response (Exod 17:1-7; Deut 6:16; Ps 106:12-15; cf. Ps 78:56-59). The two accusations together render the deception as a direct affront to God that cannot be countenanced. Both Ananias and Sapphira fall to the ground dead at the words of Peter. Luke thereupon confirms in each case that the deaths produce the effect of provoking the sense of awe due the cosmic Sovereign; intense fear gripped everyone who heard about the deaths (vv. 5-11).

The second instance, in which King Herod Agrippa is devoured by worms when he accepts adulation as a god, represents a more direct challenge (12:20-25). Luke reports that Herod delivers a speech to the people of Tyre and Sidon, arrayed in royal finery. The people, eager to curry favor, shout continuously, "A god's voice, not a human one!" whereupon the angel of the Lord strikes him down, and Herod suffers a gruesome death. Usurping God's position, even indirectly, as in the Old Testament, provokes an immediate divine response. Luke sets the episode within the context of Herod's violent efforts to suppress the growth of the church by killing James, John's brother, and imprisoning Peter (12:1-19) and reports the expansion of the church following his death (12:24-25). The context thus intimates that the death of Herod is also connected with God's willingness to remove whatever resists the expansion of God's work through the followers of Jesus.

Reviewing Divine Violence in Word and Deed

The Gospel of Luke picks up the narrative thread left dangling after the debacle that ended the Davidic monarchy and relates a new divine strategy for renewing the world. In the aftermath, God steps back and disengages from the power politics and social contests that govern the world. When the story resumes in Luke, God reveals a plan to reengage the world but in an entirely different way. Through various messengers at various locations, God reveals that God is not done with kings entirely but will not work with available rulers nor within the system that supports them. Instead, the messengers proclaim that God will establish a king outside of and apart from the monarchical systems of the man-made world. God will no longer identify with a nation or work with a king, but that does not mean that God will not identify and work with humanity. The messengers describe a reversal in the order of things and tell of a king whose reign will overturn human structures of power. God's king will identify with those who suffer from the decisions of kings.

This move to the outside is crucial for understanding why God, through Jesus, his Son and king, refuses to meet force with force and violence with violence. God no longer works through available people and systems but now turns the system upside down by sending the Son of God. God has stepped back

GOD MOVES TO THE OUTSIDE

from the human system that drew God into the web of human violence. Because God stands outside, because God will carry on redemptive work primarily through the powerless, because God's king will reign over a freed humanity, because God stands against the high and mighty, God is free to embody and establish a new humanity. God's complete disengagement from the system allows God in a sense to start over and to fully manifest divine character and objectives through the person of God's Son.

Luke's gospel also demonstrates the challenges that Jesus faces as he announces and establishes God's new approach to renewing the world through humanity. The world Jesus addresses knows little else than the application of and resistance to the power and violence that supports the aims of the high and mighty. The disciples and the crowds cannot think of God's king in any other terms than what they know and experience, and so meet Jesus with the hope that he will restore Israel to a position of national eminence (Acts 1:6). The disciples also, even though walking with Jesus, cannot grasp the magnitude of the difference between God's kingdom and the kingdoms of the world; they argue with each other about who should enjoy power and position even as Jesus prepares to offer himself for the world (Luke 22:24-27).

Jesus himself refuses to acknowledge or engage the earthly powers in any way. To say or do anything that could be even remotely viewed as a call for insurrection would only validate the worldly system that Jesus's kingdom opposes, to say nothing about the brutal suffering that Rome would inflict at the slightest hint of rebellion. Jesus does not play the game of power nor allow himself to be drawn into it. He remains steadfastly detached from any operation that maintains the system and from any hint of allegiance with the devilish power that upholds it, even to the point of suffering the full force of the system's malevolent violence and meeting it with forgiveness rather than retaliation. The cross, then, indeed represents the definitive manifestation of divine love and thus "the thematic center of everything Jesus was about."[6]

The extension of the story past the resurrection, however, reveals that God does not turn from the strategic use of violence to advance divine purposes or, as in the Old Testament, to display divine supremacy when challenged by human powers. God strikes down adherents who deal falsely and a king who receives acclaim due only to God. Moreover, God utilizes human and spiritual agents to do so, just as was the case in the Old Testament. The fact that God still harms

---

6. Gregory A. Boyd, *The Crucifixion of the Warrior God: Interpreting the Old Testament's Violent Portraits of God in Light of the Cross* (Minneapolis: Fortress, 2017), 1:170.

people in tandem with chosen agents, after the full disclosure of divine love at the cross and for the same reasons God metes out violence in Israel's narrative, suggests that God remains resolutely engaged with the world as it is.

The teachings of Jesus represent the full and unmitigated revelation of God's person and work necessary to shape the new humanity's vision and life. That is, Jesus's teachings and his death on the cross reveal the fullness of God's loving commitment to creation and convey God's vision for human flourishing in its ideal and purest form. *The divine ideal can only be embodied outside of and apart from the systems of the world.*

Jesus articulates his teachings on violence and retaliation in absolute terms. They reveal the essential character and disposition of God and present God's ideal for human living in the world. Does this mean that the trajectory they set requires absolute adherence in practice? Perhaps, but not necessarily. Jesus's words unambiguously transform perspectives and attitudes and inculcate godly dispositions in his followers. Does it follow then that living out his teachings requires a categorical refusal to participate in violence for any reason? Might believers who love as God loves find it necessary, as God does in the Old Testament, to adapt and accommodate divine ideals to the operations of a world driven and defined by violence and power? Does the ideal constitute an uncompromising stance, or does it primarily establish a trajectory?

Our overview of Jesus's teachings on enemy love and nonretaliation suggests that an interpretive openness is warranted. They may be understood as injunctions that forbid followers to take up violence in any form and for any reason. Yet the different versions and settings of the teachings suggest that there are other interpretive options. Luke's version is set within a literary context that presents the teachings as manifestations of God's justice addressed to those on the fringes of power, and within a historical context that suggests the possibility that they express pragmatic and healing practices for oppressed and traumatized people. Matthew's version, on the other hand, sets the sayings within a discussion of what fulfills God's righteousness as expressed through the law of Moses and therefore might suggest that they function as ideals that orient attitudes and practices. The point to be made is that *Jesus's teachings on enemy love and nonretaliation possess an interpretive slipperiness that renders them an unstable foundation upon which to base absolutizing pronouncements.*

There is no doubt that Jesus's teaching and ministry constitute a new and radical turn in God's self-disclosure and engagement with the world. God's disengagement from worldly systems and identification with the powerless manifest a divine strategy to establish a new humanity apart from and in opposition to the kingdoms of the world and to abandon the project to renew the warped human system from the inside out. Disentangled from the system, God is free to display the fullness of divine love through the life, teachings, and death of Jesus. Does it follow then that followers are bound to live out this ideal fully as they undertake God's renewing mission in the world?

The teachings of Jesus that construct the framework of God's opposing kingdom, the basis of which is love of God and love for others under the reign of God's chosen king, can be understood to articulate a categorical rejection of violence in all its forms, as an opposing witness to the sinful mechanisms of violence that infest human interactions in the world. Yet, as this brief overview has demonstrated, a strong case can also be made that Jesus's teachings on nonretaliation and neighbor love comprise ideals meant to reorient perspective and behavior. The interpretive openness of the New Testament narrative presses the question of what faithful followers are to do with the whole of the narrative testimony. How are present-day disciples to read the narrative as a vision for thinking and acting in relationship to the God who is still at work in a violence-saturated world? We turn to this question in the final chapter.

9

Interpreting Divine Violence

This book began with the proposal that we can best address the issue of divine violence by approaching the Bible as the definitive and revelatory text that speaks the truth about God, humanity, and creation. I have suggested that approaches that address the problem of divine violence based on reconstructions of the Bible's historical context and culture, or on reconstructions of the thoughts, worldview, or intentions of those who wrote the Bible, situate the discussion on an unstable foundation. Specifically, I have suggested that we may effectively address the violence of the biblical God by focusing on the way the Bible tells the story of God's involvement with humanity.

The biblical text, in all its complexity—as opposed to putative narratives about what authors and redactors were thinking when they wrote it—should stand at the center of Christian conversation about divine violence. Dismissing difficult or offensive portraits of God by arguing that they are human contrivances, or perhaps are even mistaken, is too simple a way of addressing the problem. Approaches that make a text and a particular interpretation definitive for assessing the rest of the canonical testimony (such as Jesus's teachings on enemy love or the crucifixion) are no more effective. According privileged texts and interpretations an incontrovertible status leads to questionable acts of hermeneutical legerdemain and tends to flatten out the tensions and paradoxes that stand at the core of the biblical testimony. The Bible sets before faithful readers a vision of extraordinary complexity and frustrating dissonance. The challenge for interpreters, I have suggested, is to resist the impulse to get God off the hook for the violence that God perpetrates and instead to grapple with the theological challenges the Bible presents to the followers of the Prince of Peace.

As a step in this direction, I have read the story of God as it is narrated from Genesis through 2 Kings and into Luke and Acts. My attention has been drawn to five instances, early in the narrative, where God is said to descend into the world, that is, to instances when God's decision to work within the world is directly stated. Yahweh's descent to Babel marks Yahweh's initial decision to enter the world and work within it, as opposed to remaining aloof and above the world. Yahweh's descent to Abraham outside of Sodom confirms Yahweh's decision to bless the world, by resetting the human/divine relationship on its original footing, and draws Yahweh into a deep identification with the human partner. Yahweh's descent into Egypt frees a people, who will manifest God's ordering work in the world, and announces Yahweh's decision to enter the contest of nations, rulers, and deities that characterizes a warped human system. At Sinai, Yahweh descends to bind the divine self to a nation through a covenant, thereby fully identifying with a nation and taking on the responsibility for the nation's welfare and safety. Also at Sinai, Yahweh descends a second time to reaffirm covenantal commitment to Israel after Israel violates the covenant.

As a whole, the narrative portrays God's participation in violence as a consequence of God's decision to enter a violence-saturated world and to work with human partners within it. It begins with the creation of a world where violence is not present. There humanity and all living things live in harmony under the blessing of the Creator, who has so ordered the world that life may flourish. God gives humanity the mandate and authority to manage the world God has created; human beings care for the earth and exercise the Creator's authority over the animals that God creates to populate it (Gen 2:15, 19-20). Human beings, therefore, occupy an exalted place in the creation by virtue of their role and relationship with the Creator, but they are also to live in obedience to the Creator (Gen 2:16-18).

The original vision rendered by the creation narratives presents the hierarchy that must be maintained if life is to flourish in the way that God intends: God / humanity / the earth and all that is in it. As the psalmist puts it, God has made human beings "a little less than God and crowned them with glory and honor," putting them in charge of God's works and subjecting everything to them (Ps 8:5-6). There are no hierarchies of power evident in the human community. Sexual difference does not entail the subjugation of one sex to another, intimating that differences among human beings are bound up in an original unity that expresses no exertion of power over one another.

Human beings, however, violate the original hierarchy of creation. Placing themselves on an equal footing with God, they take it upon themselves to decide what is good for creation, something that only the Creator truly knows. As a result, human beings transform creation into an ungodly mess. Violence results from human hubris. It grows in intensity, leading ultimately to the dissolution of the boundaries that configure creation and the destruction of all that is, save for a family of human beings whom God preserves in order to begin anew. God plays a decisive role in the destruction of the world, accelerating the process of disintegration and afterward reordering the world through a righteous man. Re-creating the world through Noah, who has lived righteously in the violent, corrupt world humans have made, raises hope that the re-created world will not fall into the destructive patterns of the corrupted one. Yet once again things go awry, culminating in a human attempt to create unity by building a city and tower that can elevate them into God's space. The human community's aspiration to restore unity by its own means and devices draws God into the world, now to undo a man-made unity maintained by achievement and pride.

God next enters the world to initiate a relationship with a particular man and his family, whom God chooses to be the agents of blessing for all humankind. The relationship, however, pulls God into the maelstrom of human conflict. God's decision to identify with Abraham and his descendants eventuates in a dramatic demonstration of power, as Yahweh asserts divine supremacy over the oppressive regime of Pharaoh and makes a name by means of brute force. Yahweh's identification with Israel at Sinai precipitates a series of decisions in which Yahweh adapts to the conventions and structures of earthly power in order to promote the welfare of the nation. Yahweh utilizes mass violence to subdue Pharaoh and launch a war of conquest against the kings of Canaan. Yahweh's awesome demonstrations of power over those at the apex of human power shatter the human fiction that kings rule and prevail through their own will and power. Yahweh enters the world, frustrates the calculus of kingship, and demands the recognition and respect due to the Creator and Sovereign of the world.

The decision to acquiesce to Israel's request for a king, however, draws Yahweh into collusion with the monarchical system Yahweh had previously opposed. Thereafter, Yahweh's work through Israel is tightly bound to the affairs and disposition of the kings. Yahweh's way of dealing with kings, however, does not change. The kings of Israel and Judah take up the forms of violence that characterize their counterparts in the nations around them, but Yahweh participates only to defend the nation or to uphold Yahweh's role and reputation. Yahweh will not countenance a break in the reciprocal choosing that defines the relationship and responds forcefully to royal flaunting of human power. In the end, Israel's kings manifest the same determination to remake the world that brought creation down in the first place. The program ends with kings blatantly defying Yahweh and seeking direction from other sources, leading to the deterioration and eventual destruction of Jerusalem and the exile of the nation.

After a long hiatus, God reenters the world with a new strategy. Now disengaged from human principalities and powers, God begets a different kind of king, and carries on the divine work of renewal from the edge of the system rather than the center. God no longer works within the systems of power that define kings and empires but rather establishes an alternative kingdom that reverses the power polarity. The divine move to the outside enables the revelation and embodiment of the fullness of God's love through Jesus Christ, who models and proclaims the original vision for human beings in relation to God and each other. The ministry of Jesus orients adherents to justice, self-giving, and love for others, and steadfastly rejects entanglement with the world and the retaliatory violence that infuses it. The teachings of Jesus define the ways that followers are to live out the self-giving love of God in the world, reversing the will to power that configures human systems. The crucifixion, finally, presents the ultimate and clearest demonstration of God's new way, while the resurrection confirms God's victory over the powers of destruction and gives birth to a new humanity who will be the agents of God's saving activity in the world.

Divine Violence and Human Agents

In the Old Testament, God engages in violence to advance God's work in the world, to announce and establish unassailable power and authority, and to the correct the waywardness of the covenant people. During the exodus and the invasion of Canaan, Yahweh undertakes wholescale violence against entire populations in order to release the Israelites and establish them in the land promised to their ancestors. Yahweh employs human agents in these instances to initiate violence in Egypt and to perpetrate violence in Canaan; divine violence is part and parcel of Israel's origins. Yahweh's violence is thereafter, as in these instances, focused and targeted, in some cases defending Israel against its enemies and in others assailing kings who turn to other deities, thus neglecting the reciprocal choosing that forms the core of Israel's identity. The New Testament, while testifying to different rules of divine engagement, also hints that Yahweh has not altogether abandoned violence as a means of dealing with human defiance.

One conclusion that can be drawn from the whole of this narrative testimony is that God's acts of violence in the Old Testament are for the most part associated with a failed project. Yahweh decides to restore creation by initiating a relationship with Abram that reestablishes the divine-human relationship on the original footing. Yet this divine descent into the world sets off a series of decisions and accommodations, made for the sake of relationship and mission, which implicate God ever more deeply in the world's violence. The project proves futile, prompting God to give up working through the covenant and its kings and to reengage by constructing an alternate and opposing system, with the Son of God at its head. One can, on this reading, argue that the Old Testament reveals the futility of working within human systems. After the whole arrangement comes crashing down, God disengages from this way of renewing the world.

On this reading, God's decision to reenter the world in opposition to its violent systems can be interpreted as an implicit rejection of the former project altogether, in favor of a better means of redemption. In the New Testament, God still identifies with Israel but primarily with its travails and sufferings. When God reengages with Israel, God identifies with the victims rather than the purveyors of royal power. Jesus's ministry and preaching represent a direct challenge to the oppressive mechanisms of empire and a rejection of the violence that maintains it. Jesus's teachings on neighbor love and nonretaliation are thus to be taken as definitive marks of God's new, restorative work. God rejects participation in the imperial system of violence, embodies this rejection through the self-giving love of Christ, and bids Jesus's followers to do likewise.

Following this line, God learns from the experience with Israel and undertakes a new way that establishes a new people as the divine agent of blessing in the world. This people, like the Lord they follow, rejects all forms of violence in order to draw humanity out of its endless captivity to violence and into the alternative set of relationships that is the only true path to a restored creation. God's people, by implication, are to take a stand outside of and opposed to the systems of the world, manifesting a radical, true witness to God's love and God's reign on the earth. As a consequence, God's people follow Jesus in refusing to engage the principalities and powers, and resist being drawn into the violent mechanisms of a corrupted world.

Yet this is not the only faithful way to read and appropriate the narrative. Must God's work within the system, as related in Israel's narrative, necessarily denote a failed project that has yielded to a better way? Does God's decision to move to the outside, through Jesus, necessarily entail the abandonment of corrupted human systems? We have already noted that God's move to the outside frees God to reveal the fullness of the divine character and to promote a vision for human flourishing that was not possible when God was enmeshed within the systems of human power. Does this clarified ideal then necessarily require followers to adopt it in its entirety? Or might it serve primarily to orient vision and practice in the midst of a complex world fraught with situations in which there is no good decision? Might the Old Testament narrative, in its depiction of God's accommodation to the reality of human sinfulness and violence, clarify how God's people should engage with corrupted systems? In short, does God's work and teaching through Jesus mean that followers should not work within human systems, or is God still at work within the systems and bidding followers to participate?

It is important in this respect to note the different positions that God occupies to restore the world and to create order out of the chaos of human conflict. In the Old Testament, God works from multiple locations within Israelite society, but primarily from the center. Yahweh identifies with the nation and takes on the responsibility of protecting it and ensuring its well-being. Although Yahweh sometimes speaks and works in the nation through prophets who stand outside the established leadership, Yahweh works prominently through interaction with Israel's leaders. With the dynastic promise to David and the agreement to abide in the temple, Yahweh adopts and works within the monarchical structures that configure the societies of the time. Yahweh's decision to work within monarchical structures binds kings so tightly to Yahweh that the fortunes of the nation stand and fall according to the king's devotion or disobedience to Yahweh. In the New Testament, however, God operates from the margins, in the person of an indigenous peasant whose people are suffering under imperial oppression. In the New Testament, God stands in radical opposition to the human powers in the world.

To simplify, the Old Testament presents God at work primarily at the center of society, while the New Testament presents God at work primarily at the margins. The question, following on this observation, has to do with whether one views the Old Testament as a narrative that must be rejected because it testifies to a failed divine approach or one that displays the messiness and accommodations that must be navigated by those who believe that God still works at the center of power as well as its periphery.

An alternative way of reading, in other words, sees in the canon a number of different depictions of God's working in human society and of those through whom God works. Within the sweep of the narrative, God responds to the brokenness of the world, and the violence it generates, in different ways and from different positions within human communities. God's presence and work within multiple social locations throughout the Bible resists the imposition of an absolutizing template. The New Testament's testimony to the God who establishes an alternative kingdom through Jesus Christ may indeed reveal the true and full disclosure of God's character and disposition, but the testimony may be viewed as an ideal that is to orient Christian thinking and practice. From this perspective, the Old Testament can be viewed as a full and true depiction of the world of sin and violence that confronts God and God's agents, and of the kinds of adaptations that must be made to work redemptively within the world's systems.

Those who believe that God continues to work within human systems may therefore see the Old Testament narrative as a realistic vision of the complexity of decision-making that confronts Christians who are called to work within human systems of power. If God indeed continues to be present and at work at the centers of power as well as at the edges, then the Old Testament presents an unvarnished view of the system, the decisions, and the dangers that face those who respond to God's call to work with God in those spaces. It testifies that even God had to adapt ideals to reality and participate in violent systems in order to accomplish redemptive purposes. As Peter Craigie aptly observes, God "acts in the world as it is, for if the prerequisite for divine action were sinless men and sinless societies, God could not act through human beings and human institutions at all."[1]

How one reads the diverse canonical depictions of God's participation in violence thus ultimately depends on the ecclesiological and theological convictions one brings to the reading of Scripture. Are Christians to stand apart from the sinful systems of the world and embody God's vision for humanity as a radical alternative to the world's ways? Or are Christians called to work redemptively within the corrupted systems, knowing well that accommodations will have to be made to advance God's restorative purposes? Is the example and teaching of Jesus so different from the work of God in Israel that it must be followed strictly, or does Israel's narrative continue into the gospel narrative so that the former calls for a more nuanced understanding of the latter?

---

1. Peter C. Craigie, *The Problem of War in the Old Testament* (Grand Rapids: Eerdmans, 1978), 96.

INTERPRETING DIVINE VIOLENCE

From Debate to Dialogue

My intent in this brief reflection on the biblical narrative has not been to suggest that one interpretive stance is better or more faithful than the other. I have aspired, instead, to argue that there are multiple faithful ways of thinking about how the story of God's violence can or should inform Christian thought and practice, particularly as it pertains to understanding the pervasive violence of God in the Old Testament in the light of the teachings and life of Jesus Christ. The multiplicity of readings that the story makes available, not to mention the diversity of canonical perspectives, indicates that a conversation on divine violence among Christian readers of different perspectives may be preferable to debates about who reads rightly and who does not.

I propose that the Bible, in its complexity and diversity, models the kind of reading community that is to interpret it faithfully. That is to say, the biblical canon may serve faith and mission best when it generates a dialogue among faithful readers who read and think differently about God's violence and what Christians should make of it. The Bible can be conceived as the testimony of a great cloud of witnesses, bound by covenant and devotion to the one true God, who nevertheless do not see things the same way and whose perspectives sometimes markedly disagree. Inspiration does not necessarily mean uniformity, as is amply demonstrated in church council meetings today when Spirit-filled servants of Christ experience strident disagreement over important decisions! The biblical canon reflects the church and urges faithful readers past the binary categorization and totalizing that characterize modern thinking and into dialogue with faithful readers of various locations and commitments. It calls for a community committed not so much to winning principled arguments as to hearing opposing perspectives and discerning together how God is at work within the mess to make all things new.

Engaging in an open conversation among respectful listeners may be a worthy interpretive practice in and of itself. I draw this idea from the late Palestinian-American literary critic Edward Said, whose tenure at Columbia University spanned forty years. Said observed that the interpretation of literary texts in Western society is an exercise in power, which privileges dominant voices and suppresses others. As an alternative, he envisioned ensembles of readers, defined by mutuality and dialogue rather than contests of interpretation. These ensembles move interpretation away from a right/wrong polarity in which individual interpreters strive to win arguments and toward a process that sees interpretation as a conversation oriented toward maintaining relationship. The reconfiguration of interpretation along relational lines creates a non-hierarchal arena that values all contributions to the interpretive enterprise. Since the goal of interpretation is no longer focused on determining the one right interpretation, the interpretive process invites participants into an ongoing dialogue and relational unity. Thus conceived, interpretation can provoke a lively interchange between interpreters, who speak from the particularities of their own perspectives and recognize that all participants are dependent on each other to understand a literary work.

Said applies the phrase "contrapuntal reading" to this communal reading strategy. The phrase is drawn from Baroque music, which intertwines independent melodic lines in counterpoint to each other to create a complex, unified fabric of sound. "Various themes," he writes, "play off one another, with only a positional privilege given to any particular one; yet in the resulting polyphony there is a concert and order, an organized interplay that derives from the themes, not from a rigorous or formal principle outside the work."[2] As in the musical work, so in interpretation. Strongly held convictions may be fervently expressed, not as a means of bending other voices to a single, agreed-upon melody, but rather as an expression of distinct voices in a complex conversation that becomes greater than the sum of its parts.

I believe Said's notion of interpretive ensembles offers a promising model for Christian conversation about divine violence and its implications for faith and practice. It has the potential to prompt Christians to listen and learn from those who differ and to enhance rather than diminish the relational connection we share with each other and Jesus Christ. The practice would require interpretive humility among Christian readers and a willingness to receive different readings as valuable contributions to one's own understanding. Instead of holding and defending one's own position, participants would recognize their *interdependence* on each other and each other's interpretations. The process of dialogue would remind participants of the complexities that must be taken into account as one discerns how to live faithfully in a violent world. Finally, approaching the interpretation of divine violence as a practice of community may enhance Christian unity rather than harden Christian division. Decisions about how the Bible guides Christian response to violence will always have to be made and lived out by individuals and Christian communities. Contrapuntal reading would allow for conclusions to be clarified and nuanced by insights gained from an ongoing conversation with other faithful followers who respect each other.

2. Edward Said, *Culture and Imperialism* (New York: Vintage, 1993), 51.

I believe, however, that a transposition of Said's contrapuntal metaphor into a different musical idiom works even better. The contrapuntal melodies that characterize Baroque music are the product of a single composer and are meant to be performed as written. Biblical interpretation, however, is a fluid and provisional process, as Christians respond to myriad challenges and changes in culture, experience, and thinking. Christian interpretation, in other words, is both determined and improvisational, not unlike jazz. Jazz integrates diverse melodies into a holistic musical experience that values the voice of each musician as a necessary component of the unified musical enterprise. Jazz requires that musicians listen carefully to the other musicians in the ensemble and follow the flow of the musical conversation. When this is done well, the result is a unified musical work, which nevertheless preserves the distinct voices in the ensemble.

Debates about the rightness and wrongness of interpretations perpetuate the antagonistic character of modern society, abet a smug assurance that one occupies the biblical high ground, and maintain divisions between Christian confessions. Conversations among disparate Christian parties, as an ongoing corporate exercise in discernment, however, underscore the relational bond that all followers of Jesus share, remind participants of the complexity of ethical decision-making in a sinful world, and may even yield new, Spirit-inspired insights. Interpretive jazz ensembles would allow all perspectives to be heard but would not demand that anyone change one's views—only that one listens actively, with respect, and with the sense that one's understanding of the biblical witness and its relevance for contemporary problems is enriched by the conversation.

Interpretive Parameters

Ensemble interpretation does not entail an interpretive free-for-all. Jazz musicians commonly improvise off a chart that contains chord and rhythm notations. In a similar sense, the dialogue on the Bible and violence that I propose does not presume that *all* interpretations are valid. Some will be off-key or discordant. The biblical text, however, provides the notations that direct the interpretive conversation. I conclude with some of the notations that might direct an interpretive ensemble riffing on the violence of the biblical God.

First: Yahweh's acts of violence do not emanate from the caprice or anger of a petty deity who has taken personal offense and seeks satisfaction. The narrative testimony confirms that Yahweh is "slow to anger and abounding in steadfast love." Although anger is sometimes associated with Yahweh's violence, many instances—notably in the cases of Pharaoh and the kings of Canaan—recount the full force of Yahweh's destructive power but do not associate the violence with divine anger. In the narrative corpus we have explored, Yahweh's anger is directed toward Israel for singular offenses that break the fundamental covenant relationship defined by reciprocal choosing and by Israel's submission to Yahweh.

Second: In the narrative literature of the Old Testament, Yahweh rarely employs violence to judge other nations. Yahweh utilizes violence as a punitive measure against Israel but rarely is said to do so against other nations. When Yahweh does take up violence against other people, it is to accelerate the deterioration of a situation whose end is already apparent (as in the cases of the flood and Sodom and Gomorrah), to release Israel from slavery and establish the nation in Canaan, and to defend Israel against its enemies. The exception that proves the rule may be the Amalekites, who attack Israel in the wilderness (Exod 17:8-16) and who Yahweh declares will in turn be erased from memory (Deut 25:17-19). Saul's failure to complete Yahweh's command to wipe out the Amalekites results in Yahweh's rejection of Israel's first king (1 Sam 15:1-35).

A case can be made that Yahweh's plagues against Egypt are acts of judgment for oppressing the Israelites, but neither Yahweh, Moses, nor the narrator directly mentions judgment as a rationale for the violence. Rather, the narrator emphasizes Yahweh's faithfulness to divine promises and Yahweh's determination that both Israel and Egypt recognize Yahweh's power and supremacy. Likewise, the argument that the Canaanites are to be wiped out as divine judgment for their sinfulness is nowhere stated and must be inferred from a few conspicuously indirect texts concerning the fate of the Canaanites. Those texts that do give a rationale for the extermination of the Canaanites focus either on Yahweh's faithfulness to divine promises (as in the Exodus account) or on the necessity of giving Israel a place in which to live out its covenant with Yahweh. In most other cases, Yahweh's *punitive* violence is directed toward Israel and in response to Israel's refusal to honor Yahweh or adhere to Yahweh's commandments.

Third: The narratives we have explored in this book are best taken as testimonies and not templates. Biblical narratives tell the story of God's determination to restore a world ruined by human arrogance and defiance. Our study has highlighted the decisions God makes as a consequence of the decision to utilize human partners as agents of renewal. These decisions are made at discrete moments in human experience and for particular purposes. The implications of each decision, as they play out in the reciprocal choosing between God and human partners, precipitate accommodations that draw God ever more deeply into the maelstrom of human violence. The episodes of the narrative are points in God's story and not templates to be replicated by readers in their times.

In particular, the salient instances of divine violence in Egypt and Canaan constitute divine actions undertaken, first to establish the covenant people and secondly to announce God's sovereign presence and power to the nations of the world. Yahweh frees Israel from slavery in fulfillment of a divine promise to Israel's ancestors and for the singular purpose of establishing a covenant relationship that resets the divine-human relationship on its original foundation. The biblical testimony thus associates the most horrific instances of divine violence with Israel's beginnings; nothing on the scale of those instances follows at any point thereafter (although Yahweh's slaughter of Sennacherib's army approaches them). It follows, then, that no interpretation of those instances can justify similar programs of mass violence, whether past or present.

Fourth: Expanding on the above, biblical narratives cannot be rightly appropriated to justify wars that advance national or group agendas. Yahweh directs wars to establish Israel as a nation and later as a dynastic monarchy. These are singular instances of violence necessary to accomplish divine objectives at the time. Yahweh overcomes the kings of Canaan through Joshua and enables David to defend himself against his enemies (1 Sam 17:38-54; 2 Sam 5:18-25). David himself initiates campaigns to take the city of Jerusalem for himself (2 Sam 5:6-10) and expand his influence and prestige past the borders of Israel (2 Sam 8:1-14; 10:1-11:1; 12:26-31)—these also the narrator attributes to the enabling power of Yahweh (2 Sam 8:14b). In the case of subsequent kings, however, Yahweh participates directly in warfare only in defensive operations (e.g., 2 Kgs 13:22-23; 18:13-19:37), although Yahweh also withdraws protection and authorizes coups against kings who violate the covenant partnership (1 Kgs 14:15-16; 2 Kgs 9:1-10; 13:1-23; 21:10-15). In a singular instance, Yahweh precipitates a war with the Arameans in order to remove Ahab (1 Kgs 22:1-40). In this case, Yahweh directs a lying spirit to entice Ahab into a battle at Ramoth-Gilead, where the king meets his death (vv. 19-23). Micaiah the prophet reveals that Ahab's decision to recover the city was actually prompted by Yahweh and that Yahweh had already decreed disaster for the king.

All of these instances of divine working within warfare derive from Yahweh's identification with a nation that Yahweh intends to be an agent of blessing to the nations of the world. The kingdom that God establishes through Jesus Christ, however, stands outside and reverses the operations of the systems that govern the world humans have made. In Christ, God no longer identifies with a nation or accommodates nationalist or monarchical objectives. Although Yahweh's defense of Israel leaves open the question of whether defensive wars may be legitimate, there is no question that violence in collusion with nationalist aims is illegitimate.

Fifth: The narrative thread we have explored offers no justification for retaliatory violence. The teachings of Jesus forbid retaliation for wrongs done to oneself or others; violence that seeks redress cannot be condoned. Here Jesus explicitly overturns a practice that Yahweh earlier affirmed with reference to the Amalekites. The Amalekites' attack during the wilderness wandering provokes a blood feud that continues for centuries (Exod 17:8-16). When Israel transitions to a monarchy, Yahweh directs Saul to wipe out the Amalekites, in the same terms Moses had employed to call for the annihilation of the peoples of the land (1 Sam 15:1-35). Yahweh also gives the rationale: "I have intervened because of what Amalek did to Israel, what he did to him when he came up out of Egypt" (v. 3). The verb I have translated "intervened" commonly signifies direct divine activity, which may be taken either as punitive or retaliatory in this context. The scenario represents the singular occasion in which Yahweh not only allows but promotes a blood feud between people. Jesus's words reveal this directive to be a singular divine accommodation to the world of the time.

Sixth: Christian interpretation on biblical violence takes place within the context of a legacy that has looked to the Bible to legitimize war and violence throughout the church's history. Quick recourse to violence and justification of the same has been more the rule than the exception among Christianized societies and nations. The most egregious acts of violence have arisen, for the most part, from the church's collusion with the oppressive systems of the world. The Crusades, the wars of the Reformation, and Western colonization are but the most well-known instances of a deep-seated Christian impulse to justify violence in pursuit of Christian aims and with the Bible's support. Christians should not underestimate the significant influence this interpretive legacy exerts on contemporary discussions about biblical violence.

Facile recourse to violence and facile biblical justification for it has been the church's default mode of operation across ages and cultures. The example and teachings of Jesus, however, demand otherwise. While there may be different views on whether violence can ever be condoned by Christian believers, there is no question that an orientation toward nonviolence and a critique of the mechanisms and instigators of violence must instead define Christian faith and practice. In this respect, the force of the contemporary nonviolent critique must be taken into account. Jesus's teaching on nonretaliation and neighbor love must be affirmed tenaciously as the nonnegotiable starting point of all Christian response to the world's violence. Although it may be argued that war or violence are sometimes necessary, the resort to violence should come, as it does for Yahweh with Israel, only as the very last resort. The call for a fundamental reversal of the Christian default mode—from justification of violence to resistance to violence—requires nothing less than a corporate soul-searching as the first step in undoing centuries of acculturated attitudes, perspectives, and practices.[3]

I return, finally, to questions I raised earlier. Are Christians then to disengage from all complicity, participation, and collusion with the violent systems of the world? To stand apart from the world as radical witnesses to the reign of the Prince of Peace? Is a thoroughgoing disengagement possible? Alternatively, are Christians to bring the presence and testimony of Christ into the violent systems of the world, working within them and making accommodations as higher values demand, all the while resisting the pull toward the destructive and oppressive? Is that even possible?

Much has been made of late of the so-called Constantinian shift, wherein the Roman emperor Constantine ensconced Christianity as the religion of the empire. The shift, put simply, transported Christians from the margins of imperial society to the center of power and decision-making. The shift had a significant impact on the church's thinking about nonviolence. No longer did the church stand in radical opposition to the empire. Instead, Christians now bore responsibility for the well-being of the empire. The responsibilities of central leadership changed Christian perspectives on violence, as Christians were now responsible for the welfare and defense of millions of people. It is one thing to practice nonviolence, and to be willing to die for one's beliefs. It is quite another to make others vulnerable to death for the sake of one's beliefs. In a violent world, citizens look to their governments to defend them. How were Christians to speak and act faithfully from the center?

This shift and its repercussions led to a process analogous to that which bound God more tightly to the mechanisms of kingship. Christian identifi-

---

3. As a critical resource toward this end, see Eric A. Seibert, *The Violence of Scripture: Overcoming the Old Testament's Troubling Legacy* (Minneapolis: Fortress, 2012). Seibert presents a range of hermeneutical and practical steps that can be taken up to reset Christian dispositions in a nonviolent mode.

cation with the empire implicated Christianity in the mechanisms of empire and the violence it generated. Some Christians regard the ensuing relationship between Christianity and the empire as a catastrophic tragedy or a lapse into apostasy from which the followers of Christ have never recovered. Others view the association as a divine moment in the life of the church, which required Christians to rethink their ethical responsibilities and practices, now from the center rather than the periphery of political systems.

One prominent thread of the contemporary discussion about divine violence seeks to recover and live out the pristine, pre-Constantinian commitment to nonviolence that prevailed among Christians when they occupied the outskirts rather than the center of power. From this perspective, theological reflection and practice from the Constantinian shift onward reflect a devil's bargain and, as demonstrated by Christianity's consistent and massive recourse to violence, an ungodly collusion with fundamentally un-Christian structures of power. Another thread sees a shift but not a radical break, nor a turn from biblical teachings. From this perspective, God adapts as God has always done in concert with human partners and within human systems throughout the ages; Christians are to work within the system because God continues to be present within the system. Ethical reflection takes place within a complex of factors that require those at the center to make hard decisions that affect thousands of lives.

This dichotomy is admittedly overdrawn, as there are many nuanced perspectives between the poles. All perspectives, I have suggested, need to be voiced and taken seriously, not to determine or refine a principle or position that holds true for every Christian in every situation, but rather to engage in a conversation with others who are respected as equally faithful, thoughtful, and sincere. Adherents of principled nonviolence can sharpen Christian witness for those working within political systems by reminding them of the propensity toward sanctioned violence that has often defined the collusion between church and empire and by holding them accountable to pursue peace when peaceful alternatives remain viable. Those who see God at work in the systems of empire may in turn raise the challenge to adherents of radical nonviolence that ethical lines are not always clear and that the pervasive sinfulness of human society creates a complex ethical environment in which hard decisions may require flexible ideals. More importantly, conversations marked by sincere listening, conversation, and respect among Christians of different perspectives may model practices of unity and peacemaking that themselves bear the light of Christ to an increasingly polarized world.

Select Bibliography

Armstrong, Karen. *Fields of Blood: Religion and the History of Violence.* New York: Anchor Books, 2014.
Baker, Sharon L. *Razing Hell: Rethinking Everything You've Been Taught about God's Wrath and Judgment.* Louisville: Westminster John Knox, 2010.
Baloian, Bruce Edward. *Anger in the Old Testament.* New York: Peter Lang, 1992.
Bekkenkamp, Jonneke, and Yvonne Sherwood, eds. *Sanctified Aggression: Legacies of Biblical and Post-Biblical Vocabularies of Violence.* New York: T&T Clark, 2003.
Bergman, Michael, Michael J. Murray, and Michael C. Read, eds. *Divine Evil? The Moral Character of the God of Abraham.* New York: Oxford University Press, 2011.
Bertholet, Katell, Joseph E. David, and Marc G. Hirshman, eds. *The Gift of the Land and the Fate of the Canaanites in Jewish Thought.* New York: Oxford University Press, 2014.
Birch, Bruce C. *Let Justice Roll Down: The Old Testament, Ethics, and the Christian Life.* Louisville: Westminster John Knox, 1991.
Boyd, Gregory. *The Crucifixion of the Warrior God: Interpreting the Old Testament's Violent Portraits of God in Light of the Cross.* 2 vols. Minneapolis: Fortress, 2017.
Brueggemann, Walter. *An Unsettling God: The Heart of the Hebrew Bible.* Minneapolis: Fortress, 2009.
———. *Divine Presence amid Violence: Contextualizing the Book of Joshua.* Eugene, OR: Cascade, 2009.
———. *Old Testament Theology: An Introduction.* Nashville: Abingdon, 2008.
———. *Theology of the Old Testament: Testimony, Dispute, Advocacy.* Minneapolis: Fortress, 1997.

SELECT BIBLIOGRAPHY

Carroll, R. P. *Wolf in the Sheepfold: The Bible as a Problem for Christianity*. London: SPCK, 1991.
Carroll R., M. Daniel, and J. Blair Wilgus, eds. *Wrestling with the Violence of God: Soundings in the Old Testament*. BBRSup 10. Winona Lake, IN: Eisenbrauns, 2015.
Collins, John J. *Does the Bible Justify Violence?* Minneapolis: Fortress, 2004.
Copan, Paul. *Is God a Moral Monster? Making Sense of the Old Testament God*. Grand Rapids: Baker Books, 2011.
Copan, Paul, and Matthew Flannagan. *Did God Really Command Genocide? Coming to Terms with the Justice of God*. Grand Rapids: Baker Books, 2014.
Cowles, C. S., Eugene H. Merrill, Daniel L. Gard, and Tremper Longman III. *Show Them No Mercy: Four Views on God and Canaanite Genocide*. Grand Rapids: Zondervan, 2003.
Craigie, Peter. *The Problem of War in the Old Testament*. Grand Rapids: Eerdmans, 1978.
Creach, Jerome F. D. *Violence in Scripture*. Interpretation: Resources for the Use of Scripture in the Church. Louisville: Westminster John Knox, 2013.
Crossan, John Dominic. *How to Read the Bible and Still Be a Christian: Is God Violent? An Exploration from Genesis to Revelation*. New York: HarperCollins, 2015.
Davies, Eryl. *The Immoral Bible: Approaches to Biblical Ethics*. New York: T&T Clark, 2010.
Dell, Katharine, ed. *Ethical and Unethical in the Old Testament: God and Humans in Dialogue*. New York: T&T Clark, 2010.
Desjardins, Michel. *Peace, Violence and the New Testament*. BibSem 46. Sheffield: Sheffield Academic, 1997.
De Villiers, Pieter, and J. Henten. *Coping with Violence in the New Testament*. Studies in Theology and Religion 16. Boston: Brill, 2012.
Dozeman, Thomas. *Joshua 1-12*. AB. New Haven: Yale University Press, 2015.
Eisen, Robert. *The Peace and Violence of Judaism: From the Bible to Modern Zionism*. New York: Oxford University Press, 2011.
Enns, Peter. *The Bible Tells Me So: Why Defending Scripture Has Made Us Unable to Read It*. New York: HarperOne, 2014.
Eller, Vernard. *War and Peace from Genesis to Revelation*. Eugene, OR: Cascade, 2003.
Fitzgerald, John T., Fika J. van Rensburg, and Herrie F. van Rooy, eds. *Animosity, the Bible, and Us*. Atlanta: Society of Biblical Literature, 2009.
Fretheim, Terence E. *God and World in the Old Testament: A Relational Theology of Creation*. Nashville: Abingdon, 2005.

———. *The Suffering of God: An Old Testament Perspective*. OBT. Minneapolis: Fortress, 1984.

———. *What Kind of God? Collected Essays of Terence E. Fretheim*. Edited by Michael J. Chan and Brent A. Strawn. Winona Lake, IN: Eisenbrauns, 2015.

Girard, René. *Things Hidden Since the Foundation of the World*. Translated by Stephen Bann and Michael Metteer. Stanford, CA: Stanford University Press, 1987.

Goldingay, John. *Israel's Life*. Volume 3 of *Old Testament Theology*. Downers Grove, IL: InterVarsity, 2009.

———. *Israel's Gospel*. Volume 1 of *Old Testament Theology*. Downers Grove, IL: InterVarsity, 2003.

Hamilton, Adam. *Making Sense of the Bible: Rediscovering the Power of Scripture Today*. New York: HarperOne, 2014.

Hawk, L. Daniel. *Joshua*. Berit Olam. Collegeville, MN: Liturgical Press, 2000.

Hess, Richard S., and Elmer A. Martens, eds. *War in the Bible and Terrorism in the Twenty-First Century*. BBRSup 2. Winona Lake, IN: Eisenbrauns, 2008.

Hill, Jim, and Rand Cheadle. *The Bible Tells Me So: Use and Abuses of Holy Scripture*. New York: Doubleday, 1996.

Hobbs, T. R. *A Time for War*. Wilmington, DE: Glazier, 1990.

Jenkins, Philip. *Laying Down the Sword: Why We Can't Ignore the Bible's Violent Verses*. New York: HarperCollins, 2011.

Jersak, Brad, and Michael Hardin, eds. *Stricken by God? Nonviolent Identification and the Victory of Christ*. Grand Rapids: Eerdmans, 2007.

Kelle, Brad E., and Frank Ritchel Ames. *Writing and Reading War: Rhetoric, Gender, and Ethics in Biblical and Modern Contexts*. SymS 42. Atlanta: Society of Biblical Literature, 2008.

Lamb, David T. *God Behaving Badly: Is the God of the Old Testament Angry, Sexist and Racist?* Downers Grove, IL: InterVarsity, 2011.

Leithart, Peter J. *Defending Constantine: The Twilight of Empire and the Dawn of Christendom*. Downers Grove, IL: InterVarsity, 2010.

Levenson, Jon. *Creation and Persistence of Evil*. Princeton: Princeton University Press, 1988.

Lind, Millard. *Yahweh Is a Warrior: The Theology of Warfare in Ancient Israel*. Harrisonburg, VA: Herald Press, 1980.

Longman, Tremper, III, and Daniel G. Reid. *God Is a Warrior*. Grand Rapids: Zondervan, 1995.

Love, Gregory Anderson. *Love, Violence, and the Cross: How the Nonviolent God Saves Us through the Cross of Christ*. Eugene, OR: Cascade, 2010.

Lüdemann, Gerd. *The Unholy in Holy Scripture: The Dark Side of the Bible.* London: SCM, 1997.
Matthews, Shelly, and E. Leigh Gibson, eds. *Violence in the New Testament.* New York: T&T Clark, 2005.
Matties, Gordon H. *Joshua.* Believers Church Bible Commentary. Harrisonburg, VA: Herald Press, 2012.
McConville, J. Gordon, and Stephen N. Williams. *Joshua.* THOTC. Grand Rapids: Eerdmans, 2010.
McDonald, Patricia M. *God and Violence: Biblical Resources for Living in a Small World.* Scottdale, PA: Herald Press, 2004.
McEntire, Mark. *The Blood of Abel: The Violent Plot in the Hebrew Bible.* Macon, GA: Mercer University Press, 1999.
Nelson-Pallmeter, Jack. *Is Religion Killing Us? Violence in the Bible and the Quran.* New York: Continuum, 2003.
Niditch, Susan. *War in the Hebrew Bible: A Study in the Ethics of Violence.* Rev. ed. New York: Oxford University Press, 1993.
Niebuhr, Reinhold. *Moral Man and Immoral Society: A Study in Ethics and Politics.* New York: Scribner's Sons, 1942.
Penchansky, David. *What Rough Beast? Images of God in the Hebrew Bible.* Louisville: Westminster John Knox, 1999.
Pitkänen, Pekka. *Joshua.* AOTC. Downers Grove, IL: InterVarsity, 2010.
Römer, Thomas. *Dark God: Cruelty, Sex, and Violence in the Old Testament.* New York: Paulist, 2013.
Schlimm, Matthew Richard. *This Strange and Sacred Scripture: Wrestling with the Old Testament and Its Oddities.* Grand Rapids: Baker Books, 2015.
Schwager, Raymund. *Must There Be Scapegoats? Violence and Redemption in the Bible.* Translated by Maria L. Assad. 3rd ed. New York: Crossroad, 2000.
Schwartz, Regina M. *The Curse of Cain: The Violent Legacy of Monotheism.* Chicago: University of Chicago Press, 1997.
Seibert, Eric. *The Violence of Scripture: Overcoming the Old Testament's Troubling Legacy.* Minneapolis: Fortress, 2012.
———. *Disturbing Divine Behavior: Troubling Old Testament Images of God.* Minneapolis: Fortress, 2009.
Sparks, Kenton. *Sacred Word, Broken Word: Biblical Authority and the Dark Side of Scripture.* Grand Rapids: Eerdmans, 2012.
Spong, John Shelby. *Sins of Scripture: Exposing the Bible's Texts of Hate to Reveal the God of Love.* San Francisco: HarperSanFrancisco, 2005.
Strauss, Mark L. *Jesus Behaving Badly: The Puzzling Paradoxes of the Man from Galilee.* Downers Grove, IL: InterVarsity, 2015.

SELECT BIBLIOGRAPHY

Thatcher, Adrian. *The Savage Text: The Use and Abuse of the Bible.* Malden, MA: Wiley-Blackwell, 2008.
Thomas, Heath, et al., eds. *Holy War in the Bible: Christian Morality and an Old Testament Problem.* Downers Grove, IL: InterVarsity, 2013.
Travis, Stephen. *Christ and the Judgment of God: The Limits of Divine Retribution in New Testament Thought.* Milton Keynes: Paternoster, 2008.
Weaver, J. Denny. *The Nonviolent God.* Grand Rapids: Eerdmans, 2013.
Wink, Walter. *Engaging the Powers: Discernment and Resistance in a World of Domination.* Minneapolis: Fortress, 1991.
Wright, Christopher J. H. *The God I Don't Understand: Reflections on Tough Questions of Faith.* Grand Rapids: Zondervan, 2008.
Wright, N. T. *Evil and the Justice of God.* Downers Grove, IL: InterVarsity, 2006.
Yoder, John. *The Politics of Jesus.* Grand Rapids: Eerdmans, 1972.
Yoder, Thomas. *Killing Enmity: Violence and the New Testament.* Grand Rapids: Baker Books, 2011.

Author Index

Bandstra, Barry, 32
Barton, John, 106
Betz, Hans Dieter, 181
Bock, Darrell L., 179n1, 184
Boyd, Gregory, 10-14, 15, 191
Brueggemann, Walter, 16n24, 17, 88n12, 102-3, 142n3

Clines, David J. A., 48n1
Collins, John J., 19n29
Cotter, David, 57n4
Craigie, Peter C., 16n23, 200
Creach, Jerome F. D., 9-10, 13, 73n2

Davies, Eryl W., 7n4
Dozeman, Thomas, 100

Fokkelman, J. P., 40n6
Fretheim, Terence, 17, 18, 24, 56n3, 72n1, 73nn2-3, 78, 79n7, 80n8, 81n9

Goetz, Ronald, 141n2
Goldingay, John, 17, 31n2, 88n11, 156

Heschel, Abraham, 107
Horsley, Richard, 179n2

Origen, 3, 4, 140n1

Philo, 4

Reventlow, Henning Graf, 6n3

Said, Edward, 201-3
Seibert, Eric, 8-9, 13, 207n3
Shaw, Garry J., 92
Smith, Anthony D., 142n4
Sparks, Kenton, 16
Stone, Lawson G., 159

Tertullian, 3
Tindal, Matthew, 5n2, 6n3

Wenham, Gordon, 40
Wright, Christopher, 144-45

Younger, K. Lawson, 158n7

Subject Index

Aaron, 15, 71, 72-77, 80, 93, 96-98, 106, 148, 151, 165
Abel, 29-30, 57
Abimelech, 62-63
Abner, 121
Abram/Abraham; agent of blessing, 26, 45-65, 89, 66 150, 171, 195, 196, 198; ancestor, 38, 69, 175, 90; intercession, 71, 72, 96; land promise, 141, 144-45, 172
Absalom, 126
Achan, 152, 161, 163-64, 166, 168, 189
Adam, 25-29, 35, 40, 41, 43, 63, 67, 79, 141
Adonijah, 127
Ahab, 136, 205
Ahithophel, 126
Ai, 154, 159, 160-61, 163-64
allegorical method, 4-5, 11, 16
Amalekites, 10, 109, 119, 120, 121, 204, 206
Ammonites, 113, 117, 121, 126, 146
Amorites, 51, 144, 149, 162, 166
Ananias and Sapphira, 189-90
angel of Yahweh, 113, 146, 148, 190
anger, divine; and love, 102-4; and sorrow, 31, 61, 131; as a problem 3, 5-6; as punishment, 72, 91, 94, 102, 104-8; response to covenant infidelity, 96-98, 112-13, 136, 139, 149; slowness to, 57, 88, 101, 102, 186; vocabulary of, 135
anger, human, 29, 98-99

Apep, 73
Aram/Arameans, 121, 133-34, 136, 142-43, 205
Assyria/Assyrians, 134-35, 138, 143, 205
Augustus, 170

Baal, 112, 136
Baal Peor, 106
Baasha, 135-36
Babylon/Babel, 37-42, 45, 47, 52, 55, 57, 58, 68, 95, 169, 195
Bathsheba, 123, 126
Bethel, 47, 132, 136
blessing, 25, 27, 37, 45-46, 48, 53, 54, 56, 63, 66-67, 68, 87

Cain, 29, 30, 31, 44
Canaan, 47, 48, 49, 51, 86, 92, 109, 115, 140-68, 196, 197, 204-5
Canaanites; killing of, 2, 8, 13, 21, 111, 113, 140-68; separation from, 103
Christocentric hermeneutic, 9
covenant, 143; as definitive of Israel, 117, 126, 147, 164, 168, 198; as reciprocal, 112, 129, 135, 149-50, 159, 165, 166; at Sinai, 91-104; faithfulness, 143, 186; renewal ceremony, 137, 152, 154; transgression of, 137, 138, 163; with Abraham, 31, 51-53, 169; with Noah, 35, 36; with the Gibeonites, 161, 163
crucifixion, 11-12, 187-88

Damascus, 50, 121, 188

216

SUBJECT INDEX

Dan, 114, 132, 136
Daniel, 21
David, 119-27, 135, 137, 138, 171, 205
Deborah, 113
Deists, 5-6
devil, 173-74, 189

Eden, 25-29, 41, 44, 49, 141, 185
Edom/Edomites, 86, 121, 145-46
Eglon, 112, 113
Egypt/Egyptians; Abram's journey to, 47-49; deliverance from, 21, 96-97, 109, 111, 146-48, 137, 163; demonstration of Yahweh's supremacy over, 66-90, 104, 126, 143, 151, 162, 165, 195, 197, 204-5; killing, 1, 12, 135; oppression in, 34, 57, 115, 145
Ehud, 113
El Elyon, 50
El Shaddai, 52
Eli, 114, 119
Eliezer, 50
Elijah, 174
Elizabeth, 171-72
Elymas, 189
Ephraim/Ephraimites, 114, 152
Eve, 25-29, 35, 41, 43, 63

flood, 30-37, 60, 86, 96, 103, 104

Gabriel, 171
Galilee, 171, 175, 178-80
Gerar, 62, 63
Gibeah, 114
Gibeon/Gibeonites, 152, 154, 160-61, 163, 168
Gideon, 113-14
Gilgal, 119, 131
Goliath, 119-20
Gomorrah, 55, 56-57, 59-61, 63, 65, 68, 71, 72, 96, 104, 105
good, 23-24, 26, 27, 28, 29, 43, 57
Goshen, 76, 77

Hannah, 114, 172
Herod Agrippa, 190
Herod (the Great), 170, 187
Hezekiah, 134-35
Holy Spirit, 170, 172, 173, 189
Hophni and Phinehas, 114

Horus, 75

Ishbosheth, 121
Ishmael, 53

Jacob/Israel, 26, 47, 67, 68, 69, 70, 165, 171
Jehoahaz, 135, 136, 139
Jehoiachin, 169
Jehoshaphat, 133
Jehu, 136
Jephthah, 113-14
Jericho, 152, 154, 159-61, 163, 189
Jeroboam I, 131-33, 135
Jerusalem, 121, 125, 127-32, 134, 137, 139, 171-73, 187
Jesus, 173-88, 190-93, 196, 198-203
Jethro, 67
Joab, 121, 127
John the Baptist, 172, 173, 177, 185, 186
Jonathan, 120
Jordan River, 147, 152, 153, 162
Joshua, 110, 130, 151-65, 205
Josiah, 13, 14, 137
Judah, 113, 137, 139
judges, 113-16

Levites, 98, 107, 114, 170, 185
Lot, 49, 59-61
love, 104-6, 107, 177-82, 192-93

Manasseh (king), 135, 137, 139
Marcion, 3-4
Mary, 171-72, 177
mercy, 29, 31, 59, 102, 104-6, 107, 162, 168, 178-79, 181
Merneptah, 158
Midianites, 113
Miriam, 15, 106
Moab/Moabites, 86, 113, 121, 133-34, 145
Moses, 144-51; commands, 86, 130, 149-51, 152, 155, 163; covenant mediator, 93-108, 163; declarations, 166; deliverer, 67-90, 146, 148, 160, 165; in the wilderness, 109-12; mistaken, 14, 15; philosopher, 4; reviewing history, 144-45, 153-54; teacher, 177, 180
Mount Sinai, 91-108

Naaman, 143, 174

217

SUBJECT INDEX

Nathan, 122, 123-24
Nazareth, 171, 174, 178
Nile, 72-74
Nimrod, 38-39, 45
Noah, 31, 33-37, 38, 45, 51, 57, 171, 196

Og, 153, 162

paradox, 7, 16
Paul. *See* Saul/Paul
Peter, 182-83, 189-90
Pharaoh; arrogance of, 126, 171; defeated, 66-90, 93, 126, 127, 138, 147, 165, 187-88, 196; oppression by, 116, 196; symbol of evil, 10; with Abram, 48-49
Philistines, 113, 114, 119, 121
Phinehas, 107
Pilate, 187
progressive revelation, 7-8

Queen of Sheba, 128

Ra, 73, 77
Rabshakeh, 134-35, 138
Rahab (Canaanite deity), 85
Rahab (Canaanite prostitute), 152, 154, 160-63, 168

Rehoboam, 132, 135
retaliation/nonretaliation, 177-82, 192-93
Rome/Romans, 1, 178, 179-80, 187-88, 191

Samaria, 133, 134, 136, 143, 175
Samson, 113-14
Samuel, 115-18, 131
Sarai/Sarah, 26, 47-49, 53, 55, 62, 66, 91
Saul (king), 116-21, 123, 130, 131, 204, 206
Saul/Paul, 188-89
Shechem, 154
Sihon, 153-54, 162
Sinai, 90-103, 109, 111, 148-49, 195, 196
Sisera, 112, 113
Sodom, 49, 55, 56-57, 59-61, 62, 63, 65, 68, 71, 72, 96, 104, 105, 195
Solomon, 127-32, 133, 135, 137, 139

Tamar, 126

Uriah, 123, 126

Zadok, 127
Zechariah (father of John), 171, 172
Zipporah, 67

Scripture Index

OLD TESTAMENT		8:21	35	23:1–20	142
		9:20–27	37	24:7	142
Genesis		10:1–32	38	25:9–10	142
1:1	78	10:8–10	38	26:3	142
1:1–2:4	23–25	11:1–9	37–42, 95	26:25	142
1:2	85	11:4	66, 68	33:20	142
1:6–10	85	11:5	23	34:2	154
1:26	23, 24	11:6–7	57	35:6–7	142
1:27	35	11:10–32	45	35:19–20	142
1:28	17, 41	12:1	141	40:31	142
1:28–30	25	12:1–2	42, 66	50:1–15	142
2:4–25	25–27	12:1–3	45		
2:8	45, 141	12:3	69	**Exodus**	
2:15–20	195	12:7–8	47, 142	1:1–14	68
2:16–17	26	12:10–20	47	2:10	67
2:17	45	13:2	49	2:23	84, 85
2:19–20	41	13:14–18	49	3:1–22	69
2:28	68	13:18	142	3:1–15:21	126
3:1–24	27–30	14:1–24	49–50	3:7	91
3:9–13	30	14:21–23	147	3:7–9	68
3:20	41	15:1–21	50–52	3:8	66, 146
3:23	29	15:13–14	145	3:11	72
4:3–17	29–30	15:16	144, 166	3:13	70, 72
4:10	57	17:1–27	52–53	3:14	69
6:1–8	30–35	17:3	55	3:19–20	71, 80, 81
6:1–9:17	147	18:1–33	55	4:1–13	72
6:5–7	57	18:17–19	56	4:2–4	73
6:6–7	31	18:20–21	45, 56	4:10	82
6:7	34, 119	18:21	54, 55	4:13–16	104
6:9	35, 51	18:23–25	58	4:14–15	72
6:11–13	31, 60	18:27–32	59	4:21	72, 81, 82
6:17	31	19:1–29	59–61	5:1	95
7:23	34	19:30–38	61	5:2	70
8:1	34	20:1–18	62–64	5:9	82

SCRIPTURE INDEX

6:1–13	69	12:32	85	20:22	166
6:6	84	12:32–36	135	20:22–24	145
7:1	71, 89	12:33	85	21:10	98
7:3	72, 81, 82	12:34	89	24:20	181
7:4	84	14:4	71, 81, 82	27:12	26
7:5	71	14:8	81, 82, 85	27:14	26
7:9	72	14:14	15, 86	27:28–29	155
7:9–10	73	14:17	81, 82, 85		
7:13	81, 82	14:18	71, 85	**Numbers**	
7:14	81, 82	14:25	85, 86	3:3	98
7:14–22	73	15:1–18	86	11:1–35	106
7:17	71	15:22–25	99	12:1–9	106
7:20–21	148	16:1–12	99	12:6–8	15
7:22	74, 81, 82	16:1–36	96	14:1–25	110–12
8:1–15	74	16:1–17:7	104	14:6	142
8:5–16	148	17:1–7	96, 99, 189	14:17–18	111
8:10	71	17:8–16	109, 204, 206	14:18	148
8:13, 14	81	19:1–24:18	90	14:21–22	111
8:16–17	148	19:4–6	91	25:1–18	106
8:16–22	74	19:11	90	25:6–13	115
8:18	81	19:13	93	25:11	93
8:19	81, 82	19:18	93	32:33	25
8:20	82	19:20	93	33:55–56	149, 157
8:22	71	20:1–23:33	18		
8:23	72	20:5–6	102	**Deuteronomy**	
8:32	80, 81	21:24	181	1:39	26
9:1–7	75	22:22–24	84, 94	2:1–23	145–46
9:3	82	23:20–33	148, 157	2:24–3:11	153–54
9:7	81	24:9–11	94	5:17	1
9:8–12	75	28:41	98	6:1–14	150
9:12	81, 82	29:9	98	6:4–5	159
9:13–35	75	29:20	98	6:10	142
9:14	71	32:1–35	92, 95–99	6:16	189
9:14–16	76	32:7	105	6:18	142
9:16	86	32:25–29	107, 115	6:24–25	117
9:17	76	33:1	142	7:1–6	155–56, 167
9:20–21	76	33:1–6	99	7:1–8	145
9:29	71	33:7–11	100–101	7:1–26	149
9:34	81, 82	33:11	15, 99	7:2	152
9:35	81, 82	33:19	100–101	7:9–14	117
10:1	81, 82	34:1–2	92	8:1–6	117
10:1–2	72	34:1–35	101–4	9:1–6	144
10:1–20	77	34:5	168	9:5	166
10:14	82	34:5–7	101	9:7	145
10:20	81, 82	34:6	111, 139	10:12–13	117
10:27	81, 82	34:10	102	11:9	142
11:1–10	83	**Leviticus**		11:21	142
11:9–10	72	16:1–12	143	11:29	152
11:10	81, 82	16:32	98	12:29–31	145
12:29–30	148	18:1–30	166	17:17	130
12:29–36	83	18:27–28	145	19:21	181
12:30	85			20:15–18	150

220

SCRIPTURE INDEX

20:16–17	1	24:1–28	154	18:10–11	120
20:16–18	145, 167	24:19–24	152	18:14	121
21:15–16	94			19:1–7	120
25:17–19	204	**Judges**		20:1–42	120
26:3	142	1:1–36	154	23:1–14	120
27:1–13	152	1:4	113	25:1–13	120
27:11	163	2:11–23	112	25:37–42	121
28:1–13	143	2:14	113	30:26–31	120
28:61	159	2:14–15	112		
29:20	93	3:8	113	**2 Samuel**	
31:26	159	3:10	113	1:1–10:19	122
34:10	15	3:28	113	5:6–25	205
		4:2	113	5:21	127
Joshua		4:14	113	7:1–11	122–23, 124–25
1:1–12:24	153–55	4:15	113	7:10	123
1:6	142	6:1	113	7:12–16	130
2:1–12:24	159–64	6:15	113	7:26	127
2:10–11	162	8:3	113	8:1–14	205
2:18–19	163	8:7	113	10:1–11:1	205
3:1–4:18	152	10:7	113	11:1–12:23	123–26
3:1–4:24	147	11:29	113	12:26–31	205
4:22–24	147	11:32	113	13:1–18:17	126
5:1–12	152	14:6	113	15:25	127
6:1–21	152	14:19	113	16:12	127
6:25	152	15:8	114	24:1	135
7:1	166	15:14	113		
7:1–5	152	17:1–13	114	**1 Kings**	
7:1–26	189	19:22–30	114	1:1–2:46	127
7:6	166	20:1–48	114	3:1–11:27	127–131
8:30–35	152	21:1–24	114	10:1–13	128
9:1–27	152			11:9	135, 139
10:40	140	**1 Samuel**		11:28–40	131–32
10:40–42	151	2:12	114	12:1–14:24	132–33
11:12	151	2:27–36	115	13:3	139
11:16–27	151	8:1–22	115–16	14:15–16	132, 205
11:19	152	8:7–8	116	14:22	93
11:20	83, 148	8:20	120	15:27–16:10	135–36
12:1–24	152	9:1–11:15	116–17	16:21–33	136
13:1	157	10:9	83	17:8–24	174
13:1–6	152	12:1–25	115, 117–18	18:10–11	170
13:1–19:46	185	12:7–10	123	18:32–35	134
14:12	157	12:17	116	19:10	93
15:63	157	12:22	109	20:23	143
17:10	152	13:8–15	118–19	20:28	134
17:12–13	152, 157	15:1–35	119, 131, 204, 206	21:21–29	136
17:14–18	152, 157			22:17	139
18:1	25	15:28	131	22:53	136
21:43–45	144	16:1	131	23:26	139
22:10–34	152	16:7	131		
23:1–10	157	17:26	119	**2 Kings**	
23:12–13	130	17:38–54	205	3:1–27	133
23:13	152	17:45–47	119–20	5:1–27	174–75

221

SCRIPTURE INDEX

5:17	143
8:7-15	135
9:1-10	205
10:1-30	136
10:16	93
13:1-23	205
13:1-25	136
13:3	135, 139
13:22-23	205
14:27	136
16:4	128
17:9-11	128
17:11	137
17:17-18	137
17:18	135, 139
17:26	143
19:31	93
18:1-19:36	134-35
18:13-19:37	205
20:1-34	133
21:1-8	137
21:10-15	205
21:14-15	137
22:1-40	205
22:1-23:25	137
22:13-17	135
22:17	139
22:53	135
23:26	135
24:20	135
25:27-30	169

1 Chronicles

22:18	25

2 Chronicles

28:10	25

Ezra

6:16-18	170

Psalms

2:1-11	128
8:5-6	195
11:4	95
29:10	32
46:1-11	128
48:1-14	128
69:2	32
69:10	93
69:15	32
78:3-4	86

78:56-69	189
106:12-15	189
124:4	32
136:2	74

Proverbs

8:6	94
22:22-23	84

Ecclesiastes

12:14	26

Isaiah

5:1-7	185
42:13	93
43:21	86
45:7	80
49:18	100
51:9-10	85, 147
56:7	184
63:1-6	8
63:15	93
66:1	95

Jeremiah

7:11	184
32:21	74
51:13	32n4

Ezekiel

7:2-7	32n4
16:8-14	100
16:37	94
23:40	100

Joel

2:18	93

Amos

8:2	32n4
9:7	146
5:15	94

Micah

3:2	94

Nahum

1:8	32

Zechariah

8:2	93

Malachi

1:2-3	94

NEW TESTAMENT

Matthew

5:1-7:27	180
5:21-48	180
5:27-48	176

Mark

11:15-17	184

Luke

1:5-2:52	170-73
3:4-6	177
4:1-27	173-74
4:16-21	178
6:17-36	177
6:27-36	176
6:28-29	169
8:26-39	175
9:51-56	175
10:3-4	183
10:17-22	183
10:25-37	175
16:19-31	175
19:45-56	184
20:9-16	185
20:20-26	175-76
22:24-27	191
22:35-38	182-83

John

2:13-22	184

Acts

1:6	191
5:1-11	189
9:1	188
12:1-25	190
13:1-12	189

Romans

9:7	86
12:18-21	181

1 Corinthians

5:1-13	181

2 John

10-11	181

www.ingramcontent.com/pod-product-compliance
Lightning Source LLC
Chambersburg PA
CBHW020647300426
44112CB00007B/276